Salesforce CPQ Implementation Handbook

Configure Salesforce CPQ products to close more deals and generate higher revenue for your business

Madhu Ramanujan

BIRMINGHAM—MUMBAI

Salesforce CPQ Implementation Handbook

Group Product Manager: Alok Dhuri
Publishing Product Manager: Shweta Bairoliya
Senior Editor: Nisha Cleetus
Content Development Editor: Rosal Colaco
Technical Editor: Maran Fernandes
Copy Editor: Safis Editing
Project Coordinator: Manisha Singh
Proofreader: Safis Editing
Indexer: Subalakshmi Govindhan
Production Designer: Shyam Sundar Korumilli
Marketing Coordinator: Deepak Kumar

First published: March 2022

Production reference: 1090322

Published by Packt Publishing Ltd.
Livery Place
35 Livery Street
Birmingham
B3 2PB, UK.

ISBN 978-1-80107-742-2

www.packt.com

To my parents and siblings, who taught me the value of education. To my husband and daughters, for their support and inspiration throughout my writing journey.

Contributors

About the author

Madhu Ramanujan has been extensively using the Salesforce platform for almost a decade now. She finds that her substantial experience and work on multiple implementations has helped her easily transition between various roles in renowned corporations. She is a certified Salesforce Application Architect and System Architect and is an aspiring CTA with 14x certifications. She enjoys giving back to the community through volunteering as a RAD Women coach. She is passionate about designing secure, scalable, reliable, and high-performing solutions using cutting-edge technologies and helping customers in their transformational journeys.

I want to thank the following people from the Packt team, who helped make this book that you are holding in your hands a reality: Alok Dhuri, for having faith in my ability to write this book, as well as Storm Mann, Vaishali Ramkumar, Prajakta Naik, Aaron Lazar, Shweta Bairoliya, Nisha Cleetus, Rosal Colaco, Maran Fernandes, and Deepak Kumar. A big thanks to the reviewers, Brad Gross and Mitch Colyer, for their invaluable suggestions and helpful feedback. I would also like to thank all of my friends and colleagues who helped me in this wonderful process. A virtual high-five and a lot of gratitude from me to all of you!

About the reviewers

Brad Gross has been working in IT since the 20th century. In 2000, he developed one of the first Salesforce organizations and then turned his attention to helping others learn Salesforce. His work in the community led to his induction into the first class of Salesforce MVPs and the first-class Salesforce MVP Hall of Fame. For the past decade, he has been a leading industry consultant, working for several firms and even founding his own firm, Information Logistics. Currently working as the principal strategist for revenue cloud at Traction on Demand, his focus is on Sales Cloud and revenue operations.

When he is not developing the next generation of Salesforce leaders, he spends his time biking, skiing, and cooking for his family.

Mitch Colyer is a principal quote-to-cash consultant, specializing in Salesforce CPQ, Salesforce Billing, and other non-Salesforce product implementations. His experience inside and outside of the Salesforce platform lends him a unique perspective on how to best bring a Salesforce CPQ solution to light. Throughout his time working on the Salesforce platform, Mitch has led partner enablement training both domestically and internationally, been a Dreamforce speaker, and assisted in Salesforce CPQ and Billing rollouts in the United States and Europe. He lives with his wife, Brooke, in Montana, where he enjoys being outdoors, fishing, and trail running in his free time.

Table of Contents

3
Configuring CPQ Products

4
Configuring CPQ Pricing

5

Generating and Configuring Quote Templates

Section 2: The Next Stage of the CPQ Journey

6

Configuring Guided Selling

7
Creating Contracts, Amendments, and Renewals

8
Configuring CPQ Package Settings

Section 3: Advancing with Salesforce CPQ

9
The CPQ Data Model and Migration Concepts

Preface

Now more than ever before, customers have become the focal point of businesses around the world. Not to be left out, companies both big and small want to invest in digital transformations that can drive growth and improve operational efficiencies. These in turn help businesses accelerate their sales and see revenue growth. The sales teams need technology that can help them with responsive and flexible customer needs and automate the quote-to-cash process. Salesforce CPQ helps reshape the business relationship between sales organizations and customers.

Salesforce CPQ is a configure, price, quote tool that helps businesses automate the quote-to-cash process in a unified platform. Using the CPQ application allows sales organizations to focus on selling, while the tool can help with complex product configurations, accurate pricing, and helping sales reps generate precise quotes in minutes. CPQ is a native app built on Salesforce, the world's number-one cloud-based **Customer Relationship Management** (**CRM**) software for managing customer relationships and integration with other systems.

This book will start with an outline of the quote-to-cash process, present an overview of CPQ, and provide the details of when a business needs to implement CPQ. We will explore how CPQ helps configure complex products and bundles and helps apply accurate pricing and discounts. Then, we will learn how to automate the approval process and generate a professional quote and send it to customers.

After the initial sales have been closed, you will learn how a contract can be generated. The customer relationship gets stronger as the sales process progresses further and amendments can help make any changes to existing contracts. You will understand the renewal process that will generate revenue for your business for both subscription-based and non-subscription-based products and services. You will also learn how package configurations help in controlling the configurations and automation at the Salesforce org level.

Then, you will explore Industries CPQ and the types of businesses that need to implement this. This book provides insights into how Salesforce Billing replaces the multiple systems typically used by finance to create orders, send invoices, and collect payments. By the end of the book, you'll have gained CPQ knowledge that can be utilized to configure and customize various kinds of use cases for CPQ implementation in any type of industry.

Who this book is for

This book is intended for Salesforce professionals who have standard Salesforce platform knowledge and readers who are interested in learning about CPQ. This book helps administrators, business analysts, functional consultants, sales managers, and Salesforce architects understand CPQ configurations and customizations. This book also provides the foundational knowledge needed for any CPQ implementation project. Most of the CPQ concepts are explained using simple use cases.

This can become your go-to reference material that can be applied to any implementation as needed. Reading these chapters will also help those aspiring to gain Salesforce CPQ certifications. Working knowledge of the Salesforce ecosystem is recommended to get the most out of the book. It is recommended to create a Salesforce CPQ test instance and follow along with the examples provided in this book.

What this book covers

Chapter 1, Getting Started with Salesforce CPQ Implementation, provides a high-level overview of the quote-to-cash process for any business. This chapter describes the basic concepts of what CPQ is in Salesforce. Each Salesforce object concept (opportunities, quotes, products, price books, and quote templates) will be explained clearly and the high-level CPQ data model will be discussed. The details of how to configure these in Salesforce will also be covered. The decision as to when a Salesforce CPQ is needed will be explained. The different types of CPQs present in the market today will be briefly touched upon. The advantages of using Salesforce CPQ from a business perspective will be discussed. You can practice all these concepts using a free Salesforce developer org. Instructions for creating a free developer organization and CPQ installation will be provided.

Chapter 2, Configuring Opportunities and Quotes, walks you through, having understood what Salesforce CRM is and what you gain by implementing Salesforce CPQ in your organization, what Salesforce opportunities, quotes, and orders are. Using an example, you will understand the relationship between opportunities/quotes and products. Then, you will be guided with an overview to configure the opportunity and quote objects in Salesforce. You will explore the **Quote Line Editor** (**QLE**) in detail and understand several out-of-the-box features of QLE, including QLE customizations for different use cases. This chapter also provides the knowledge to implement advanced approvals and their advantages. Configuring advanced approvals for CPQ quotes will be explained in detail.

Chapter 3, Configuring CPQ Products, having understood creating and configuring Salesforce CPQ opportunities, creating quotes, and creating orders, will take you to the next step, which is understanding how to configure products. Product configuration is the bedrock upon which many CPQ configurations and automations can be built. Whatever the type of the business, either B2B or B2C, defining a product structure is very important. This chapter will help you understand what product options, features, and bundles are. You will also understand the power of CPQ product rules to automate business processes. All of these can be achieved with configurations and no Apex coding is required. As a power user, you are now ready to create custom CPQ actions and use custom filters for automating different business requirements. This chapter also provides the concept of the twin field feature in CPQ.

Chapter 4, Configuring CPQ Pricing, helps you to automate pricing and discounting. You will understand the CPQ pricing methods and the configuration. By the end of this chapter, you will understand how to define pricing, price structure, how multi-currency use cases can be handled, configuring price rules, discounts, and multi-dimensional quoting, and will be able to set up all these configurations in Salesforce using different use cases. Each concept will be explained by providing the Salesforce navigation path so that you can practice these in the test environment.

Chapter 5, Generating and Configuring Quote Templates, walks you through how Salesforce CPQ generates PDF quotes to send to customers. You will understand how dynamic templates can be used for quote generation. You will also learn the advantages of using quote templates. For sending quotes to the customer, you will learn how DocuSign, or any other third-party integration tool, can be used for the automation of quote signing by customers.

Chapter 6, Configuring Guided Selling, helps you understand how to use guided selling and its advantages. You will explore a guided selling use case and configuration details.

Chapter 7, Creating Contracts, Amendments, and Renewals, helps you understand why we need amendments and how to create amendments, amendment opportunities, and amendment quotes. You will also understand what Salesforce assets are. You will learn how to configure CPQ renewal opportunities and quotes automatically and be able to customize them for business-specific needs. You will also understand how evergreen contracts and autorenewals work.

Chapter 8, Configuring CPQ Package Settings, helps you understand what CPQ package configurations are and how some of these settings control the other configurations. This chapter also provides details on the prorate multiplier and how CPQ provides different options to configure the prorated pricing for subscription products.

Chapter 9, The CPQ Data Model and Migration Concepts, helps you understand how Salesforce CPQ objects are related to each other and how you can perform a data migration from a legacy system into Salesforce, as well as the order in which the objects need to be migrated. You will understand the CPQ Data Model and use Salesforce Schema Builder to view and configure object relationships. You will also be advised on CPQ deployment from one Salesforce org to another.

Chapter 10, Salesforce Billing, provides an overview of Billing, installation details, and the advantages. You will understand how Billing enhances CPQ capabilities with invoice generation, payment, and revenue recognition functionalities. You will learn how Billing implementation provides the ability to create quotes, orders, and invoices all on a single platform.

Chapter 11, Understanding Industries CPQ, provides an overview of Industry Cloud and where Industry CPQ falls within Industry Cloud. This chapter outlines high-level differences between standard Salesforce CPQ and Industries CPQ. You will learn the key features of Industries CPQ. You can create an Industry CPQ training org to further explore the features.

Chapter 12, CPQ Implementation Best Practices, provides you with some of the best practices recommended by Salesforce for getting optimal CPQ performance. Also, you will learn some of the standard implementation guidelines. Any tool that you use should be used efficiently. Salesforce CPQ is no exception; with proper implementation, you will reap the benefits. Otherwise, you will hit performance bottlenecks.

To get the most out of this book

You will get the most out of this book by practicing the examples and CPQ configurations in a Salesforce test instance or training instance.

Salesforce provides a pre-installed CPQ developer org for 90 days. You can get a free training org here: `https://developer.salesforce.com/promotions/orgs/cpqtrails`.

Alternatively, you can install the CPQ package in any Salesforce developer org. To create a developer org, sign up here: `https://developer.salesforce.com/signup`. Follow the instructions provided in *Chapter 1, Getting Started with Salesforce CPQ Implementation*, for installing CPQ.

For advanced approvals, install the package from this link: `https://install.steelbrick.com`. Follow the instructions provided in *Chapter 2, Configuring Opportunities and Quotes*, for installing CPQ.

You can create a test environment for configuring sample use cases and examples using Industries CPQ; refer to the Industry Cloud documentation on Vlocity University: `https://help.salesforce.com/s/articleView?id=000357469&type=1`. You can request a training environment by filling in the form at `https://vlocitytrial-prod.herokuapp.com/?templateid=SFI_IPQ`. This is a free instance that is available for a limited amount of time.

Download the color images

We also provide a PDF file that has color images of the screenshots and diagrams used in this book. You can download it here: `https://static.packt-cdn.com/downloads/9781801077422_ColorImages.pdf`.

Conventions used

There are a number of text conventions used throughout this book.

`Code in text`: Indicates code words in text, database table names, folder names, filenames, file extensions, pathnames, dummy URLs, user input, and Twitter handles. Here is an example: "Similarly, add the other product picklist API names (in this example, `Hardware type` and `Laptop type`) that you created in the product object."

A block of code is set as follows:

```
<apex:page standardController="SBQQ__Quote__c"
extensions="QuoteExtController" action="{!onRecall}">
<apex:pageMessages />
```

Bold: Indicates a new term, an important word, or words that you see onscreen. For instance, words in menus or dialog boxes appear in **bold**. Here is an example: "To configure contracted pricing, navigate to **App Launcher → Account → Related → Contracted Prices → New**."

Tips or Important Notes
Appear like this.

Get in touch

Feedback from our readers is always welcome.

General feedback: If you have questions about any aspect of this book, email us at customercare@packtpub.com and mention the book title in the subject of your message.

Errata: Although we have taken every care to ensure the accuracy of our content, mistakes do happen. If you have found a mistake in this book, we would be grateful if you would report this to us. Please visit www.packtpub.com/support/errata and fill in the form.

Piracy: If you come across any illegal copies of our works in any form on the internet, we would be grateful if you would provide us with the location address or website name. Please contact us at copyright@packt.com with a link to the material.

If you are interested in becoming an author: If there is a topic that you have expertise in and you are interested in either writing or contributing to a book, please visit authors.packtpub.com.

Share Your Thoughts

Once you've read *The Salesforce CPQ Implementation Handbook*, we'd love to hear your thoughts! Scan the QR code below to go straight to the Amazon review page for this book and share your feedback.

https://packt.link/r/1-801-07742-8

Your review is important to us and the tech community and will help us make sure we're delivering excellent quality content.

Section 1: Getting Started with Salesforce CPQ Implementation

This section focuses on providing Salesforce CPQ foundational knowledge. You will understand the quote-to-cash process and get an overview of CPQ Using simple examples, you will learn how to create CPQ quotes from opportunities and understand the relationship between opportunities, quotes, and products. You will focus on how products can be configured and customized, how complex pricing can be automated with applicable discounts, and how to create quotes accurately. You will understand how product rules, price rules, and quote templates can be customized for any business easily.

This section comprises the following chapters:

- *Chapter 1, Getting Started with Salesforce CPQ Implementation*
- *Chapter 2, Configuring Opportunities and Quotes*
- *Chapter 3, Configuring CPQ Products*
- *Chapter 4, Configuring CPQ Pricing*
- *Chapter 5, Generating and Configuring Quote Templates*

1
Getting Started with Salesforce CPQ Implementation

In this chapter, we will learn what **Salesforce CPQ** is, as well as begin to identify situations and business needs that can be aided by Salesforce CPQ. Typically, sales personnel spend a lot of time creating quotes, calculating prices, seeking approvals, and working through multiple legacy systems. These legacy tools may not be up to date and so are inaccurate, leading to delays in closing deals as well as impacting customer satisfaction. Salesforce CPQ helps to automate and streamline sales processes and create quotes quickly and efficiently, resulting in increased business revenue, the ability to forecast efficiently, and increased customer satisfaction.

In this chapter, we will cover the following topics:

- The relationship between the sales process and cloud computing
- Understanding the quote-to-cash process
- Introducing Salesforce CPQ

- Salesforce CPQ advantages
- Salesforce CPQ versus Industries CPQ
- Installing Salesforce CPQ

By the end of this chapter, you will be able to install Salesforce CPQ either in a Salesforce test environment or in a production environment. You will also understand when your business needs Salesforce CPQ. With the examples provided in the upcoming chapters in this book, you will learn how to configure, test, and automate Salesforce CPQ.

The relationship between the sales process and cloud computing

In the past, the sales process was done manually. Sales representatives used printed catalogs and assembled quotes by hand. These quotes would then be physically delivered to customers. Changes to a quote or fixing errors in either the product or pricing meant the quote process had to be started again.

Before cloud computing, closing deals included business cards and manual processing. Over the decades, though, the **sales process** changed along with the advent of technology, and businesses started using automation as a result.

A business that hosts everything in-house is called an **on-premises** model. The on-premises model of using software also has its own challenges in the form of a lack of flexibility and agility for the sales rep. When data is disconnected, sales reps struggle to keep up with demand. Without the sales process being automated, businesses would face longer sales cycles, resulting in revenue loss.

The limitations that businesses face with an on-premises model were tackled by the introduction of **cloud computing**. Cloud computing has taken the world of software by storm and the sales process has not been left out, consequently getting a boost in the form of automation with speed, enhanced security, ease of use, centralized reporting, and an efficient sales process.

Salesforce is one of the leading **Customer Relationship Management** (**CRM**) vendors, having realized the limitations of the traditional on-premises model, leading the transformation of the sales process through their cloud computing software.

With the evolution of cloud computing, the Salesforce sales process has also benefitted. We'll explore the quote-to-cash process in detail in the next section.

Understanding the quote-to-cash process

The sales process is key for any business to be successful. Although this seems pretty simple, right from leads entering the system, generating opportunities, quotes, shipping the products or services, and invoicing the customer, this process can become complex as your business grows. The **quote-to-cash process** refers to the sales process right from **opportunity** creation to the invoice being paid by the customer.

In any business, once the marketing team completes the lead generation process, the potential leads will be handed over to the sales team. This marks the entry point of the quote-to-cash process for the sales team. The first step in the quote-to-cash process is creating an opportunity to deliver a quote to a customer. Here is a look at the high-level quote to cash process (this is a generic sales process and this can be tweaked as per the customers' business needs):

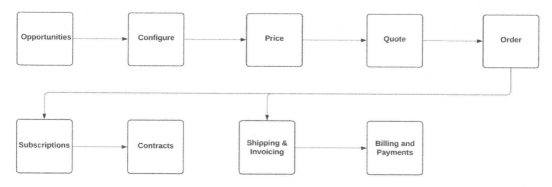

Figure 1.1 – Quote-to-cash process

The following are the major steps from *Figure 1.1* for the quote-to-cash process:

1. **Opportunities** are pending sales. You can create an opportunity in your system when the customer is interested in your business's products and services. In Salesforce, an opportunity can be created for an existing **account** or by converting a qualifying **lead**.

2. Using CPQ software, you can start **configuring** the products and services, create product bundles, and automate product selection.

3. The **price** is calculated automatically, and relevant discounts can be applied.

4. You can then present the **quote** to the customer. Multiple quotes can be generated to adjust products and prices as per the needs of the customer and the terms and conditions.

5. Once a quote is finalized and necessary approvals are completed, an **order** can be generated.

6. Based on your business model and the type of product you are selling, **subscriptions** and **contracts** can be created. For example, if there is a one-time purchase such as hardware for the products and services you are selling, there won't be a need for a subscription. If you have a warranty associated with a product, then you need to create a subscription associated with the product.

7. Once the customer agrees to place an order, it can be generated, and goods and services are **shipped** to the customer.

    Shipping and invoicing is not a pure CPQ process. Salesforce Billing can be used as an add-on to CPQ and helps customers to have an end-to-end solution on a single platform.

8. Finally, an **invoice** will be created, and the customer is ready to make a payment. Once the customer pays, **billing and payments** can be processed for the order.

In the upcoming chapters, you will learn in detail how to configure and implement Salesforce CPQ to automate this process. You will also see how **renewals** can be combined with **cross-selling** and **upselling** to increase revenue and continue selling to new and existing customers.

From the preceding brief description, you will realize the important role that the quote-to-cash process plays, from quote creation to payments for your products and services.

When the quote-to-cash process is part of an integrated system, it will result in the following:

- Revenue growth for the business
- Speed and accuracy in the sales cycle using automation
- Increased customer satisfaction
- Improved overall productivity and accuracy
- Profitability for the business

Important Note

All technical references in this book will be with respect to Salesforce only. You will be advised otherwise if a non-Salesforce-related topic is being discussed.

Now that you understand the elements of Salesforce CPQ and the quote-to-cash process, we will dive deeper into each of the components of **CPQ**.

Introducing Salesforce CPQ

CPQ is cloud-based Salesforce software standing for **Configure, Price, Quote**. This tool can be used to create a structured and scalable sales process for your company and can provide your customers with accurate pricing for your business's products and services.

Salesforce CPQ was originally called SteelBrick, which was a managed package. CPQ uses most of the standard Salesforce objects, including opportunities, products, and price books. Here are some of the key concepts of the Salesforce business process that will help us have a better understanding of CPQ:

- **Opportunities** are potential revenue-generating deals for your business. Opportunities go through different stages before the deal is either **Closed Won** or **Closed Lost**.

- **Accounts** are companies that you are doing business with, and **Contacts** are the people who work for them, while **Leads** are potential customers that may be people or companies. In B2B business scenarios, leads convert into a business account, contact, or opportunity. For B2C business scenarios, leads convert into a personal account and opportunity.

- **Products** and services are the items that your company sells. Each of these products can exist in single or multiple price books based on your business model. A **price book** contains the prices related to these products and services. We will explore these concepts further in *Chapter 3, Configuring CPQ Products*, and *Chapter 4, Configuring CPQ Pricing*.

When a CPQ package is installed, custom objects, including subscriptions and quote lines, are added, which extends the native functionality of Salesforce **Sales Cloud**.

In this section, we are going to dive into CPQ as a concept. This will help us to understand how accurately you can configure products and combine the right products into a single bundle or separately. You can also apply discounts and complex pricing to your products to generate a quote for your customer.

Let's start by exploring C for Configure.

Configure

You need to first **Configure** the product your company is going to sell to its customers. Typically, CPQ is used when the product configuration is more complex than what standard Salesforce can support. When there is a need for product bundling, validations, automatic pricing, and discount calculations, standard Salesforce requires heavy customizations that are hard to maintain. In addition, a simple error in adding a product can delay the sales process. If an error occurs, the rep will need to start the quote all over again and add the right products.

Using Salesforce CPQ, product configuration becomes simple and easy. This configuration can be achieved by answering a few questions related to what the customer wants to buy, including the type of product, quantity, and configuration. When these questions are answered, the related products will be displayed. Using out-of-the-box CPQ configurations products can be bundled together with related products or services, and reps can add the configuration with a few clicks. Bundles can also be configured based on a customer's specific needs.

For example, if your company is selling laptops, the rep does not need to remember the configuration of the laptop and the prerequisites.

Product managers can bundle the following:

- The hardware (laptop), power cables, mouse, and keyboard can all be bundled together
- The warranty, which will be a subscription product based on the customer selection

The rep can then add the configured bundles in one click. When the company has customers across different regions, based on the locations you are selling in, bundles can be adjusted accordingly.

For example, a laptop bundle sold in the US will include a US power cord and a US keyboard. The same bundle, when sold in EMEA, will contain a UK power cord and a UK keyboard.

Product configuration can also provide soft alerts or hard errors. When the rep is configuring and they forget to add an optional component, the system generates a soft alert: *Do you need to add a mouse pad?* The CPQ can force hard errors on the product configuration when the rep forgets to add a mandatory product such as the power cord.

Automations such as bundling accessories according to the geography and providing alerts if a mandatory component is missed while configuring the products can be configured in a timely manner with Salesforce CPQ. Using CPQ, sales reps will always generate error-free quotes and make the sales process a better customer experience.

In *Figure 1.2*, a sales rep can use previously created bundles with all the relevant products to create a quote. With one click, the bundle can be added to the quote, and all the products in the bundle will be added automatically.

	PRODUCT CODE	PRODUCT NAME	PRODUCT FAMILY	PRODUCT DESCRIPTION	LIST PRICE
☐	INTERIORBADGEREADER	Interior Badge Reader	Hardware		$65.00
☑	INTERIORCAMERA	Interior Camera	Hardware		$100.00
☐	INTERIORKEYPAD	Interior Keypad	Hardware		$55.00
☐	KEYBOARDUK	Keyboard UK Layout	Hardware		$50.00
☐	KEYBOARDUS	Keyboard US Layout	Hardware		$50.00
☐	Laptop 13 inch	Packt Laptop 13 Inch			$0.00
☐	LAPTOP13	13" Laptop	Hardware	13" Laptop	$1,300.00
☐	LAPTOP15	15" Laptop	Hardware	15" Laptop	$1,500.00
☑	LAPTOPCART	Laptop Charging Cart	Miscellaneous		$1,100.00
☑	LASERPRINTER	Laser Printer	Hardware		$275.00
☑	LDWARRANTY	Loss and Damage Warranty	Support		$0.00
☐	LTEHOTSPOT	LTE Hotspot	Hardware		$125.00

Figure 1.2 – Product Selection

In the **Product Selection** page, both standalone products and bundles can be selected as required.

Price

Reps do not have to burden themselves with memorizing the **Price** of products or referring to a third-party tool or a pricing catalog. They also do not need to waste time on spreadsheets and calculators for complex discount calculations. In addition, they do not need to refer to any additional details to provide extra discounts.

All the pricing logic and discounts can be configured in CPQ, which does all the complex math for you. As a result, reps can stop worrying about the calculations and concentrate on each customer's needs.

If the rep wants to apply discounts or make changes to any of the quantities, the quote can be updated in a matter of a few seconds with the click of a button. With prices changing dynamically for any business, CPQ can automatically pull the active price from the Salesforce **price book**.

A price book is similar to a catalog with the list of products and services that your company is selling, and the corresponding price associated with them. Salesforce provides two types of price books:

- **Standard price book**: This contains a list of all the products and services that your company is selling and their default standard prices. A Salesforce admin needs to create a price book entry whenever a new product is created. Also, if the product needs to be sold in multiple countries with different currencies, a price book entry is required for each currency.

- **Custom price book**: This contains all of, or a subset of, the products from the standard price book with custom prices called list prices. Custom price books are created to offer products at different prices based on region, market segment, or specific customers. For example, we can have one price book for all the products sold in the Americas and another for selling the same products in Asia or Europe.

CPQ allows different pricing methods based upon the type of product. Using the number of units purchased and the discounts applied by the rep, the quote's total price is automatically calculated by the CPQ engine.

Quote

When a sales rep is negotiating an opportunity, there can be multiple quotes. However, there can be only one quote that is marked as *primary*. A **primary quote** is a quote that will most likely be accepted by the customer, and this gets converted to an order. At any time, all the quote lines from the primary quote are synced to the opportunity.

It is now time to generate a **Quote** for the previously created product(s). Out of the box, Salesforce CPQ supports generating **doc** and **PDF** versions of a quote using a pre-built template. This quote template can also have the company logo embedded to create a professional quote. Dynamic quote templates can be used to change the quote's terms and conditions. We can also dynamically add sections to a quote. This can be integrated with e-signature software (for example, DocuSign) to send the quote to the customer in a matter of minutes and close deals faster.

Shorter sales cycles and more accurate data result in greater customer satisfaction day by day.

What does a quote template contain?

A quote template is a PDF document that contains the products and services that you are selling. It contains the prices associated with these products, including the discounts and the totals. It also includes the terms and conditions specific to your business.

To generate a PDF quote, navigate to a Salesforce org, App Launcher → Opportunity → Quote → Generate Document.

The quote template can be emailed directly to the customer. A sample CPQ PDF quote has been generated next using out-of-the-box Salesforce CPQ functionality:

AW Computing   Quotation

1 Market St, San Francisco, CA 94105, United States
Phone: (650) 987-6543 Fax: (650) 987-6544
Email: info@awcomputing.com

Quote #:	Q-00048
Date:	Mar 4, 2021
Expires On:	Apr 2, 2021

Ship To
Edge Communications
312 Constitution Place Austin, TX 78767 USA
Austin, TX

Bill To
Edge Communications
312 Constitution Place Austin, TX 78767 USA
Austin, TX

SALESPERSON	EXT	EMAIL	DELIVERY METHOD	PAYMENT TERMS
John Doe	x	@gmail.com		Net 30

QTY	PRODUCT	DESCRIPTION	UNIT PRICE	DISC (%)	EXTENDED
10.00	13" Laptop	13" Laptop	$1,000.00	10.00	$9,000.00
10.00	SSD Hard Drive 128GB		$50.00	10.00	$450.00
10.00	CPU 1.6GHz i5		$200.00	10.00	$1,800.00
10.00	Keyboard US Layout		$50.00	10.00	$450.00
10.00	Warranty		$300.00	10.00	$2,700.00
				TOTAL:	$14,400.00

Terms & Conditions

This quote is presented to the customer under the condition that it remains a valid quote for only 15 days after the stated Quote Date, after which the quote becomes null and void.

Signature: _____   Effective Date: ____/____/____

Name (Print): _____   Title: _____

Please sign and email to John Doe at   @gmail.com

THANK YOU FOR YOUR BUSINESS!

Figure 1.3 – CPQ PDF quote

You can preview the quote template before emailing it to the customer and change the terms and conditions as needed. You can also customize quote templates.

CPQ high-level object flow

While there are many aspects of Salesforce CPQ, the main objects are **products, pricebooks, accounts, opportunities, opportunity products, quotes, quote lines, orders,** and **contracts**. The following diagram shows a high-level CPQ object model:

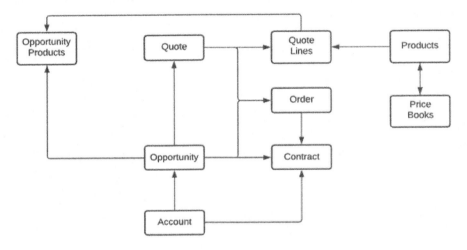

Figure 1.4 – High-level CPQ object model

Opportunity is created from an **account**. Once the **products** are added to the **quote** and the quote is made **primary, quote line products** sync to **opportunity products**. An **order** can be created from an opportunity or quote. Based on the products added to the quote, contracts and subscriptions can be created either from an opportunity or an order. We will learn about object relationships and the data flow in *Chapter 9, The CPQ Data Model and Migration Concepts*.

Salesforce CPQ Return on Investment Calculator

The decision to implement Salesforce CPQ for your business can be methodically calculated by using the **Return on Investment (ROI)** calculator, provided by Salesforce. This tool asks you to answer a set of questions that will help you make an informed decision. The questionnaire includes basic questions about your business, such as the number of invoices raised, the number of quotes generated, the number of sales reps, the hourly rates of sales reps, the gross profit margin of your products, and the annual revenue of your business.

The results of the ROI calculator will provide insights into your business regarding increased sales productivity, a reduction in invoicing costs, an increased win rate, and improvements in cash flow, to name a few. These indicators will help you make informed decisions for your business to be successful.

Here is the link for the Salesforce CPQ ROI: `https://www.cpqbillingcalculator.com`.

Now that you have an understanding of Salesforce CPQ, let's explore the advantages of implementing CPQ.

Salesforce CPQ advantages

Out-of-the-box Salesforce may not always support all your business needs. Sales reps sometimes struggle to sell complex products with their associated pricing. They resort to the manual generation of quotes to be sent to the customer. Generating quotes that are accurate is one of the biggest challenges that companies face. When the sales process is dependent on accurate data that the rep does not have access to or the quote does not reflect the products and services being sold to the customer, the following may occur:

- **A disconnected sales process**: When the data used by the sales rep during the sales process is disconnected, it is hard for the sales rep to refer to isolated product catalogs and price catalogs. This sales process will have data discrepancies when the information is stored locally if the source changes, (Microsoft Excel or Microsoft Word is referred to as the local copy). Referring to product codes or product names that have changed may result in the pricing not being accurate during the sales process.

- **Revenue impact and quote correction**: Generating quotes with information that does not reflect accurate pricing of products impacts revenue for the business. Furthermore, retracting such quotes could result in a longer deal closure and a loss of revenue as well.

- **Approval and bad customer experience**: Sales reps need to chase approvers manually for updated quotes, resulting in potential delays for the customer to receive these quotes. The sales organization may also see a bad customer experience when quotes are retracted, or when quote information needs to be corrected.

- **Sales forecast and lack of visibility**: The sales org will struggle to forecast the buying habits of the customer accurately and to keep optimal product inventory, resulting in revenue loss for the business.

- **A solution that is not scalable**: When customized solutions are implemented, the sales process is not scalable. Data will reside in silos and will depend on individuals for access and the retrieval of information.

To address the aforementioned shortcomings and to give more flexibility to the sales organization, Salesforce CPQ is the way forward.

Some of the obvious advantages of using Salesforce CPQ include, but are not limited to, the following:

- **A predefined process**: The disconnected sales process discussed in the previous section can be addressed using Salesforce CPQ. Salesforce CPQ helps you close complex deals quickly. Sales reps can use CPQ to apply discounts, automate product configurations, and create quotes. Salesforce CPQ serves as an internal e-commerce platform. Sales reps can add, modify, and delete items from the cart. The Salesforce CPQ configuration can help sales reps tailor product configuration. It will also act as a guard rail in providing the right products to the right customers.

- **Quote change and approval**: When the customer requests a change, the sales rep can generate quotes with the company branding and update and/or modify the quotes. Negotiations with the customer become easy for the sales rep, as multiple quotes can be created within a short time. With automation in place using Salesforce CPQ, approvals happen when the criteria are met. Changes to existing contracts that are to be shared with customers can be made easily with add-ons or amendments. Sales reps can generate quotes in Microsoft Word or PDF and can also share them with customers.

- **Pricing**: Pricing is part of the integrated system and sales reps do not need to refer to a third-party system. They can automatically apply discounts based on volume or customer tiers (for example, premium customers). Sales reps will be provided with proactive suggestions by the CPQ engine, which looks at the buying patterns of customers. These can be added to the cart and quotes will be updated accordingly.

- **Customer visibility and customer satisfaction**: The sales organization gets a 360-degree view of the customer and works on improvements if gaps are identified. By integrating third-party tools such as DocuSign, deals can be closed faster for better customer satisfaction. Salesforce CPQ is often referred to as the heart of the sales process, ensuring that business rules and technical rules are enforced in every transaction that goes through the system.

In the next section, we will look at Industries CPQ and when it can be used.

Salesforce CPQ versus Industries CPQ

Apart from Salesforce CPQ, the other CPQ used for specific business needs is Industries CPQ. Industries CPQ, formerly known as Vlocity, was acquired by Salesforce in 2020, and it is built on the force.com platform. The solutions that Industries CPQ provides are for specific industries that include telecoms, health, insurance, media, and entertainment. Industries CPQ requires a typically extensive programming effort and is not a direct competitor to CPQ. They serve different needs entirely, even though the end result is generating a quote. Industries CPQ helps companies with complex business models overcome the challenges that are unique to their industries.

Industries CPQ with Salesforce Service Cloud helps companies deliver a personalized solution. For example, in the insurance industry, combining Salesforce Service Cloud's omnichannel capabilities with Industries CPQ helps deliver a personalized and seamless retail experience. For the media and entertainment industry, Industries CPQ can provide a complete industry solution across subscriber and advertising sales life cycles for both B2B and B2C customers. Pre-built modules can be downloaded, deployed, and integrated, with Salesforce removing the burden on the business to come up with new solutions.

In *Chapter 11, Understanding Industries CPQ*, we'll cover more use cases and Industries CPQ tools and features.

Installing Salesforce CPQ

Having covered the need to implement Salesforce CPQ, as well as the advantages it offers, it is now time to install it.

Before the full implementation is deployed in the production environment, all the required configurations can be done in a test environment. The advantage of using a test environment is that deploying these configurations into production following thorough testing and approval by the business will leave little room for error. All use cases in this book will be demonstrated in a developer org using **Salesforce Lightning**. Let's get started.

> **Tip**
> You can skip the installation if you just need to practice CPQ configurations. Salesforce provides a pre-installed CPQ developer org for 90 days. You can get a free training org here: `https://developer.salesforce.com/promotions/orgs/cpqtrails`.

Before installing Salesforce CPQ, you will need to create a developer org. The developer org comes with sample data for all the Salesforce standard objects. To create a developer org, sign up here: `https://developer.salesforce.com/signup`. You can then verify your account via email and set up a password.

> **Important Note**
> Salesforce CPQ is a managed package and it needs to be separately installed on any Salesforce org.

Once you have created a developer org, you are ready to install Salesforce CPQ. The following steps can be followed to install CPQ in any Salesforce org:

1. Log in to the Salesforce org where the CPQ package needs to be installed.

2. If email deliverability is not enabled, you will not receive any email notifications. These could include notifications for the package installation status, for example, completed or failed. Before installing, make sure the **email deliverability** option is enabled for all users. Navigate to **Setup → Email Administration → Deliverability → Access level → All email → Save**.

3. To install Salesforce CPQ, go to `https://install.steelbrick.com`.

4. The latest version of the CPQ package is found under the **Package Installation Links** tab. The current Salesforce CPQ is **Spring '22** at the time of writing this book.

5. In the **Package Installation Links** tab, under **INSTALLATION LINKS**, there are two options: **Production** and **Sandbox**.

    I.   Click on the **Production** link to install in the production instance and click on the **Sandbox** link to install in the sandbox instance.

    II. To install the CPQ package in the developer org, click on the **Production** link under **INSTALLATION LINKS**. This will prompt the Salesforce login screen.

6. Log in to the Salesforce org by providing your credentials.

7. After logging in, you will be taken to the **Installation** screen (**Upgrade Salesforce CPQ**). Click on **Install for All Users** and then click **Install**.

8. From here, click **Approve Third-Party Access** and then click **Continue**.

9. The installation will begin, and it will take few minutes to complete. If the installation of the app takes longer, a notification will be sent to the registered email, once the installation is complete. You can close the **Upgrade Salesforce CPQ** installation window or leave it as is.

10. Verify the installed package by logging in to your developer org or the org where you have installed the CPQ package. Navigate to **Set up → Installed packages → Salesforce CPQ**.

11. After the package is verified, a new calculation service needs to be authorized in the CPQ package settings before configuring the CPQ automation. To do this, navigate to the **Set up → Installed packages → Salesforce CPQ → Configure → Pricing and Calculation** tab, and then click **Authorize New Calculation Service**. An *Authorize new calculation service* message will be displayed until the configuration is selected and completed, as shown here:

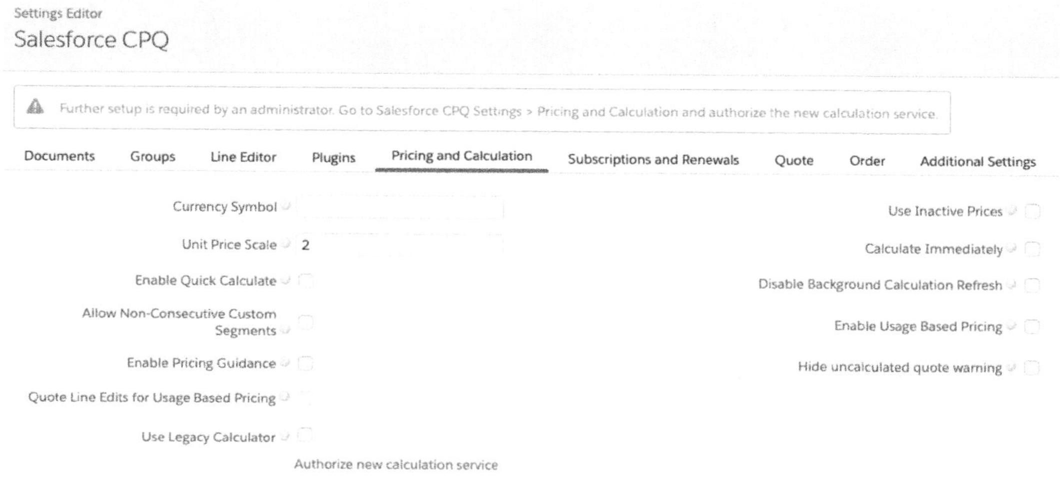

Settings Editor
Salesforce CPQ

⚠ Further setup is required by an administrator. Go to Salesforce CPQ Settings > Pricing and Calculation and authorize the new calculation service.

Documents	Groups	Line Editor	Plugins	Pricing and Calculation	Subscriptions and Renewals	Quote	Order	Additional Settings

Currency Symbol

Unit Price Scale   2

Enable Quick Calculate

Allow Non-Consecutive Custom Segments

Enable Pricing Guidance

Quote Line Edits for Usage Based Pricing

Use Legacy Calculator

Use Inactive Prices

Calculate Immediately

Disable Background Calculation Refresh

Enable Usage Based Pricing

Hide uncalculated quote warning

Authorize new calculation service

Figure 1.5 – CPQ package pricing authorization

Now that the package installation is complete, you are ready to configure CPQ as per your business requirements.

Summary

Great work! In this chapter, you gained an understanding of the stages through which a quote that is generated by the sales rep gets converted to cash. You also learned about situations where Salesforce CPQ has not been implemented and the difficulties that sales reps undergo with a sales system that does not support closing deals on time and with accuracy.

We have covered in detail what Salesforce CPQ offers to the sales organization in particular, and to your business in general. We also covered the individual components of **C**onfigure, **P**rice, and **Q**uote, its meaning, and how it fits into the sales process. We covered the advantages and the ROI for your business organization when CPQ is implemented. We also outlined the steps that are necessary for installing the Salesforce CPQ package. You will be able to utilize the full potential of quote-to-cash automation in the following chapters.

In the next chapter, we will cover how to configure opportunities and quotes, and how to automate approvals.

2
Configuring Opportunities and Quotes

Customers often ask for more than one quote when buying products or services. They compare the quotes' total prices and often spend more to get an additional discount. Alternatively, a sales representative can provide more than one quote to a customer to provide various options and close the deal faster. When the customer's budget is unknown, the sales rep will provide multiple quotes with different combinations of products and pricing. This chapter will help you understand how Salesforce CPQ can help create multiple quotes. You will also learn about the relationship between quotes, opportunities, and products or services, creating orders and returns in CPQ, and the advantages of using Salesforce CPQ Billing.

CPQ Billing can be used as an add-on to carry out end-to-end customer engagement that can be managed in Salesforce. Accounting systems can focus only on general ledger accounts. This facilitates having the end-to-end quote to cash process in Salesforce itself.

Upon completion of this chapter, you will be able to create an opportunity, associate it with a primary quote, submit the quote for approval, and complete the approval process. Optionally, you will also be able to create an order for the customer.

In this chapter, we will be covering the following topics:

- Salesforce opportunities, quotes, and products
- CPQ quotes and the quote line editor
- CPQ Advanced Approvals and configuration
- Creating orders from a quote

Salesforce opportunities, quotes, and products

Opportunities are potential revenue-generating deals for the sales org. They can be created from a lead conversion process, or a sales rep can create them manually from accounts in Salesforce. When a customer needs a quote, the sales rep can quickly use CPQ to generate the quote, add products using CPQ automation, generate the quote PDF, and then send it to the customer. If a customer already exists, then Salesforce **amendments** can be used. *Chapter 7, Creating Contracts, Amendments, and Renewals*, describes in detail amendments and renewals.

Let's learn how to create opportunities and quotes and add products in Salesforce CPQ.

Opportunities

Opportunities progress through different stages as the deal progresses from **Prospecting** to **Closed Won** or **Closed Lost**. Each opportunity stage is associated with a probability and these stages can be customized as per the business needs. As the stages progress, the probability of winning the sale will increase. We can also have a separate sales process for each type of sale (B2C versus B2B). These probabilities can also be used in **sales forecasting**.

For example, John Doe from Packt Communications is interested in buying laptops from you. Let's create an opportunity for Packt Communications:

1. Log in to your Salesforce organization and navigate to **Opportunities** → **New**.
2. Fill in the mandatory fields: **Opportunity Name**, **Stage**, **Close Date**, and so on.
3. Associate the account and click **Save**.

In the Salesforce Lightning experience, interactive tools such as the sales path *interactive visual representation* can be used to track deal progress and close deals faster.

The following figure shows an opportunity created in Salesforce CPQ and the corresponding stages:

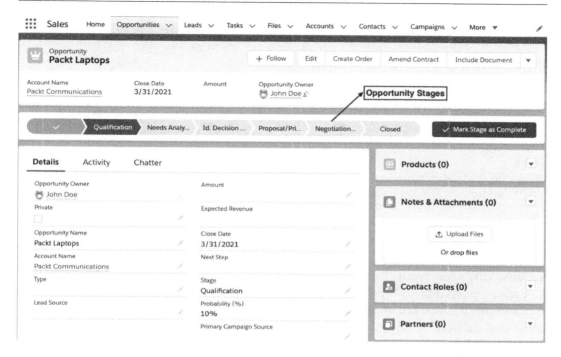

Figure 2.1 – Creating an opportunity

Each stage in the sales path can be marked as closed upon completion. The sales path can also be customized to show reps the mandatory fields that are required to move to the next stage level.

Now that you have created an opportunity, you are ready to create a quote.

Quotes

A quote contains the information on all products and services, including the pricing details.

During the negotiation phase, multiple quotes can be created for an opportunity. At any point in time, only one quote can be made primary. The primary quote has a special relationship with the opportunity. When the quote is marked as primary (by selecting the **Primary Quote** checkbox), all the quote lines will automatically be synced to the opportunity product lines.

Products

Products are goods and services that your company will be selling to its customers.

The following figure shows the relationship between **Opportunity → Quote → Product**:

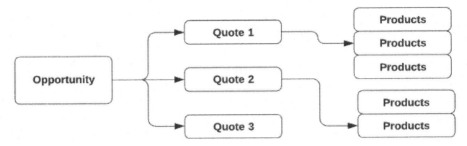

Figure 2.2 – Opportunity-Quote-Product

In *Figure 2.2*, **Quote 1** was initially marked as primary. Quote lines store the information about the products added to the quote. Products associated with **Quote 1** will be synced to opportunity products. If the customer does not agree with the initial quote, they may ask to modify a few products or to make some changes to the product quantity of **Quote 1**. A sales rep can quickly create another quote and change that to the primary quote. When **Quote 2** is marked as primary, all the products related to it will be synced to opportunity products.

Opportunity products contain information related to the products that you are selling, their quantity, price, discount details, and so on. You can add opportunity products as a related list to the opportunity page layout.

When a quote is marked as primary, Salesforce will sync the following fields from quote to opportunity products:

Quote Line Field	Field API Name	Opportunity Product Field API Name	Field Name
Net Unit Price	SBQQ__NetPrice__c	Sales Price	UnitPrice
Product Code	SBQQ__ProductCode__c	Product Code	ProductCode
Effective Quantity	SBQQ__EffectiveQuantity__c	Quantity	Quantity

Table 2.1 – Quote line to opportunity product mapping

Additional fields can be synced by using the **twin fields** functionality. A twin field is CPQ functionality that can be used for certain objects. Two fields can be called twin fields when they have the same data type and **API** names. Creating a twin field will automatically sync the data from one object to the other. Creating a twin field between the quote line and the opportunity product line will automatically sync the quote line value to the opportunity product.

The total price (the `TotalPrice` API name) on the opportunity product is calculated by multiplying the opportunity product quantity by the sales price (`Unit Price`).

When a customer requests a quote, the sales rep can provide multiple quotes, as applicable, from the opportunity. In the next section, we will see how reps can create multiple quotes and how Salesforce administrators can configure the quote creation process as per specific business needs.

Introducing CPQ quotes

In this section, we will discuss the one-time prerequisite to enable permissions that CPQ admins perform after the package installation. When your customer asks for a quote, they are looking for details about the products and services that they are planning to buy. Sales reps can create and modify quotes as per the customer's requirements.

Enabling CPQ permission set licenses

After installing the CPQ package, the Salesforce administrator needs to enable the **Permission Set Licenses** (**PSLs**) for configuring and customizing CPQ:

1. Users are required to have the PSLs assigned for interacting with Salesforce CPQ or **Advanced Approvals** (**AA**) related objects. To enable the CPQ PSL for a user, navigate to **Setup → Users**, click on the username for who you want to enable the CPQ permissions for, click **Permission Set License Assignments → Edit Assignments**, and select the **Salesforce CPQ AA License** and **Salesforce CPQ License** options.

Figure 2.3 shows enabling PSL assignment to user John Doe in a Salesforce test environment:

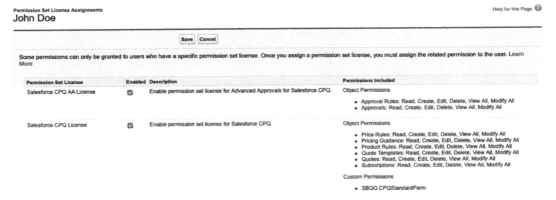

Figure 2.3 – CPQ permission sets

Enabling PSL assignments is an important step and without this, the user will not be able to use CPQ.

Salesforce administrators can execute **SOQL** queries in the Developer Console Query Editor to view the list of PSL assignments either for Salesforce CPQ or AA. PSLs are not available for standard Salesforce reports.

Admins can run these queries in the Developer Console and view the results to see who has access to these PSLs:

- **SOQL query to view a list of PSL assignments for Salesforce CPQ:**

```
select Assignee.Id, Assignee.Name,
  PermissionSetLicense.MasterLabel from
    PermissionSetLicenseAssign
Where PermissionSetLicense.MasterLabel in
  ('Salesforce CPQ License')
```

- **SOQL query to view list of PSL assignments for an AA package:**

```
select Assignee.Id, Assignee.Name,
  PermissionSetLicense.MasterLabel from
    PermissionSetLicenseAssign
Where PermissionSetLicense.MasterLabel in
  ('Salesforce CPQ AA License')
```

The next step is to assign CPQ permission sets to specific users who need to access CPQ.

To do this, navigate to **Setup → Quick Find → Users** (select the user for whom you need to enable the permission sets) **→ Permission Set Assignments → Edit Assignments** and add the **Salesforce CPQ Admin** and **Salesforce CPQ User** permission sets.

The CPQ object and field permissions (create, read, update, and delete) can be controlled by using the permission sets. *Figure 2.4* shows an admin user who has been assigned both the **Salesforce CPQ User** and **Salesforce CPQ Admin** permission sets:

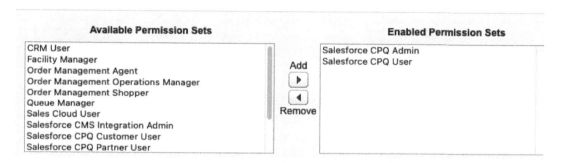

Figure 2.4 – Assigning CPQ permission sets to a user

The **Salesforce CPQ Admin** permission set can be assigned to only admins who maintain the system. End users who are not administrators need only the **Salesforce CPQ User** permission set. These two permission sets must be manually adjusted to include the necessary objects and fields to perform the correct tasks.

After enabling CPQ configurations, you are now ready to create a CPQ quote. Admins need to enable these configurations for users, and this is a one-time implementation task. Let's see how reps can create a quote.

Creating a quote

Salesforce administrators can assign PSLs to all the users who need to use CPQ. A CPQ quote can be created, modified, and edited using the **Quote Line Editor** (**QLE**). Implementation consultants and administrators can configure and customize the QLE in Salesforce. This will help reps to create quotes effectively and accurately. Any user with an active PSL and the CPQ permissions can now create a CPQ quote. Quotes are closely related to opportunities:

1. A quote can be created from the related list on the opportunity or the **New Quote** button in the opportunity. From here, navigate to an opportunity for which you would like to create a quote.

2. A Salesforce **custom action** can be used to create the quote. For this example, the custom action button **New Quote** has been created on the opportunity. In the **Opportunities** tab, click **New Quote** and the screen shown in *Figure 2.5* will be displayed. From here, select the quote's related opportunity and account details:

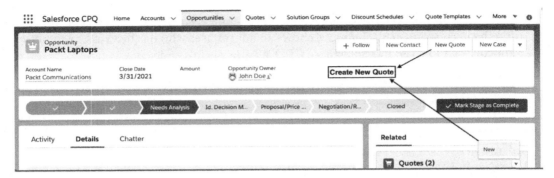

Figure 2.5 – Creating a quote from an opportunity

Mark the quote as **Primary** and click **Save** as shown here:

New Quote

Information

Quote Number   Opportunity ⓘ   ↺
                                              👑 Packt Opportunity   ✕

Primary ⓘ   ↺   Account ⓘ   ↺
☑   📇 Packt Communications   ✕

Type ⓘ   Primary Contact ⓘ
Quote   ▼   Search Contacts...   🔍

Status ⓘ   Sales Rep ⓘ
Draft   ▼   Search People...   🔍

Expires On ⓘ   Owner
6/15/2021   📅   👤 John Doe

ApprovalStatus
--None--   ▼

SubmittedDate

                         Cancel   Save & New   Save

Figure 2.6 – Creating a quote

3. Saving the quote will link the quote to the related opportunity for which it was created. To add products to the quote, open the quote, and click **Edit lines**. If this is the first quote, the system will prompt you to choose a **price book**. Select the price book. Any new quotes created after the first quote will use the price book that was already used for the first quote. The price book is set on the opportunity and all the quotes related to that opportunity must use the same price book.

4. Editing the quote lines will take you to the QLE. Open the quote and click on **Edit Lines**. This will open the QLE as shown here:

This quote has no line items. Click on Add Products button to select products.

Figure 2.7 – QLE

5. To add products and services to the quote, click on the **Add Products** button. This will display all the products that are associated with the selected price book. You can select products from the list. Alternatively, the products can also be searched using keywords:

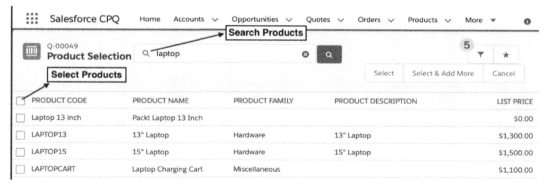

Figure 2.8 – Selecting products in the QLE

The filter icon can be used to show the search filter box while selecting products. This can be used to search by **Product Code**, **Product Name**, and **Product Description** by default. We can add or remove standard and custom fields by editing the product objects search filter field set.

6. Click **Save** after the products are added.

7. Because the quote is marked as primary, product lines from the quote will automatically sync to the opportunity.

Now that you have learned how to create opportunities and quotes and add products to quotes, in the next section, we will learn more about the QLE and how to configure and customize it.

The Quote Line Editor

The QLE is the user interface that Salesforce CPQ provides to reps for adding, deleting, and editing products. The QLE can be configured and customized as per your business needs. We can also apply discounts and markups and calculate the pricing.

Some of the Salesforce CPQ out-of-the-box QLE features that can be customized with configurations without using code are as follows:

- Additional columns can be added to the QLE header or lines using **field sets**.
- We can dynamically change the column headers and adjust the column width.
- Default buttons on the QLE can be customized as per the business needs using quick actions.

Products can be grouped together and related product images can be associated as required.

The following figure shows a sample QLE with the quote header, quote line fields, and default buttons:

	#	PRODUCT C...	PRODUCT NAME	QUANT...	LIST UNIT PRICE	ADDITIONAL DISC.	NET UNIT PRICE	NET TOTAL
☐	1	Laptop 13 inch	∨ Packt Laptop 13 Inch	10.00	$0.00	10.00 %	$0.00	$0.00
	2	LAPTOP13	∨ 13" Laptop	10.00	$1,000.00	10.00 %	$900.00	$9,000.00
	3	CPU16GHZI5	CPU 1.6GHz i5	10.00	Included		$0.00	$0.00
	4	RAM8GB	RAM 8GB	10.00	Included		$0.00	$0.00
	5	SSD128	SSD Hard Drive 128GB	10.00	$50.00	10.00 %	$45.00	$450.00
	6	CPU16GHZI5	CPU 1.6GHz i5	10.00	$200.00	10.00 %	$180.00	$1,800.00
	7	KEYBOARDUS	Keyboard US Layout	10.00	$50.00	10.00 %	$45.00	$450.00
	8	WARRANTY	Warranty	10.00	$300.00	10.00 %	$270.00	$2,700.00
							SUBTOTAL:	$14,400.00

Figure 2.9 – QLE quote header, quote lines, and products

Using the QLE, changes can be made at the quote header or quote line level. Fields on the header are stored in the **quote object** and fields on the lines are stored in the **quote line object**.

Let's learn how to customize the quote line header and line fields using field sets and customize different column and field visibility, as well as sorting. We will also learn how to customize the out-of-the-box QLE buttons and create new buttons.

Field sets

Fields that are displayed in the quote header or quote lines can be modified by customizing **field sets**.

Field sets are used to add or remove columns from the QLE. For example, based on the business process of your company, you may have a specific requirement where you want the sales rep to modify the *start date* and *end date* at the line level. Using the field set configuration, you can add these fields from the quote lines. To configure this in Salesforce CPQ, navigate to **Setup → Object Manager → Quote Line Object → Field Sets → Line Editor**, as shown here:

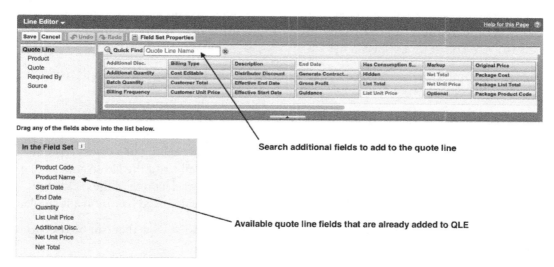

Figure 2.10 – Line editor field set

You can see the default available fields in the field set section of the QLE. You can also search for specific fields in the line editor and add those fields to the field sets. For example, if you would like to add the **Start Date** and **End Date** fields, search for them in the quick find, drag and drop the fields into the field set section, and click **Save**. In *Figure 2.10*, you can see that the start date and end date fields have been added to the quote line field set. This is similar to editing the Salesforce page layouts.

When you go back to the QLE and refresh the screen, you can see the new fields added.

Similarly, to customize the fields in the quote header section, the header field sets need to be configured. To configure quote header fields, navigate to **Setup → Object Manager → Quote → Field Sets → Line Editor**.

As per your business process, you can decide which fields are at the quote header level versus the line level. When there is a need for a particular field to be applied to all the lines, for example, the **Additional Disc.** field, we can add this to the header (the quote information section). Instead of editing each line of the quote, an update at the header level will apply to all the lines. A particular field can be added to both the quote header level and the line level. Sales reps can use these fields as required for editing.

Dynamically changing CPQ QLE column headers

The quote line object field set controls what columns are displayed in the QLE. When you add columns to a field set, these new columns will always be displayed. To dynamically change the visibility of these columns, we can use a list view or a **formula** field on the QLE header.

The quote field set controls what columns are displayed in the quote header section. Quote header columns can be dynamically changed using the Salesforce CPQ `HeaderFieldSetName` special field.

The QLE columns can be changed dynamically as per the business requirements using the Salesforce CPQ `EditLinesFieldSetName` special field.

For example, say your sales rep sells your product to both direct customers and distributors. When selling to distributors, you want to display an additional *distributor discount* field and this field should not be visible when you are selling to a direct customer. To do this, you can create a new **custom view** picklist value and add the **None** and **Distributor_view** picklist values. The rep can then manually select one of the picklist values in the QLE header, or this field can be automatically calculated based on a formula.

The following figure shows a sample QLE with a custom picklist view that can be used to dynamically change the quote line columns:

Figure 2.11 – Line editor field set

In the next section, we will see how administrators can configure the custom view values on the quote line header so that the quote line columns can be changed dynamically.

Dynamically changing the QLE list view using a picklist value

To change the QLE list view using a picklist value, create a new *distributor view* field set in the quote line object by navigating to **Object Manager → Quote Line Object → Field Set → Create New Field Set**.

Create a new picklist value (**custom view**) on the quote object. Based on the picklist value, the QLE view can be changed dynamically. Set a field label and the field name as EditLinesFieldSetName. The picklist values for this field need to be the API names of the field set that you have created on the quote line object. Field set API names do *not* contain __C.

To make this picklist value available in the quote information section, navigate to the quote line object line editor field set and add this new picklist field. The user can change this picklist value manually to modify the field sets and display the columns accordingly.

Dynamically changing the QLE list view using a formula

To change the QLE list view automatically, instead of creating a picklist field, create a formula in the quote object and set the return type as text. Based on the formula evaluation output, the corresponding field set will be displayed for the user.

Quote line drawers

Quote line drawers can be used to reduce horizontal scrolling on the QLE when you have many columns. Drawers will help you create a collapsible view for QLE columns.

The following figure shows a sample QLE with quote line drawers; clicking the > symbol in the QLE opens the quote drawer and displays additional fields (such as **Pricing Method** and **Original Price**):

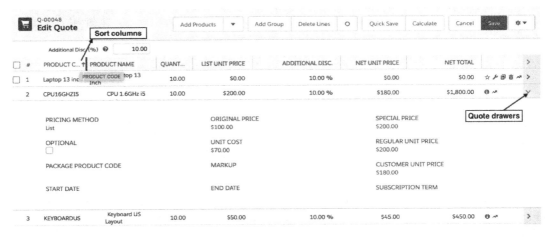

Figure 2.12 – QLE sorting columns

In the preceding figure, you can see that the important fields can be on the main view and the remaining fields can be moved to the drawer.

To create a drawer, navigate to **Setup → Object Manager → Quote Line Object → Field Sets → Standard Line-Item Drawer**. Add and delete QLE fields as needed.

Sorting QLE line columns

The columns in the QLE can also be sorted by clicking the up arrow shown in *Figure 2.12* next to the **PRODUCT CODE** field. Text columns can be sorted alphabetically, and numerical columns can be sorted ascending or descending. This feature is helpful for finding a specific quote line when there are a large number of lines.

Default buttons on the QLE

These are the default buttons that the Salesforce CPQ package provides out of the box. Let's see what functionality each of these buttons provides and how we can use them:

- **Add Products**: You can click on the **Add Products** button to navigate to the standard **Add Products lookup** page. All the products related to the quote price book will be available. You can select the products that need to be added to the QLE.

- **Add To Favorites**: This option can be used to add products to favorites. Reps can mark a product as a favorite product if it is sold frequently. The reps will not need to search for that product as it will be available in the favorites section. We can add previously saved favorites. In the QLE, clicking the small star icon will save that product to the favorites, as shown here:

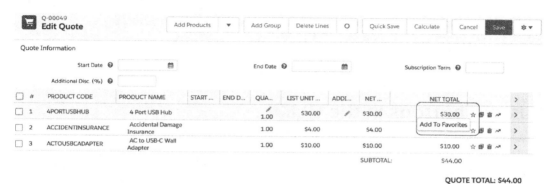

Figure 2.13 – QLE favorites

- **Add Group**: Groups help to apply discounts or obtain totals for specific sets of quote lines by organizing them into groups.

  A **quote line group** can be used to organize related quote lines. Quote line groups can also show multiple options for a customer to consider on one quote. All quote lines where the group's **Optional** field is set to **TRUE** are *not* synced to the opportunity and do not contribute to the quote total. Quote line groups are also useful if you are eventually shipping products to different locations or from different warehouses. **CPQ+** has **advanced order management**, which will split a quote into multiple orders. To create a group, from the QLE, click **Add Group**. Within the group, click **Add Products** to open the product selection page and select all the products that you would like to add. All the existing quote lines are added to group 1. A quote line group is only available for the specific quote it has been created for.

> **Tip**
>
> Quote lines with groups cannot contain any ungrouped items.
>
> Quote line groups do *not* transfer to an amendment or renewal, so should be used carefully.

To remove groups, you can click **Ungroup**.

- **Delete Lines**: This button is visible only if the Salesforce admin enables it for the specific user profile. Select all the lines that need to be deleted and click **Delete Lines**.

- **Quick Save**: Saves the record and the user stays in the QLE.

- **Calculate**: Calculates all the automation on quotes, including applying discounts, product rules, and price rules, and displays the results in the QLE. Changes are not saved to the database; changes are displayed only in the user interface.

- **Cancel**: Returns to the quote detail page without saving the changes.

- **Save**: Saves the changes to the database and returns to the quote detail page.

Custom buttons in the QLE

Custom actions can be used to create custom buttons in the QLE. These buttons can be used to customize the QLE according to the business' needs. Using custom actions, we can create a subset of products and/or a filtered view of our products from the price book.

For example, you can create a custom action to show only regional-specific products.

Imagine, if your company is selling products in multiple regions, you can create a custom button such as **US Products** or **EMEA Products**, and show only those subsets of products. We will learn more about custom actions in *Chapter 3, Configuring CPQ Products*.

Cloning a quote line

To enable the clone functionality, the CPQ package **Enable Multi Line Delete** setting must be selected. Select the clone icon to duplicate an existing line and reconfigure the product lines. We see that the quote line maintains all the field values and configurations. Any changes to the cloned quote line are not applicable to the original line.

Figure 2.14 shows a sample QLE with the **Clone Line** button:

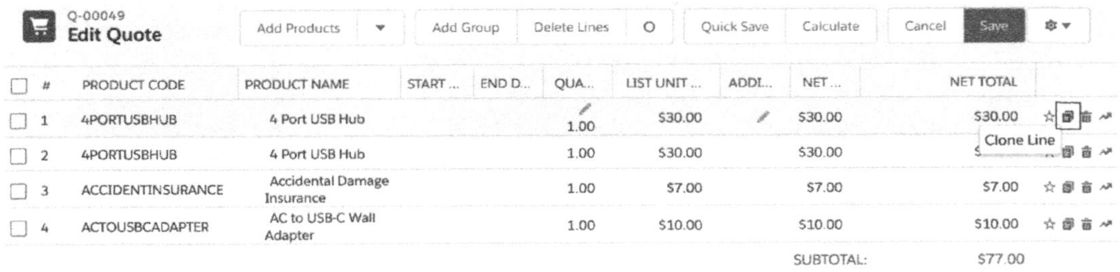

Figure 2.14 – QLE cloning lines

Customizing the QLE column width

When you have too many columns with long names, the column width can be adjusted as per the user's need to avoid horizontal scrolling. This feature was added as part of the Salesforce Summer '20 release. As we add more fields to the QLE, horizontal scrolling will be helpful.

To adjust the quote line field column width, drag the column (similar to Microsoft Excel) and save. Users can customize the layout by resizing the columns. The changes are saved automatically. Only columns can be resized and not rows. Also, the columns cannot be resized below a minimum width as users will lose complete visibility. Resizing columns will only apply to the field set you are editing and each field set needs to be resized separately. The column adjustments that you made can be reset back to the system defaults. Click on the gear icon on the QLE and click on **Reset Column Widths**:

Figure 2.15 – QLE Reset Column Widths

To enable this feature, navigate to **Setup → Installed Packages → CPQ → Configure → Line Editor → Enable column resizing** (checkbox).

You also need to give **CRUD (Create, Read, Update,** and **Delete)** permissions to the column metadata. Field set metadata object permissions are needed for the user profile.

In the next section, we will learn how to install and customize advanced approvals. When quotes created by reps need to be approved by a sales manager or a finance director, we will see how advanced approvals can be used.

CPQ approvals

The approval process in Salesforce defines how records are approved. For example, when the sales rep provides a discount that is over a certain threshold, based on your company's business process, the rep needs to get approval on the quote from the sales manager. In this section, we will learn about the approval processes available in Salesforce CPQ.

Salesforce provides two types of approvals: **standard approvals** and **advanced approvals**. Standard approvals are available as part of a Sales Cloud license. Advanced Approvals is an add-on license through Salesforce and is a part of the CPQ+ license. Let's look at these individually.

Standard approvals

The standard approval process is linear in nature. The progression through the process is dictated based on the approval of the current step. When a quote is submitted for approval, it goes through a series of approvals from the sales manager to the finance director, as shown in the following figure:

Figure 2.16 – Standard approvals

In this process, if any approver rejects the quote, the sales reps will make changes to the quote. The quote will need to be resubmitted and all the approvers will need to reapprove the quote, which delays the process.

Advanced Approvals

The approval process can be automated and customized using CPQ AA. For business scenarios with simple approval use cases, Salesforce standard approvals are usually sufficient. However, for businesses with complex approval workflows, CPQ offers AA; this allows a structure in which independent verticals, also known as **chains**, operate in parallel. These chains are independent of each other, and approvals can be triggered simultaneously for each chain.

AA works for any object in Salesforce, including standard and custom objects. Let's see an example of AA requiring approvals from multiple people, as shown here:

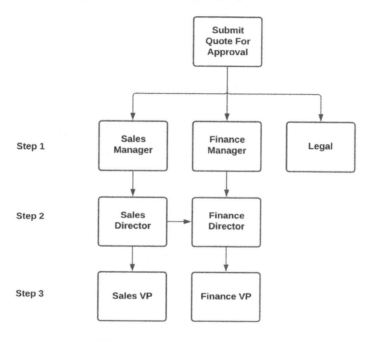

Figure 2.17 – Advanced Approvals

For example, if a quote needs multiple approvals from different stakeholders, as shown in *Figure 2.17*, it can be parallelly sent to all the approvers. The quote will be approved only if all the approvals within each chain are completed.

Reps can click the **Preview Approvals** button in the CPQ quote and view the status summary of the approvals.

Dynamic assignment of approvers is possible using advanced approvals. Following the process outlined in *Figure 2.17*, if the quote is submitted by a sales representative in the United States, it can be dynamically assigned to the United States sales manager. Similarly, if the same quote is submitted for approval by a sales rep in Europe, it can be automatically submitted to the European sales manager.

Using the smart approvals feature, if an approval is rejected by one of the approval members in the chain, Salesforce CPQ remembers the approval history. When the quote is resubmitted, the same users do not need to reapprove. Only the person who rejected the quote earlier needs to approve.

AA comes with a package that is built on top of Salesforce CPQ. AA comes with two permission sets: **admins** and **users**. Admins approve submissions and must be licensed users.

AA installation instructions

To use AA, we need to install the Salesforce AA package for our sandbox or production organization. CPQ installation is a prerequisite for installing AA. Follow these steps to install AA:

1. Open `https://install.steelbrick.com` in your browser.

2. Scroll down to **Advanced Approvals** and click **Production** or **Sandbox**, depending on where you are installing the package. Currently, Winter 22 is the latest version. Salesforce will upgrade the version automatically for installation as new releases are implemented:

Advanced Approvals

▶ PACKAGE VERSION NAME	VERSION NUMBER	RELEASE DATE	INSTALLATION LINKS	NOTES
Spring '22 *PRE-RELEASE*	236.1	2021-11-19	PRE-RELEASE DETAILS	
Winter '22	234.0	2021-07-23	Production | Sandbox	

Figure 2.18 – Installing AA

3. Follow the instructions, similar to the CPQ package instructions in *Chapter 1, Getting Started with Salesforce CPQ Implementation*, and install the package.

4. Once the installation is complete, the package will appear in the installed package list in your sandbox/production organization.

Configuring AA for a quote object

The Salesforce CPQ package enables AA for opportunities by default. In this section, you will see how Salesforce administrators can enable and configure AA for CPQ quotes:

> **AA for Other Standard or Custom Objects**
> The same instructions can be followed to enable AA for any other object.
> (Replace the quote with the object for which you want to enable AA.)

5. On the approval object, create a lookup for the quote.

    Navigate to **Setup → Object Manager → Approval Object → Fields & Relationships → New → Lookup Relationship → Next → Related to (Quote) → Field Name (Quote) → Next → Make the field visible → Next → Save**.

6. Create an **Approval Status** picklist field on the quote object.

    Navigate to **Setup → Object Manager → Quote → Fields & Relationships → New → Picklist → Field Label (Approval Status)** and set the API name as `ApprovalStatus__c`. Make sure that the API names match exactly and add the following picklist values, then click **Next → Save**.

    Lets add the following picklist values:

    - Pending
    - Approved
    - Rejected
    - Recalled

    Figure 2.19 shows the **ApprovalStatus** picklist field creation in a Salesforce test instance:

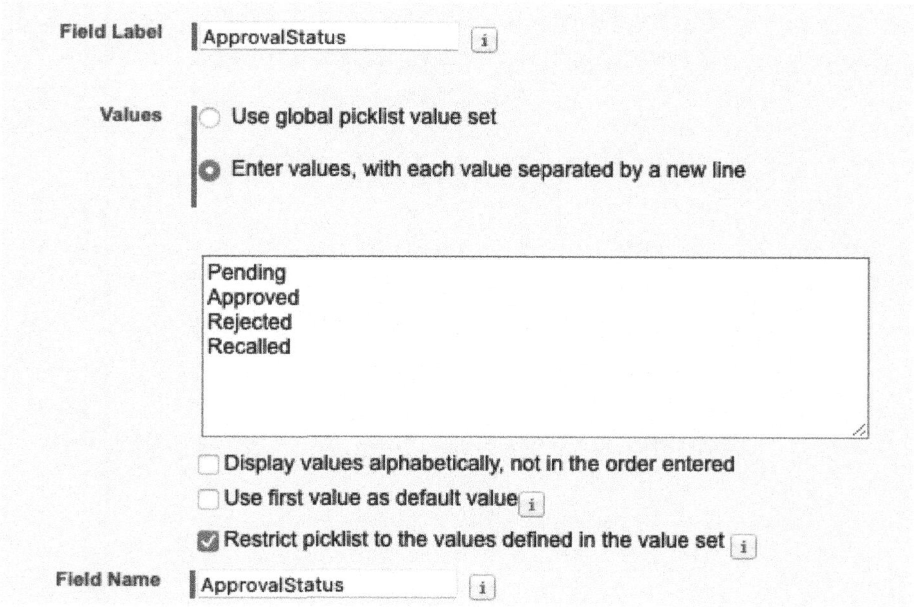

Figure 2.19 – Creating an ApprovalStatus picklist field on a quote

7. Create a **Submitted Date** date field on the quote object. Set the API name as `SubmittedDate__c`.

8. Create one more lookup field, called **Submitted User**, on the quote object. Set the API name as `SubmittedDate__c`. This lookup is related to the user object.

9. Make sure that the `Invalid_First_Segment_Term_End_Date` validation rule on the quote object is inactive.

10. Create a `QuoteExtController` apex class. To do this, navigate to **Setup → Quick Find → Apex Classes → New**, paste the `class QuoteExtController` code, and save.

`QuoteExtController` can be used in the Visualforce page where the admin can create the `SubmitQuote` and `RecallQuote` buttons:

```
public with sharing class QuoteExtController {
    private Id quoteId;
    public QuoteExtController(ApexPages
        .StandardController stdController) {
            quoteId = stdController.getId();
    }
    public PageReference onSubmit() {
        if (quoteId != null) {
            SBAA.ApprovalAPI.submit(quoteId,
                SBAA__Approval__c.Quote__c);
        }
        return new PageReference('/' + quoteId);
    }
    public PageReference onRecall() {
        if (quoteId != null) {
            SBAA.ApprovalAPI.recall(quoteId,
                SBAA__Approval__c.Quote__c);
        }
        return new PageReference('/' + quoteId);
    }
}
```

11. Create another apex class, called `QuoteExtControllerTests`, and copy the `class QuoteExtControllerTests` code. This is the test class for the `QuoteExtController` class.

This test class will help the Salesforce administrator to deploy the `QuoteExtController` code to the Salesforce production instance:

```
@isTest
private class QuoteExtControllerTests {testMethod
  static void testSubmit() {
    SBQQ__Quote__c quote = new SBQQ__Quote__c();
    insert quote;    Test.startTest();
    QuoteExtController con = new
      QuoteExtController(newApexPages
        .StandardController(quote));
    con.onSubmit();
    quote = [SELECT ApprovalStatus__c FROM
      SBQQ__Quote__c WHERE Id = :quote.Id LIMIT 1];
    Test.stopTest();    System.assertEquals
      ('Approved', quote.ApprovalStatus__c);
  }  testMethod static void testRecall() {
    SBQQ__Quote__c quote = new SBQQ__Quote__c();
    insert quote;    Test.startTest();
    QuoteExtController con = new QuoteExtController
      (new ApexPages.StandardController(quote));
    con.onRecall();
    quote = [SELECT ApprovalStatus__c FROM
      SBQQ__Quote__c WHERE Id = :quote.Id LIMIT 1];
    Test.stopTest();
    System.assertEquals('Recalled',
      quote.ApprovalStatus__c);
  }
}
```

We are now ready to create the Visualforce pages for submitting and recalling a quote. Next, we can add buttons to submit a quote for approval, recall a submitted quote, and preview the approval process. Let's learn how an admin can configure AA and add these buttons to the quote page layout.

Creating AA buttons

Sales reps can use AA buttons to submit a quote for approval, recall an already submitted approval, or preview the approval status. These buttons will be available on the CPQ quote object. Let's learn how to create these buttons using CPQ configurations:

1. Create two Visualforce pages, one for the `SubmitQuote` button, which can be used to submit a record for approval, and the other for `RecallQuote`, which reps can use when recalling submitted quotes.

2. To create the **SubmitQuote** button, navigate to **Setup** → **Quick Find box** → **Visualforce Pages** → **New**. Apply the following settings:

   - **Label**: `SubmitQuote`

   - **Name**: `SubmitQuote`

   - **Visualforce Markup**:

   ```
   <apex:page standardController="SBQQ__Quote__c"
    extensions="QuoteExtController" action="{!onSubmit}">
   <apex:pageMessages />
   </apex:page>
   ```

3. To create the `RecallQuote` button, navigate to **Setup** → **Quick Find** box → **Visualforce Pages** → **New**. Apply the following settings:

   - **Label**: `RecallQuote`

   - **Name**: `RecallQuote`

   - **Visualforce Markup**:

   ```
   <apex:page standardController="SBQQ__Quote__c"
    extensions="QuoteExtController" action="{!onRecall}">
   <apex:pageMessages />
   </apex:page>
   ```

4. Create three buttons, **Submit for approval**, **Recall approval**, and **Preview approval**, and link them to the Visualforce pages created in *steps 2* and *3*.

5. To create the **Submit for approval** button, navigate to **Setup** → **Object Manager** → **Quote** → **Buttons, Links, and Actions** → **New Button or Link**:

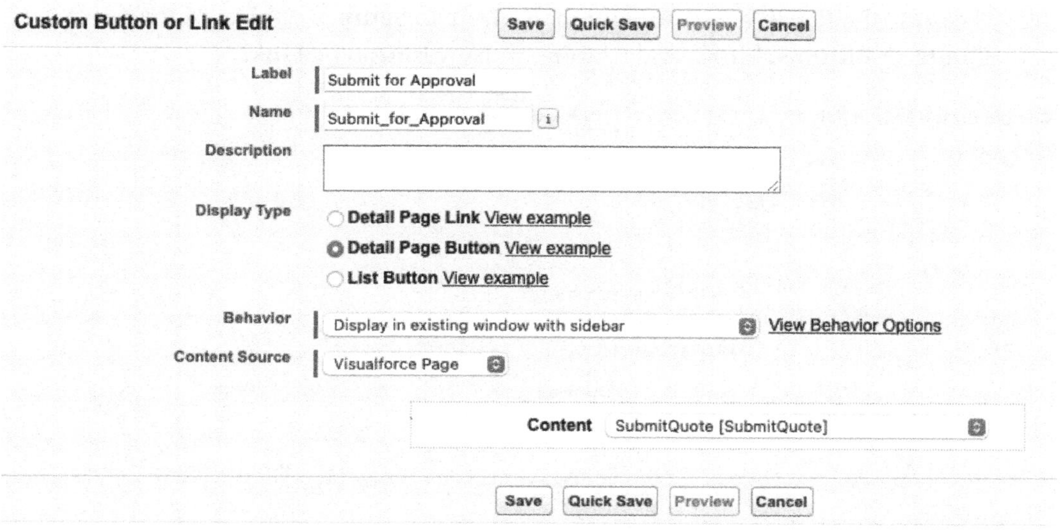

Figure 2.20 – Creating the Submit for Approval button

A Salesforce admin can create a **Submit for Approval** button as shown in *Figure 2.20*. End users can use these buttons on the quote record to perform the corresponding actions. The following settings should be filled in:

- **Label**: Submit for Approval. This will be the label of the button that will be displayed to the user on the quote object.

- **Name**: Submit_for_Approval. This unique name will be used by the API and managed packages.

- **Display Type**: This determines where the button or link appears on the page layout. Using this option, we can create a button that we can add to the heading of the quote detail page. These buttons perform an action on the record that the user is viewing.

- **Behavior**: This defines where the interface will open when the user clicks the button. For this example, we have selected to display it in the existing window with a sidebar.

- **Content Source**: This can have the values **URL**, **OnClick JavaScript**, or **Visualforce Page**. For this example, we have selected **Visualforce Page**. For this, we can use the Visualforce page defined in *step 2* with a standard controller.

- **Content**: **SubmitQuote [SubmitQuote]**. We will use the `QuoteExtController` Apex class that we have previously created.

6. To create the **Recall Approval** button, navigate to **Setup → Object Manager → Quote → Buttons, Links, and Actions → New Button or Link**:

Figure 2.21 – Creating the Recall Approval button

Create the **Recall Approval** button as shown in *Figure 2.21*:

- **Label**: `Recall Approval`. This will be the label of the button that will be displayed to the user on the quote object.

- **Name**: `Recall_Approval`. This unique name will be used by the API and managed packages.

- **Behavior**: This defines where the interface will open when the user clicks the button. For this example, we have selected to display it in the existing window with a sidebar.

- **Content Source**: For this example, we have selected **Visualforce Page**. For this, we can use the Visualforce page defined in *step 3* with a standard controller.

- **Content**: **RecallQuote [RecallQuote]**. We will use the `QuoteExtController` Apex class that we have previously created.

7. To create the **Preview Approval** button, navigate to **Setup** → **Object Manager** → **Quote** → **Buttons, Links, and Actions** → **New Button or Link**:

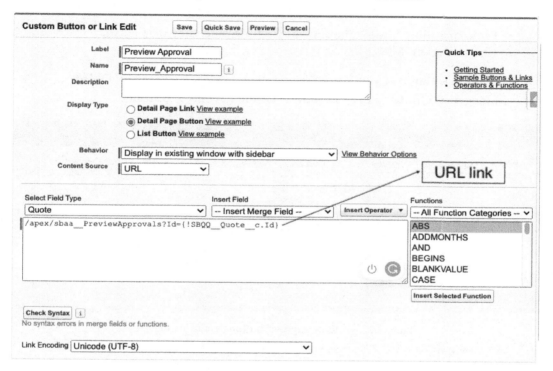

Figure 2.22 – Creating the Preview Approval button

Create the **Preview Approval** button as shown in *Figure 2.22*. Clicking this button on the quote object will redirect the user to the CPQ **Preview Approvals** page and pass the quote ID as the parameter:

- **Label**: Preview Approval. This will be the label of the button that will be displayed to the user on the quote object.

- **Name**: Preview_Approval. This unique name will be used by the API and managed packages.

- **Behavior**: This defines where the interface will open when the user clicks the button. For this example, we have selected to display it in the existing window with a sidebar.

- **Content Source**: This can have the values **URL**, **OnClick JavaScript**, or **Visualforce Page**. For this example, we have selected **URL**.

- **URL link**: For the content source URL, this field provides the URL link. Paste the URL `/apex/sbaa__PreviewApprovals?Id={!SBQQ__Quote__c.Id}` and click the **Check Syntax** button to verify the syntax.

- **Link Encoding**: Choose the encoding setting. Encoding defaults to **Unicode (UTF-8)**.

8. To add these buttons to the quote page layout, navigate to **Setup → Object Manager → Quote → Page Layout → Quote Layout → Buttons**:

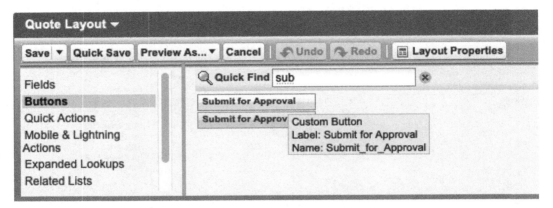

Figure 2.23 – Adding approval buttons to the quote page

As shown in *Figure 2.23*, we see two **Submit for Approval** buttons: one is the standard button and the other is a custom button for CPQ approvals.

9. Add the custom button to the quote page layout, which will be used to submit approvals. Add the other two buttons, **Recall Approvals** and **Preview Approvals**, to the quote page layout. Reps can use these buttons to perform the corresponding actions.

Setting up email services for advanced approvals

Once a record is submitted for approval, the approver can respond with an email that automatically approves or rejects the record. The keyword for approval or rejection can be set in the AA package configuration.

To set up the approval keyword for your Salesforce organization, navigate to **Setup → Quick Find → Installed Package → Advanced Approvals → Configure** to set up the **Approved Keywords** (for example, `Approved`, `Approve`, `Yes`) and **Rejected Keywords** (for example, `Rejected`, `Reject`, `Decline`, `No`).

Approvers can respond to emails with these keywords for approvals and rejections.

Setting up an email service

Setting an email service and email service address is a prerequisite for applying the email responses to AA. This email service will help approvers to receive notifications in their mailbox and they can use the keywords in their responses. The corresponding record in Salesforce will be updated with an approved status or rejected status based on the response. To configure the email service, follow these steps:

1. Make sure your **Orgs email deliverability** is set to **All Email**.

2. Navigate to **Setup** → **Email Services** → **New Email Service**. Enter email service name (`Approval Services`) → **Apex class (ApprovalEmailHandler)** → **Accept email from** (input domain details as needed, for example, mail.com) → **Failure responses section** → **Bounce message for all the fields** → select **Enable Error Routing** → **Route email** (administrator email) → **Save**.

   Refer to *Figure 2.24* for the email service configuration:

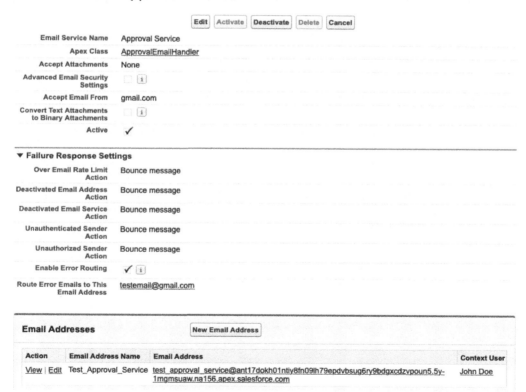

Figure 2.24 – Approval email service

The preceding approval service is set up to accept emails from Gmail. You can add other service providers, such as Yahoo or Hotmail, as needed. The email service created in *Figure 2.24* needs to be linked to the CPQ AA package setting.

Enable Error Routing

When email services cannot process an incoming email, enabling error routing in the failure response settings sends an error message to the email specified in the **Route Error Emails to This Email Address** field.

Connecting the email service to AA

To enable email approvals, copy the email address from the email service in *Figure 2.24* and update this email address in the AA approval package configuration.

Navigate to **Setup → Quick Find → Installed Packages → Advanced Approvals → Configure** and paste the email address in the **Inbound Approval Email** (Long) field and save the changes.

Setting up AA email templates

Visualforce AA email templates need to be configured to send the AA process email in response to an approval **request**, **rejection**, **recall**, or **approval**. It's recommended to create a separate email template for each of these actions. In this example, we will walk through creating an email template for setting up a request email. You can follow these same steps for creating email templates for the remaining actions:

1. First, we need to create a Salesforce Visualforce email template and then link it with an AA email template record. To create an email template, navigate to **Setup → Quick Find Box → Classic Email Templates → New Template → Visualforce → Next**. This will open the screen shown in the following screenshot:

SETUP
Classic Email Templates

New Template

Select the appropriate folder and enter the name and description for the email template below. Note that the Description field is for internal use only.

Once you have completed the Visualforce email template, check the "Available For Use" box to make this template available to your users.

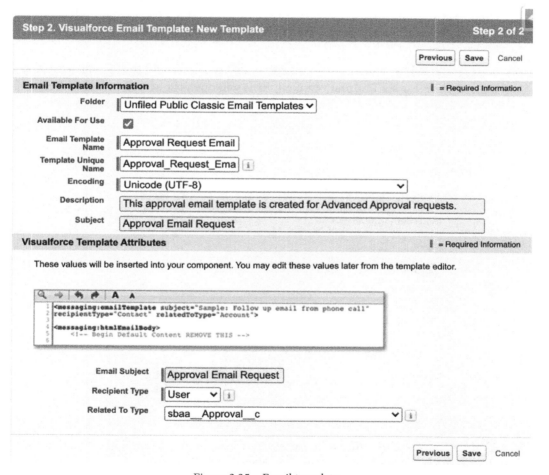

Figure 2.25 – Email template

Set the following fields:

- Choose the **Folder** where you want to store the email template.

- Select the **Available For Use** checkbox.

- Update the mandatory fields, such as **Email Template Name**, **Template Unique Name**, **Encoding**, and **Email Subject**.

- Set **Recipient Type** to **User** and **Related to Type** to **sbaa_Approval__C**. This is the object from which the email template merge fields will be selected.

2. Once you're done, click on **Save**. Edit the email template that you created, and make sure that the template contains the reference to the ID of your approval record. Add the text and any markup that you want to show in your approval request email. For example, to style the code's text color as white, the sample code is `<p> "style=color:white" "apex:outputText" value="{!relatedTo. ID}" </p>`.

3. Next, you need to create an AA email template record. To do this, navigate to **App Launcher → Email Template → New**. This will open the screen as shown here:

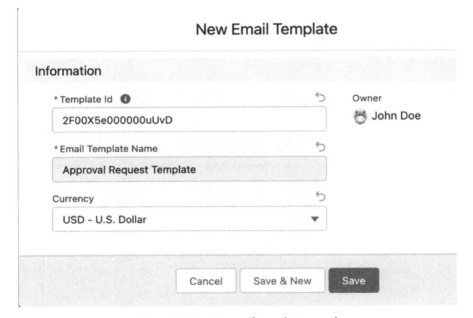

Figure 2.26 – AA email template record

4. Update **Template Id**. This is the Salesforce ID of the email template created in the first step. Set the field **Email Template Name** and click **Save**.

The AA approval email template is now ready to use.

AA objects

Once AA is configured for the quote object, the approval rules can be created as per the business needs. Installing AA creates all the related components from the package, including a few main objects:

- **Approver**: An approval request can be sent to a user or a group within Salesforce. Approvers are assigned to a rule that will fire based on one or more conditions. An approver record is typically named for the job role and not the individual. All users who will be a part of AA (including individual salespeople) must have an approver record created for them. An approver can approve or reject an approval request.

- **Approval rule**: Approval rules drive the process. Approval rules can be defined based on your business requirements. For example, if the finance manager wants to approve all quotes where the rep provides a discount that is more than 25%, we can define an approval rule with this condition. Additional conditions can be added as needed, such as when you want to fire this approval rule only for quotes where the quote total exceeds $50,000.

- **Approval condition**: All approval rules need at least one approval condition. Approval condition fields can be used to create a logical statement. For example, when we have two approval conditions, the first one based on the discount percent and the next condition based on the quote total, we can combine these two conditions with an and operator.

- **Approval chain**: An approval chain can be created when you need to send approvals in a specific sequence. For instance, say you want to send an approval to the sales manager first, and then trigger the next level to the sales director, and then to the sales vice president.

- **Approval variable**: Approval variables are child objects of approval rules. They aggregate data from child records for evaluating a condition. These variables can be used in place of standard rollups and apex triggers for aggregating data. These are evaluated in synchronous mode.

Let's see how an admin can configure approvals using these CPQ objects.

Creating a new approver

To create an approver, navigate to the approver object and click on **New**. Fill in the approver name. Then, update the **User** field, either with a single user or a user group. You can also use a delegated approver if the primary approver is on vacation.

Let's look at creating an approval rule, condition, and chain. Based on the business criteria for approvals, these configurations can be customized. When the rep adds the products to the QLE, CPQ AA will trigger in the backend. Records that need approval will be assigned to the approver automatically and the quote status will be pending approval until the approvals are completed.

Creating a new approval rule

To create an approval rule, navigate to **App Launcher** → **Approval Rules** → **New**

and follow these steps:

1. Fill in the rule name and the target object to evaluate the rule.

2. Mark it as active and fill in the approval step based on where it fits in the approval chain and update the approver to whom the request should go.

   Approval chains can send approvals to several approvers in a sequence or in parallel paths.

3. Then, set the combination of conditions the rule must meet. Email templates can be included to send the approval requests. These must be **Visualforce** based email templates.

Defining the approval condition

To define an approval condition, navigate to **App Launcher** → **Approval Rules** → **Related** → **Approval Conditions** → **New**. Then, follow these steps:

1. If the approval rule evaluates several conditions in a logical statement, provide an index value referencing each condition.

2. Select the approval condition test by choosing the tested field or tested variable.

3. Update the filter information for evaluating the conditions.

Creating a new approval chain

To create an approval chain, navigate to the **App Launcher** → **Approval Chains** → **New**.

Provide the chain name. In the target object name, provide the object for which you want to run the approval process. Click **Save**.

After the quote is approved, the sales rep can create an order for the customer. In the next section, we will learn about CPQ order management.

Advantages of creating orders from a quote

When a customer is ready to order, an order can be created from the quote. Orders contain order products for each of your quote lines. Creating orders is a prerequisite for using **Salesforce Billing**. Orders are also a great location for integrations with other services beyond Salesforce Billing. You can create invoices from an **order** object using **Salesforce Billing**. We will learn more about Salesforce Billing in *Chapter 10, Salesforce Billing*.

Advanced order management is available for customers who buy **CPQ+** licenses. With this feature, a business can provide a single quote for multiple orders, making it possible for the business to deliver the shipment to multiple locations at different times. In addition, an order object can be used to activate subscriptions after their implementation.

Enabling orders

Before users can create orders, Salesforce admins need to perform a one-time activity: enabling orders at the org level. To enable orders, log in to your Salesforce org and navigate to **Setup → Quick Find → Orders → Enable Orders → Save**.

Orders must also be configured to support negative quantity lines. To do this, navigate to **Setup → Quick Find → Order Settings → Enable Negative Quantity**.

Use Salesforce profiles or permission sets to assign user and object permissions to the appropriate users. Orders can be disabled to hide order-related data. To access the data again, re-enable orders.

Orders must be created from a primary quote. The primary quote cannot be modified after an order is created. List price, unit price, and the total price will be inherited from quote to order. Orders can be created using the **Create Order** button on an opportunity or quote. Alternatively, setting the **Ordered** field to **True** on an opportunity or quote and saving the record will automatically create an order.

For an end-to-end solution on quote-to-cash automation, both order management and Salesforce Billing can provide a lot of advantages and shorten the sales cycle.

Summary

This chapter helped you understand how you can create an opportunity, quote, and quote line items. You also learned when AA can be applied for a quote object. By applying the approval rules to CPQ quotes at various stages, you can speed up the whole approval process, as well as customize the CPQ package as per your business needs. The QLE interface helps you to create quotes easily and accurately. You have also seen the advantages of implementing orders and how to enable orders.

In the next chapter, you will learn how to configure product bundles and further automation related to product configurations.

3
Configuring CPQ Products

In this chapter, we will discuss product configurations and their crucial role in CPQ implementation. As your business grows, the complexity of operations increases. Based on your business process, you need to decide what information to capture at the product level, how to define your product catalog, and how to break up the product components. This solely depends on the type of product or service you are selling. CPQ configuration supports both products and services. Products and services can be configured as non-subscription and subscription products in CPQ.

For example, if you are selling a laptop and an associated service as warranty and support, some of these components may be mandatory and some may be optional that a rep can select, based on which the pricing will change. You cannot build a laptop without a hard drive or memory, but the size of these components can be changed by selecting different options. Each of these options will have a different price. All these components that make up the laptop need to be defined as products and Salesforce CPQ can help build the configuration by automating the product selection process and guiding the rep. Sometimes, preconfiguring all the mandatory products into a laptop bundle will be helpful. These products can be added to the quote easily, and the rep can concentrate on selling the configurations rather than having to remember their details.

If your company is selling huge medical equipment, such as an X-ray unit, you need to decide what components need to be defined as products. You cannot define every component, such as the nuts and bolts, as a product, as they will be added to the quote and it will become impossible to manage. We will see how CPQ product attributes can help organize these products.

The success of CPQ implementation depends a lot on the product master data and its configuration. In this chapter, we will learn different ways for how a product can be configured and how we can bundle products together, define options, and define product features. In addition, we will learn how a Salesforce admin can manage these configurations in CPQ so that the reps can easily add them to quotes and work efficiently to close deals faster.

In particular, we will be covering the following topics:

- Products overview
- Configuring products
- Configuring product bundles
- Creating product rules
- Creating custom actions and search filters
- Creating twin fields

Products overview

Salesforce CPQ uses the native Salesforce product object. Before a product can be added to a quote, the product needs to be configured and activated in Salesforce. Based on your company's business process, you would need to create the products and define attributes such as the product code, product name, and product family. Product attributes help organize products. Using Salesforce **custom fields**, you can create custom attributes such as recyclable products or whether a product is shippable or not on a product object. These attributes will be useful for automating things such as product rules and custom actions, which we will learn about in the next sections.

To create a product in CPQ, navigate to **App Launcher** → **Salesforce CPQ** → **Products** and click on **New**. Provide a product name, a unique product code, and a product family and activate the product. Admins can create additional custom fields on products as required. Products need to be activated and added to a **standard price book**.

> **Tip**
> To ensure fast system performance with price books, keep the number of products under 2 million.

Let's learn about product types and some of the out-of-the-box attributes that Salesforce CPQ provides.

Types of products

Products in Salesforce can be configured as **non-subscription** or **subscription** products. Non-subscription products are one-time purchases, such as a laptop or hardware, that can be converted to **assets**. Subscription products are sold as services that last for a specific period (whether that's days, months, or years). For example, Amazon Prime is a subscription product. Subscription products have a recurring payment associated with them. These models drive the **pricing**, **contracts**, and **renewal** functionalities.

Salesforce CPQ handles subscriptions with built-in proration. **Proration** is common in businesses that sell subscription products. For example, suppose you are buying a cell phone subscription for a month that costs $100. When you sign the contract on January 10, the price can be prorated for the remaining 21 days. They can be added from one contract to the next and renewals can be generated. Non-subscription products are not renewable and the price cannot be prorated. Subscription products are added to the contract as subscriptions and perpetual products become assets.

To define a product as a subscription model, there are specific custom fields on the product object and product attributes that need to be updated:

- **Subscription type**: The product subscription type field influences how Salesforce CPQ handles renewals for a subscription product. CPQ provides four picklist values, out of the box. Based on the picklist value (it is advised not to change these picklist values) selected at the product level, the functionality changes:

  - **Renewable** includes subscriptions in a renewal quote.

  - **One-time** subscriptions will not include products in renewal quotes. Note that there is a **Preserve Bundle Structure** package setting in CPQ that, when activated, adds one-time subscriptions to a renewal.

  - **Evergreen** subscriptions remain active until canceled and cannot be renewed. Note that these evergreen subscriptions cannot be on the same contract as renewable or one-time subscriptions. CPQ will always split them out automatically.

- **Evergreen/renewable** subscriptions are renewable, or evergreen, on individual quote lines in the **quote line editor** (**QLE**). These values can be manually selected or automated using Apex or a flow.

> **Important Note**
> To select the **Evergreen/renewable** picklist option for a product, first enable evergreen subscriptions in the CPQ package settings. Once enabled, these cannot be disabled.

- **Subscription pricing**: Product subscription pricing defines how the quote pricing will be calculated for the subscription products. Subscription pricing has three default picklist values: **Fixed price**, **Percentage of total**, and **None**:

  - **Fixed price**: Products get their list price from the price book.

  - **Percentage of total**: The product's list price is a percentage of either the quote, the quote line group, or a bundle's total price.

  - **None**: Not a subscription product.

- **Subscription term**: A product subscription term is the default amount of time the subscription lasts. A subscription term unit is set in the CPQ package settings. When a product is added to the quote, the quote lines subscription inherits the value from the product's subscription term. This is closely associated with the price book entry. For a fixed-price product, if the subscription term is 12 months, the price book entry should be a 12-month price. For a percent of total product subscription pricing, the percentage should reflect the term.

  Percent of total is used when you want to scale a product's price relative to another product. For example, when you go to a restaurant, a tip is an example of a percent of total price. We will learn more about this concept in *Chapter 4, Configuring CPQ Pricing*.

Now that we have discussed product types, let's see how they can be configured in Salesforce CPQ.

Configuring products

Products can be configured in Salesforce CPQ as product bundles, **Multi-Dimensional Quoting (MDQ) products**, subscription products, and usage products. Product configuration depends on the products that your company sells and how you want to price your products. Let's learn about the different product configurations that CPQ offers out of the box and how we can configure and customize them as per the specific business use cases:

- **Product bundles**: Product bundles are a collection of products that are sold together. Bundles may include options to choose from; these are like the subproducts. Product options with similar characteristics can be grouped together as features. For example, a laptop can be a bundle with a charger and a mouse as its components. The color and memory can be the options to choose from.

- **MDQ products**: Show a fixed-price subscription product in the QLE as one quote line broken into segments. Each segment that is an additional quote line represents a unit of time (quarter, month, year, or custom) and has pricing and a quantity independent of the line's other segments. They're useful if you want your sales rep to have detailed control over the pricing of specific units of time within one subscription product.

- **Subscription products**: These products are services that run for a specific period. For example, you can purchase an Amazon Prime subscription for a year or a month.

- **Usage products**: These products change based on product consumption. The price of the products will be based on the predefined rates for future consumption of the product. The rates can be defined based on the volume. The more you buy, the lower the price, and this increases revenue. For example, your cell phone consumption pricing is based on the amount of data you consume per month. CPQ will let you quote usage and create a billing table, but the pricing shown on the output doc is not going to show the billing table without a lot of customization. Usage products typically show up as zero on a quote line.

Now that we have learned about the product types, in the next section, let's learn about a few more configurations that admins can use to customize the QLE.

Creating custom actions and search filters

Custom actions and search filters are Salesforce features that we can use to customize the QLE and the **configurator** as per the business needs. They can be added as buttons in the QLE that will help the rep to easily select and add products. In this section, we will learn how admins can create them and look at examples where they are useful. Let's start with custom actions.

Creating custom actions

Custom actions are buttons that perform an action. These can be added to the QLE, configurator, or other detail pages. These actions will vary based on where the admin configures the custom actions. For example, custom actions in the QLE can delete lines, add a quote line group, save the quote, or navigate to an internal/external page. Custom actions in the configurator can load an internal/external page and apply edit rules. Custom actions in contracts can amend or renew them.

You can also create conditions for custom actions and Salesforce CPQ will not display the custom actions until the conditions are satisfied. When the rep clicks the custom action button in the QLE or configurator, the products are displayed based on the search filter parameters.

Salesforce CPQ provides a lot of out-of-the-box custom actions; the add products button and the save favorites button that we saw in earlier chapters are both custom actions. It is advisable to limit the custom actions to five or fewer.

If the sales rep wants to search only the hardware products, they can use the search filter and view products. The admin can create a button and add it to the QLE that can be used by the rep. Clicking the button will display all the hardware products.

Let's see how an admin can create a custom action.

To create a custom action, navigate to **App Launcher** → **Salesforce CPQ** → **Custom Action** → **New**. This will open the **New Custom Action** screen, as shown here:

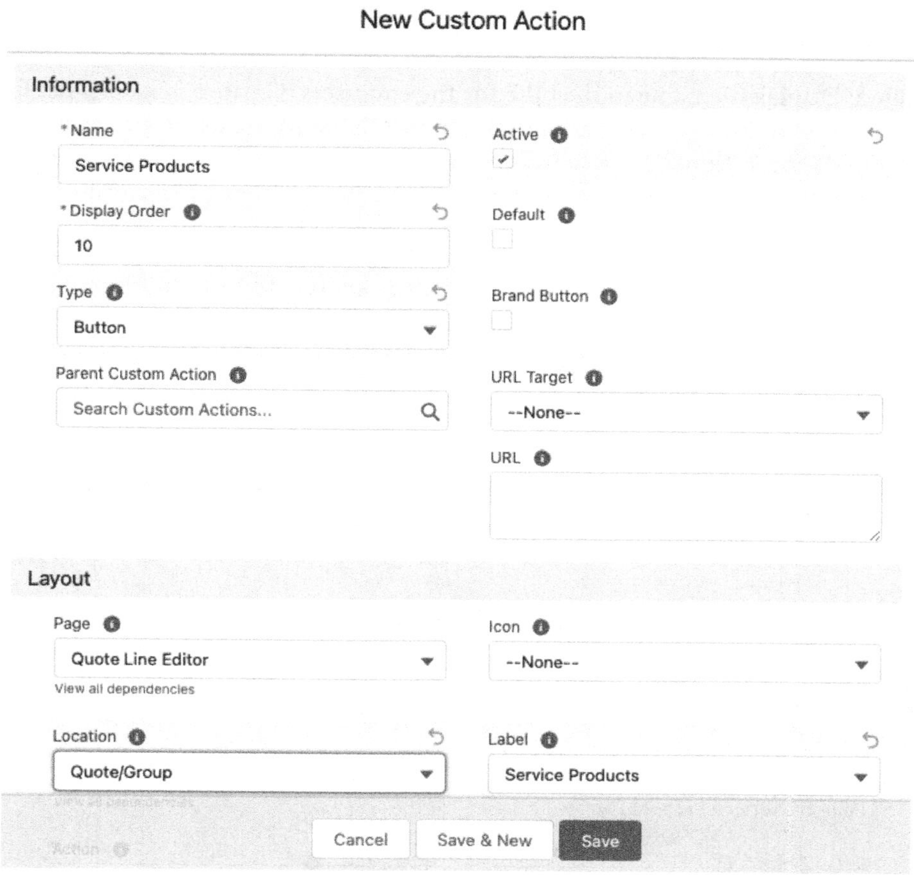

New Custom Action

Information

* Name	Active
Service Products	✓

* Display Order	Default
10	☐

Type	Brand Button
Button ▼	☐

Parent Custom Action	URL Target
Search Custom Actions... 🔍	--None-- ▼

URL

Layout

Page	Icon
Quote Line Editor ▼	--None-- ▼
View all dependencies	

Location	Label
Quote/Group ▼	Service Products ▼

Cancel   Save & New   Save

Figure 3.1 – Custom action

Some important fields in custom action creation include the following:

- **Name**: The name of the custom action.

- **Display Order**: Specifies where the custom action is displayed.

- **Type**: Determines whether the custom action is a button, menu, or separator. In this example, we are creating a button for service products.

- **Parent Custom Action**: If you want to group a child custom action under an existing custom action, then you need to select this.

- **URL Target**: If your custom action is a URL, then you can provide the link here.

- **Page**: This is where your custom action will be displayed.

- **Location**: The place where the custom action appears on the chosen page.

- **Action**: Determines the result of selecting a custom action. In this example, let's select **Add Products**.

- **Label**: Display the name in the QLE for the end users. Create a label picklist field in the custom objects by navigating to **Setup** → **Object Manager** → **Custom Action** → **Fields & relationship** → **Label** → **Values** → **New**. Add the new picklist value. In this example, we are adding `Service Product`. Once the picklist value is added, you can select that in the **Label** field here.

After entering all the required fields, save the custom action. The admin can now create a search filter. In the next section, let's learn how to create a search filter.

Creating a search filter

Search filters are used to filter products based on the search criteria. Search filters can be created from custom actions. To create a search filter, navigate to **App Launcher** → **Custom Action** (select the sample custom action service product created in *Figure 3.1*) → **Related** → **Search filter** → **New**. This will open the new search filter, as shown here:

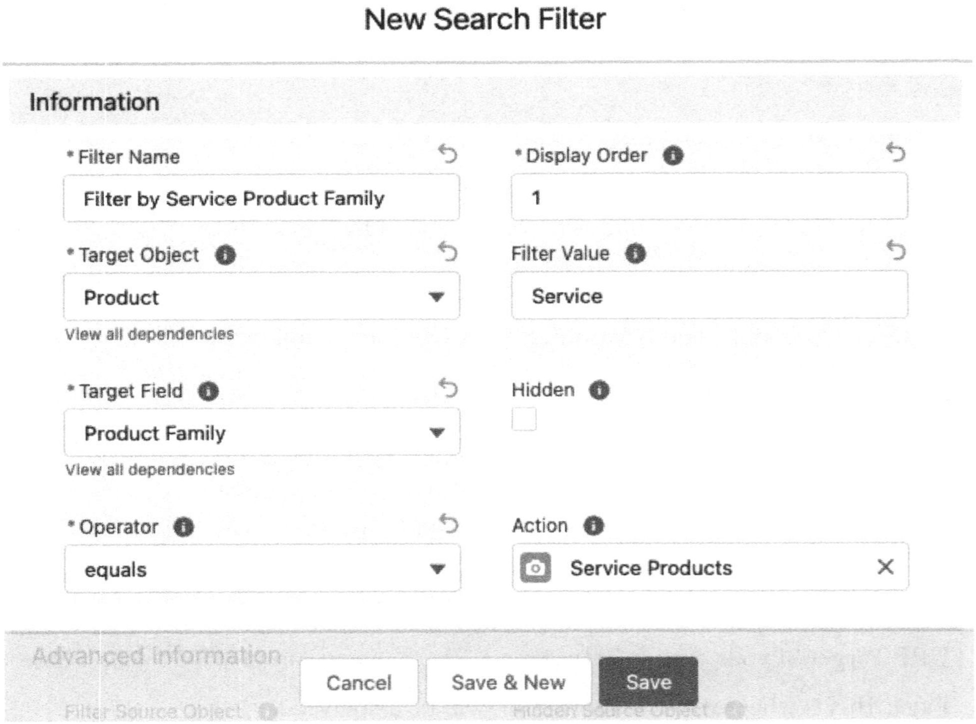

New Search Filter

Information

* Filter Name	* Display Order
Filter by Service Product Family	1

* Target Object	Filter Value
Product	Service
View all dependencies	

* Target Field	Hidden
Product Family	☐
View all dependencies	

* Operator	Action
equals	📷 Service Products ✕

Advanced Information

Cancel   Save & New   **Save**

Filter Source Object   Hidden Source Object

Figure 3.2 – Search filter

In the sample search filter created in the preceding figure, the admin is filtering all the service products.

Verifying custom actions in the QLE

Let's see how reps can benefit from the sample custom action the admin has created for service products in the previous section. To view the custom action, navigate to any quote and click on **Edit Lines**. The rep can see the new **Service Products** custom action, as shown in *Figure 3.3*. Rather than searching for service products manually, the rep can directly click this button:

Figure 3.3 – Custom action in the QLE

When you click on the **Service Products** button, only the service products will be displayed. Reps can change the filter criteria, as shown in *Figure 3.4*. If you do not want the rep to change the search filter, you can hide this by selecting the **Hidden** checkbox while creating the custom action.

Figure 3.4 – Custom filter in the QLE

The preceding figure shows the sample product selection for the service products' custom action.

Creating dynamic search filters

QLE search filters are used to filter products, assets, or subscriptions by their field values. We can navigate to **Quote → Edit Lines →** the search filter icon; a search can be based on a product code, name, or family. Additional fields can be added as required. Creating dynamic search filters makes a limited set of products available to your rep. CPQ admins can set the custom search filter using a filter source object and fields from the search filter. To create a dynamic search filter, navigate to **App Launcher → Search filter → New**. This will open the new search filter screen, as shown here:

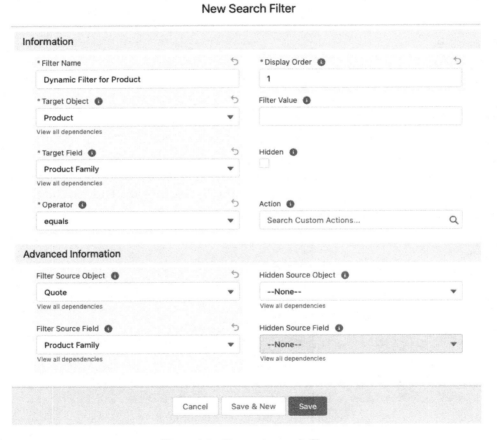

Figure 3.5 – Dynamic search filter

Admins can update all the mandatory information as shown in the preceding figure.

This search filter will display only the products that belong to the product family, region, company size, and/or seasonality selected in the quote.

A CPQ admin can create a product family field in the quote. Reps can then select this field while creating a quote. When the reps start to configure the products, only the products whose product family matches will be displayed. A rep can edit the product family and based on that, the product filter will dynamically change.

Now that we have learned how to define the products and select the products, in the next section, let's see how admins can create and configure these products in Salesforce.

Configuring product bundles

In this section, let's learn more about product bundles. This will help sales reps enforce business logic for mandatory products, a minimum quantity of a product in a bundle, and so on. For example, when you are selling a laptop, rather than the rep hand-selecting the products one by one, a preconfigured bundle can be selected that includes all the products. Adding a bundle to a CPQ quote adds all the related products automatically. Bundles are a great tool for moving to package or solution-based selling.

There are three types of bundles:

- **Static bundle**: These bundles always have the same products. In a static bundle, you want your reps to always sell the products together and they will not have an option to modify anything. A cheese pizza is an example of a static bundle as it will always have the fixed pizza crust, cheese, and tomato sauce.

- **Configurable bundle**: In a configurable bundle, some products are predefined, but others can be changed as per your requirements. This is like making a pizza with your choice of toppings. The pizza crust might be mandatory, but you can choose the type of cheese you want, choose the vegetable toppings you want, and increase the quantity as per your preferences.

- **Nested bundle**: This is a bundle inside a bundle. Nested bundles can be static or configurable. For instance, a sandwich is a bundle that contains bread, cheese, and tomatoes, which can be inside your lunch box, which is another bundle containing sandwich, chips, and juice. It becomes hard to maintain multiple levels in nested bundles, so the best practice is to keep to one or a max of two levels. Nested bundles should be avoided if CPQ is being interacted with by external systems using the CPQ API for quote configuration and amendments.

So, why do we need bundles? They will help a rep choose the right products. Bundles provide a **user interface (UI)** that will help a rep select the correct products for a situation. Without bundles, reps would need to select from a huge list of product catalogs and any error will add an incompatible product to the quote. A rep needs to thoroughly understand what products go together, which will be very difficult if the rep is new to the company. Bundles are preconfigured with all the mandatory products that are needed. These are one-time activities that admins can perform, and reps can add these bundles to any quotes.

Bundles also allow us to facilitate special pricing and discounting. For example, a charger when bundled together with a laptop can be sold at 0 dollars or at a discounted price and when sold separately as a single product, the charger will be sold at full price.

For an admin to create a bundle, all the products in that bundle need to be created in CPQ. The admin can create a bundle, add all the required products, and link them together. Products can be linked to each other by creating **options**.

For example, many laptops may use the same processor (CPU 1.6 GHz i5). The processor needs to be created as one product. All the laptop models can have this processor as a **product option**. Options can be grouped together logically as **features** for a better user experience. Features are not mandatory, but they will help organize products. **Features** are not products but containers of products. Using the **Category** field on a feature, we can organize features into categories and display these categories in separate tabs. This is a useful UI tool. For example, all the important **features** for configuring a laptop can be grouped under the **Essential** category in a tab, and all the accessories such as laptop cases and additional cables can be grouped under the **Other** category in a different tab. For instance, all the different processors (i5, i7, and so on) for the laptop can be grouped under the **processor feature**.

Let's imagine Packt Corporation is a company selling laptops and other office supply products to their customers. We will help Packt Corporation reps by creating a bundle that the company sells together with options and features that their salesperson can configure in the QLE.

Creating a product bundle in a Salesforce instance

Salesforce admins at Packt Corporation can create different bundles and combine the related products together. This helps the rep to just add the bundle to the quote without trying to remember all the components that need to be added. Admins can create many bundles as required. Let's try creating a sample bundle for a 13-inch laptop.

To create a *Packt Pro 13" Laptop* bundle in a Salesforce instance, navigate to **Product → New**, fill in **Product Name** and **Product Code**, and select the **Active** checkbox. Then click on **Product Family → Configuration type → Configuration event → Save**. This will take you to the **New Product** screen, as shown here:

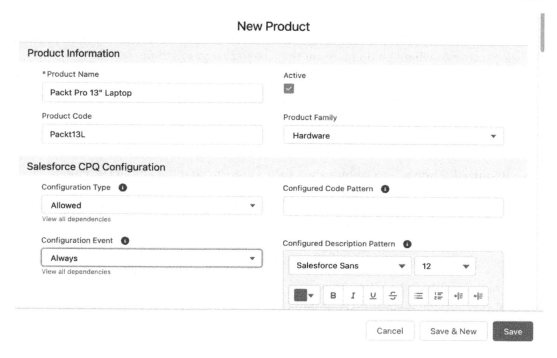

Figure 3.6 – Creating a product bundle

As shown in *Figure 3.6*, bundles are created the same way new products are created. Bundle configuration for any product is guided by business rules that validate the configuration. There are different ways admins can control how this bundle can be added to a quote and configured. This depends on the combination of the configuration type (this value determines whether a bundle requires a configuration or not) and configuration event (this value determines when to allow product configuration). Let's see what functionality each of these combinations provides:

- **Allowed/Always**: The user will first select the product bundle and will be able to configure products immediately after adding the product bundle. When you set up a bundle with this combination, the user can configure the products in the QLE by clicking the wrench icon. The user can also go back and forth as many times as they need and save the products to the QLE.

- **Allowed/Edit**: This combination skips the configuration at first, and after the bundle selection, the rep goes to the QLE page. This combination allows the rep to configure products by clicking the wrench icon in the QLE when needed. This option will be useful for scenarios where most of the time users do not need to reconfigure. But if needed, they will have the option to do so.

- **Disabled/Always**: This combination skips configuring products completely and will never allow users to configure. The bundle is static, and this option will be suitable for scenarios where we do not want the reps to change anything.

- **Allowed/Add**: This combination allows the user to configure products just one time before they go to the QLE page. This type of setting will be useful for business scenarios where there are two bundles (*nested bundles*) that the rep needs to add, and the second bundle needs to be configured based on the first bundle configuration. Hence, we do not want the rep to change the first bundle.

- **Required/Always**: This combination forces users to configure bundles, reminding them of important configuration possibilities and allowing rules and other business logic to be evaluated. The rep must click on the wrench icon and acknowledge the options. Until then, the systems will not let the user save the record. This will help in scenarios where you have nested bundles and before adding them to the quote you want the reps to validate the configuration.

For the sample *Packt Pro 13" Laptop* bundle, we have set the configuration event as **Allowed** and the configuration type as **Always** with which reps can edit the configuration as many times as needed. Most organizations choose this setting for their implementation. In the next section, let's see how admins can configure and add options to this bundle.

Creating a product option in a Salesforce instance

Product options are the glue that puts together the set of products that make the bundle. They are the junction record that places a product within the bundle of another product. A product can belong to many bundles, and bundles can have many products. There are a lot of different behaviors that we can set on product options. These behaviors control the way the products are added while configuring and adding to the QLE. To create product options (in this example, we will learn how to create an option for the i5 processor and add it to the bundle), navigate to the *Packt Pro 13" Laptop* bundle. To do that, click on the App Launcher (the nine dots in the top left-hand menu in your Salesforce instance), search products, then click **Packt Pro 13" Laptop → Related → Options → New**. This will open the **New Product Option** screen, as shown here:

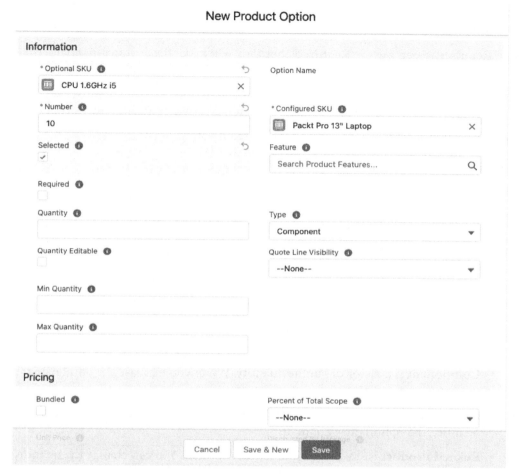

Figure 3.7 – Creating a product option

As shown in *Figure 3.7*, a few important fields in product option creation include the following:

- **Optional SKU**: This is a lookup for the product's object. Select **CPU 1.6GHz i5** – this is an already existing product (in the CPQ test environment). Optional SKU will be a product within the bundle.

- **Number**: This is the display order of the option within the feature. When the rep configures the bundles, the product options will be displayed based on this configuration. This is useful when you have several products and you want to display them in a certain order. The order is typically entered in multiples of 10 (10, 20, 30, 40) initially. This allows an admin to have space to insert additional options later in the sort order.

- **Selected**: When this checkbox is ticked, any product added to this quote will be preselected.

- **Required**: Selecting the **Required** checkbox will make the product mandatory in the QLE, and end users cannot uncheck it.

- **Quantity**: This is the product quantity that will be added to the quote. If the **Required** checkbox is selected, then you should provide a default quantity.

- **Quantity Editable**: This checkbox is selected if you want your reps to be able to edit the quantity or check the quantity editable. Alternatively, you can leave the previously discussed **Quantity** field blank. If **Quantity Editable** is turned off, a user will not be able to amend and remove the quote line on contracts.

- **Min Quantity** and **Max Quantity**: These set the limit on the number of products a rep can add to the quote.

- **Bundled**: The products in the bundle contribute to the bundle price. When this checkbox is selected, the *product option* will have a zero-dollar price regardless of the price book.

- **Type**: There are three possible option types that can be selected: **Component**, **Accessory**, or **Related Product**. These option types determine the behavior of the bundle quantity in the QLE. The various **Type** options are explained as follows:

  - **Component** is a factor of bundle quantity. When you increase the bundle quantity, the option gets multiplied.

  - **Accessory** is independent of bundle quantity. When you increase the bundle quantity, the option does *not* multiply.

  - **Related Product** is special and not used very often. You can change the quantity of the option in the QLE while the other two types are not editable. For example, I can order a burrito and a side of guacamole as a related product. I do not want the guacamole to be affected by the bundle's configuration and the guacamole is shared with everyone.

- **Quote Line Visibility**: This determines when you can see a product option. The following picklist values can be selected for quote line visibility:

  - **Always**: This option is the default setting where the product is visible in both the QLE and the output document.

  - **Editor Only**: With this option, the product appears only on the QLE and is excluded in the output document.

- **Document Only**: With this option, the product appears on the quote output document.

- **Never**: This option hides the product from both the QLE and the output document. It is used when a product serves a downstream purpose (provisioning, billing, rev-rec most commonly) but should not be viewable or modified by the rep. This option is only important to the order visibility team.

A product bundle can have as many options as needed. Similar options can be grouped together as *features*. In this example, these products (processors) can be grouped into a processor feature.

Creating a product feature in a Salesforce instance

A feature is a way to organize many options and we associate options with features. They also help enforce some business logic. For example, in the laptop bundle with i5 and i7 processors, the product feature will make sure at least one processor is selected because the rep cannot sell a laptop without a processor. In the Packt Laptop bundle, the following figure shows how a feature is used to link the product options to a bundle:

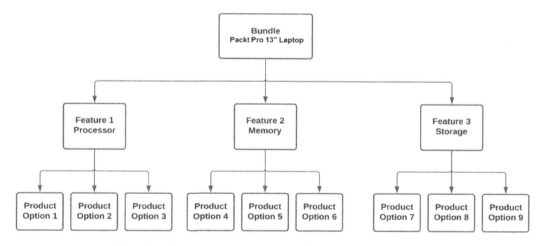

Figure 3.8 – Relationship between bundles, features, and options

To create a product feature, navigate to the sample *Packt Pro 13″ Laptop* bundle, click on the App Launcher (the nine dots on the top left-hand menu in your Salesforce instance), search `products`, then click **Packt Pro 13″ Laptop** → **Related** → **Feature** → **New**. This will open the **New Product Feature** screen, as shown here:

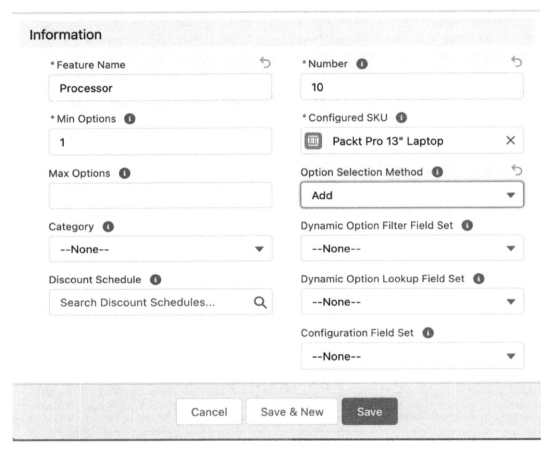

Figure 3.9 – Creating a product feature

A few important fields in product feature creation include the following:

- **Feature Name**: Provide a meaningful name. For example, as we are creating this feature for processors, let's name this `Processor`.

- **Number**: This field is used to sort features when displayed to the end user.

  Go back to the i5 processor option and update the feature lookup. Similarly, add an i7 option to the processor feature.

- **Min Options**: Minimum number of options required for this feature.

- **Max Options**: Maximum number of options that can be selected as part of the product bundle.

- **Option Selection Method**: Determines how users select options attached to a bundle product. This has three values: **Click**, **Add**, and **Dynamic**.

  - **Click** presents options with checkboxes next to them.

  - **Add** renders a button that will show the predefined options.

  - **Dynamic** renders a button that will show all the active products.

  For this example, let's select **Add**.

- **Category**: Assign a category if you want to group this feature to a specific category and display it in a separate tab.

- **Additional Instructions**: This is a special field configuration that helps your rep with some additional instructions on a feature. Create a new text field in the product feature object. Name this field exactly as `AdditionalInstructions`. This can be displayed to the rep while they're configuring products.

Let's group the previously created options in *Figure 3.2* into the features processor, memory, storage, and accessories.

The next figure shows the example bundle that the admin has created with options and features:

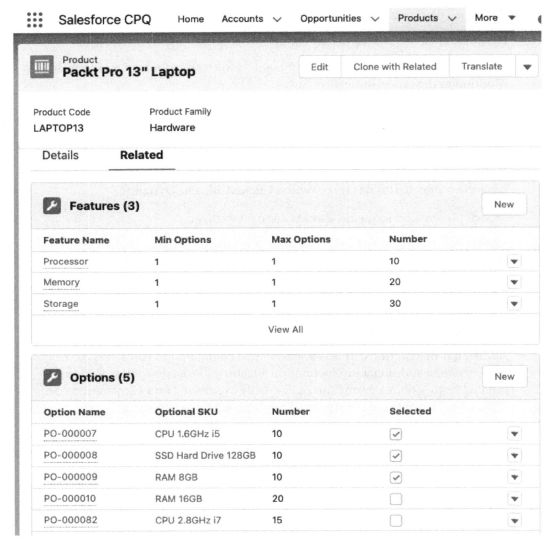

Figure 3.10 – Product bundle with options and features

Let's see how reps can add these bundles to QLE.

Adding a bundle to the QLE

When the rep adds a bundle to the quote, CPQ provides all the options related to this bundle. The rep can choose which options to add to the quote. The following figure shows the QLE where the sample bundle is added:

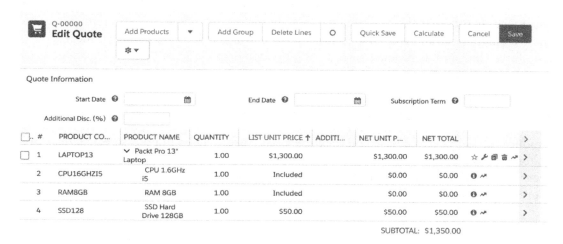

Figure 3.11 – Product bundle in the QLE

As shown in the preceding figure, bundles help reps to add products easily to the QLE without having to manually add products. Salesforce CPQ provides another functionality that will help to exclude some of the options from the bundle. It is called **option constraints**, which are used when you want to exclude one option while another one is selected for the product bundle. They are also used to preselect the dependencies or exclude them. For example, a *Wi-Fi Router* product needs to be selected before *Wi-Fi Installation* is selected. In another use case, you don't want your reps to add two options for processors: one for i5 and another for i7. Option constraints can either enable or disable an option. It is important to note that the system will not force a user to select an option that is handled by a constraint. The user must still select it. They can be used in real-time rule processing, which gives immediate feedback to the sales rep.

What if we want to automatically select products for a specific user, automatically hide or show products, and validate a user selection for a specific product or bundle? Product rules can be used to dynamically generate options based on filter logic. In the next section, we will learn how to configure product rules in CPQ.

Creating product rules

If a customer is buying a printer from your company and your sales rep forgets to add a cartridge, it costs time and energy for everyone involved in the process to buy the right combination of products. This also results in a poor customer experience. In some cases, the rep may not know the actual combination of products, which may lead to incompatible products that are included in a quote. It is difficult for a rep to remember these combinations and rules, especially when a business is selling a lot of products. Salesforce CPQ and its product rules are designed to help the rep get the right products added to the quote the first time.

Admins can work with the business to define these rules for your organization and perform a one-time configuration.

Product rules are derived based on the *if/then* structure. *If* a condition is satisfied, *then* an action will be performed. Product rules allow admins to define advanced configuration logic compared to option constraints. We can show/hide specific product options that are more resource-intensive.

There are four types of product rules:

- **Validation**: This prevents the rep from saving a record until the error is corrected. For example, when you are selling a laptop without a power cord, it stops the rep from saving the incorrect configuration until the right products are added.

- **Alert**: These are like soft alerts, where the system will warn the rep that a required product is missing but will still allow them to save the record. For example, when your rep is selling a laptop, the system will provide an alert that the mouse is missing but the sales rep can still decide whether to include a mouse, and the system will not have a hard stop.

- **Selection**: Selection rules work with the product option configurations for selected products to provide more dynamic and specific bundle configurations. It automatically performs actions on product options without displaying any message. Selection adds, removes, or hides products during bundle configuration. For instance, when a rep is selling a laptop, mandatory products such as the power cord will be automatically added to the configuration. This overrides the product bundle option while adding the products.

- **Filter**: Allows specific products in a feature that uses the dynamic selection option. For example, when a US sales rep is creating a quote, it shows only US-compatible products in the configuration.

A product rule is an object in Salesforce CPQ. It contains business logic that helps sales reps get the right products into a quote. There are some main objects that look up to the product rule. Salesforce admins use these objects to configure most of the product automation. They are as follows:

- **Error Condition**: This defines the condition for which the product rule should be executed.

- **Product Action**: This defines how CPQ changes the bundle configuration. Product Action performs an action on a product option, such as selecting or deselecting the option within the bundle.

- **Lookup Query**: This is used in product rules to query data from an object (both standard and custom objects) other than a quote. They map the data from the lookup object back to the product rule.

- **Configuration Rule**: This links the product rule with a bundle or individual product.

- **Summary Variable**: A summary variable is a way of aggregating data. Be mindful of the number of summary variables. It should not be more than 5 or 10 per rule. Excessive use may result in performance issues and governor issues.

- **Configuration Attribute**: This is a field that the sales rep can set during the product configuration. These are not part of product rules, but they are used in error conditions and sometimes in lookup queries.

In the next section, let's learn how to create the different types of product rules. Along with creating the product rule, we will see how an admin can leverage the out-of-the-box CPQ objects to configure the rules.

Creating a validation product rule

Imagine Packt Corporation is selling a warranty product named *Laptop Loss and Damage Warranty* along with the laptops. The company does not want its reps to sell a warranty quantity that is greater than the laptop quantity.

If the warranty quantity is greater, the product rule will trigger and will not allow the rep to save the record until the error is resolved. To create this rule, the admin can navigate to **App Launcher → Salesforce CPQ → Product Rules → New**. This will open the following screen:

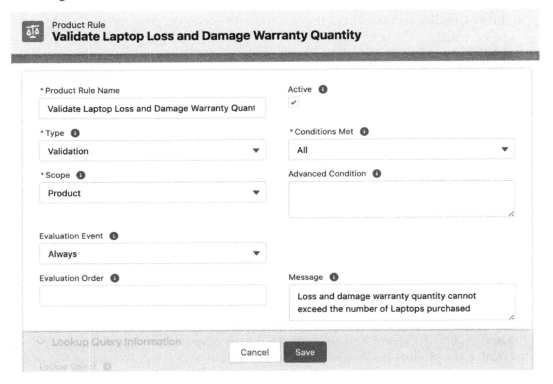

Figure 3.12 – Validation product rule

The preceding figure shows the configuration of a sample product rule in a Salesforce instance. Please refer to it while creating your product rule. The important fields in this configuration include the following:

- **Product Rule Name**: Provide a descriptive name that's easy to understand why we created this rule.

- **Type**: This is one of the four product rule types. In this example, we want to create a product rule of the **Validation** type.

- **Scope**: This field's value can be a *product* or *quote*. When **Product** is selected as the scope, the product rule will be applied to the specific bundle and will be executed during the configuration. When **Quote** is selected as the scope, the product rule will be applied to the entire quote and will be executed in the QLE.

- **Conditions Met**: Based on this value, the rule will be executed when all the conditions are met, if one condition is met, or a combination is met.

- **Advanced Condition**: When an admin has more than one condition, they can be logically grouped using advanced conditions.

- **Evaluation Event**: Determines when Salesforce CPQ runs this rule. It can have the following values:

  - **Load**: The rule will be evaluated when the product bundle is opened.

  - **Edit**: The rule will be evaluated when the product bundle is changed.

  - **Save**: The rule will be evaluated when the user saves the record.

  - **Always**: The rule will always be evaluated.

  - **None**: The rule is applied after the user clicks save.

- **Evaluation Order**: Determines the order in which the rules should fire when there are multiple rules. The best practice is to leave some gaps between the numbers so that when there is a need to add additional rules, you can do so.

- **Message**: This is the text that will be visible to the rep when the rule is triggered.

Save the product rule and navigate to the **Related** section. Error conditions can be created in the **Related** section. In the next section, we will learn how admins can create summary variables and error conditions for a product rule.

Creating a summary variable and an error condition

For the validation product rule that we want to create for Packt Corporation, whenever a rep tries to add products to the quote, we want Salesforce CPQ to calculate the warranty and laptop totals in the backend and compare them in the error condition. To create the product totals, the rep can use the out-of-the-box functionality using summary variables. These variables can be used in the error condition filter values to evaluate when the rule should fire. **Summary variables** are aggregations of products on quotes. They can be referenced in a product's rule error conditions. These are like *Salesforce rollup fields* except that you don't store these values in a field. Let's first create a sample summary variable:

1. In this product validation rule, we want to compare the total number of laptops and the total number of warranty products. To create a summary variable, navigate to **App Launcher** → **Salesforce CPQ** → **Summary variables** → **New**.

   The following figure shows a sample summary variable creation in a Salesforce instance:

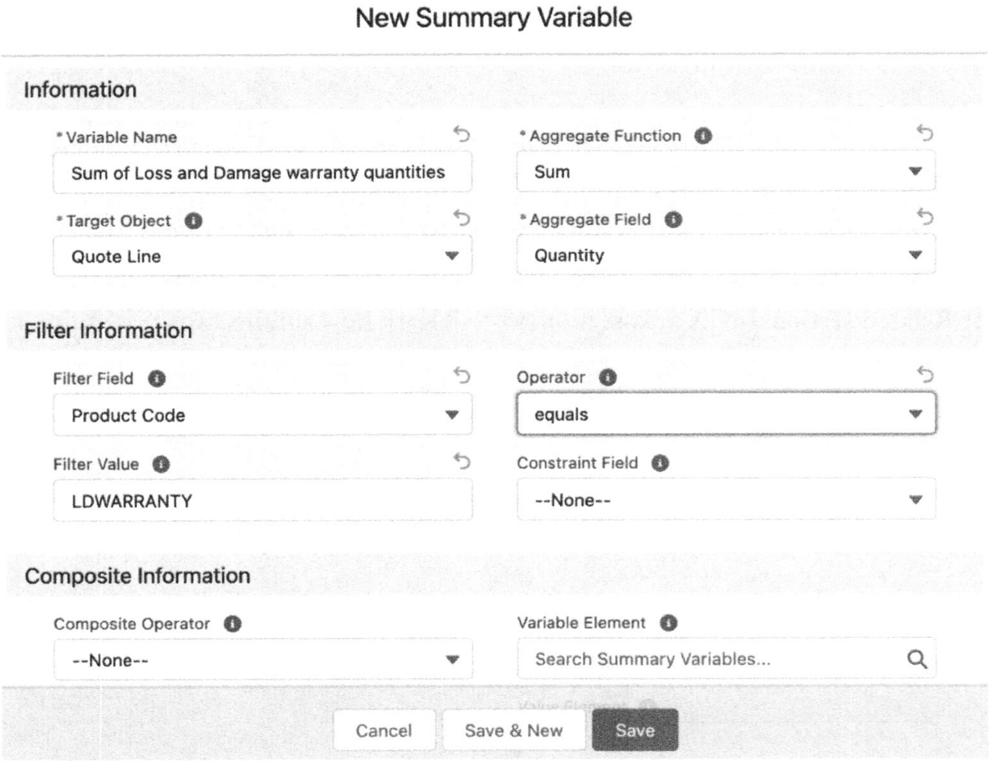

Figure 3.13 – Creating a summary variable

A few important fields in the summary variable creation include the following:

- **Variable Name**: The name of the summary variable. Provide a meaningful name.

- **Target Object**: This is the object we want to calculate the sum for. In this example, we want to sum the product quantities.

- **Aggregate Function**: There are different aggregate functions – sum, average, min, max, and count. In this example, we want to sum the total warranty products, therefore we selected **Sum**.

- **Aggregate Field**: This is the field for which we wanted to perform the aggregate operation. In this example, we want to sum up the **Quantity** field.

- **Filter Information**: Here, we want to sum all the quantities where the product code is LDWARRANTY. This is the product code associated with the *Loss and Damage Warranty* product in the Salesforce test instance.

2. Similarly, create another summary variable (**Sum of Laptop quantity**) that calculates the sum of all the laptops. You can add the filter condition based on the product family as we may have more than one hardware product.

> **Summary Variable for Custom Product Fields**
>
> If the target object is a product option and the custom field is not available, create the custom field before creating the summary variable. A summary variable is just going to query the quantity and return it to the filter condition.

These two summary variables can be used in the error condition creation. Next, let's create an error condition.

This is where we define the product rule conditions. To do this, navigate to the **Validate Laptop Loss and Damage Warranty Quantity** sample product rule created for Packt Corporation, by going to **Product Rule → Error Conditions → New**. This will land you on the screen shown here:

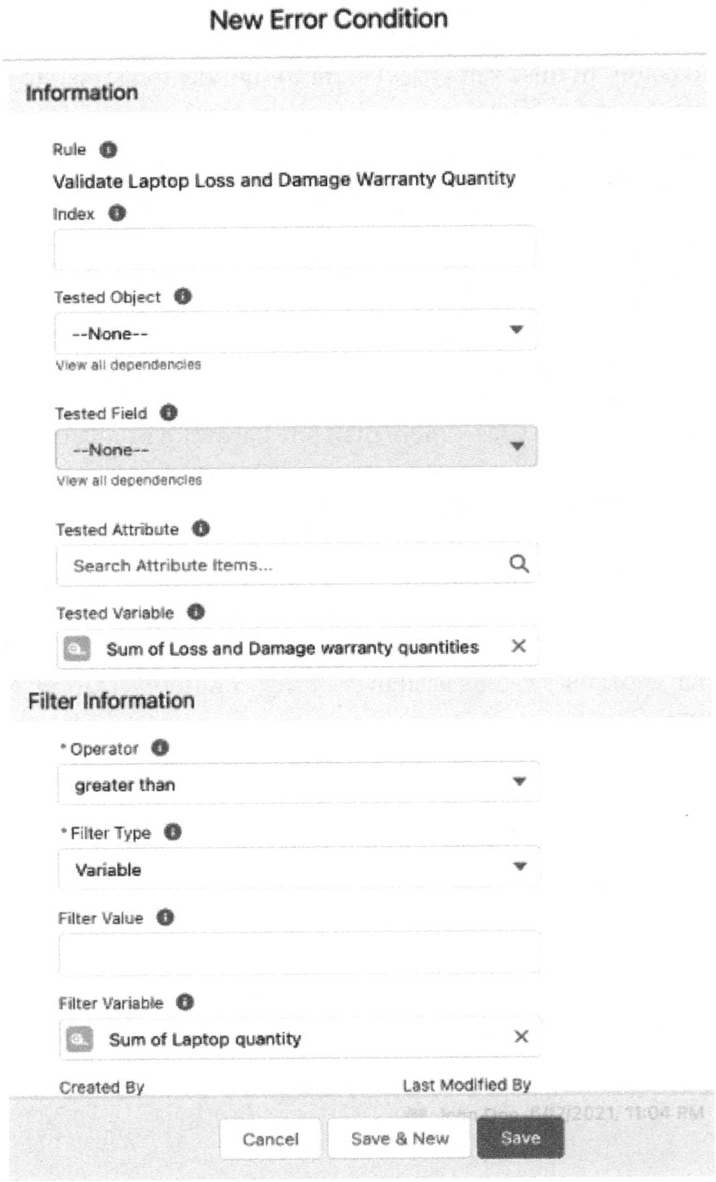

Figure 3.14 – Product rule error condition

The error condition can be created using either **Tested Object/Tested Field** or **Tested Variable**. In this example, we will learn how to create the error condition using the tested variable the summary variable created. Important fields in the error condition include the following:

- **Tested Object** and **Tested Field**: The object/field for this error condition to be evaluated. This should not be used if **Tested Variable** is populated.

- **Tested Variable**: *Look up* a summary variable that needs to be evaluated. This should be left blank if **Tested Object/Tested Field** values are used. In this example, we are using the **Sum of Loss and Damage warranty quantities** summary variable.

- **Operator**: Choose how the filtered information will be compared to the evaluated information.

- **Filter Type**: Choose this if a filter value or filter variable will be used to compare against the evaluated information.

- **Filter Value**: A manually entered value that is compared against the evaluated information.

- **Filter Variable**: Look up a summary variable such as **Sum of Laptop quantity** to compare against the evaluated information.

Associating a product rule with a product bundle

Now we can associate the product rule to the bundle using the configuration rule. This example is specific to one bundle and one rule; many configuration rules can be created to relate a single product rule to many products. Here, we want this product rule to apply only to this bundle. To do this, navigate to the **Packt Pro 13" Laptop** product bundle → **Related** → **Configuration Rules** → **New**. This will open the configuration rule screen, as shown here:

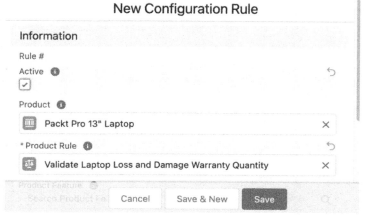

Figure 3.15 – Associating a product rule to the bundle

In the configuration rule shown in the preceding figure, we are associating the **Validate Laptop Loss and Damage Warranty Quantity** product rule with the **Packt Pro 13" Laptop** bundle.

Testing the validation product rule in the QLE

Let's learn how reps use the bundles created by admins and add bundles to quotes. We can test the product rule created for validating the warranty quantity. A rep can navigate to the QLE page to do this. Open any opportunity, then go to **Quote → Edit Lines**. This takes you to the QLE. Click **Add Products → Search Products**. Search for the **Packt Pro 13" Laptop** bundle and click **Select**. This will take you to the **Configure Products** page, where you can see all the features and options that the admin has configured in the backend.

When you try to add a warranty quantity greater than the laptop's purchased quantity, the product rule will fire and display an error message, as shown in the following screenshot:

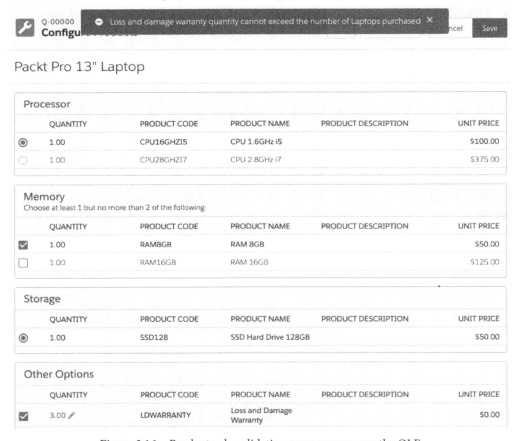

Figure 3.16 – Product rule validation error message on the QLE

As shown in the screenshot, the rep can choose from the product features and select the product options as per the customer's requirements. At the same time, the automation that the admins created using product rules will make sure that the configuration is accurate.

Creating an alert product rule

An alert is a soft validation. It displays a message for the user to acknowledge. It's at the user's discretion to continue or cancel. For instance, if your company is selling printers, when a rep is configuring a printer bundle, we would like to provide an alert to see whether the customer is interested in buying printer paper. A good admin limits the number of alerts in an org to only the most important ones. The rep can either add printer paper to the configuration or ignore it as per the customer's needs. To create an alert product rule, the admin can navigate to **App Launcher → Salesforce CPQ → Product Rules → New**. This will open the **New Product Rule** window, as shown in the following figure:

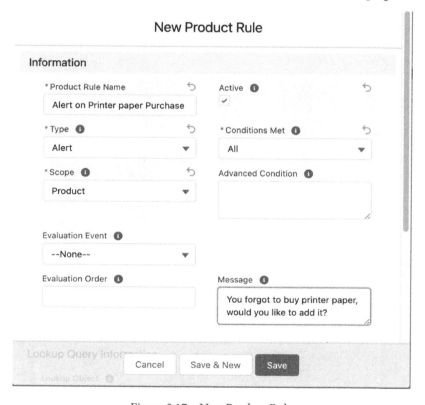

Figure 3.17 – New Product Rule

This product rule's type is **Alert** and its scope is **Product** as we would like to trigger this rule only for the laser printer bundle.

Creating an alert product rule error condition

Let's create the error condition for this alert and define the criteria to trigger this rule. To add an error condition, navigate to **Product Rule → Error Conditions → New**.

In the previous example, we created an error condition with a summary variable using the **Tested Variable** field in the error condition. Now, let's use **Tested Object** and **Tested Field** to define this condition. You can only use one or the other and based on the business requirement, you can decide whether a summary variable is needed or not. In this example, we are simply verifying whether the customer is interested in buying paper along with the printer. There is no mathematical aggregation needed and hence there is no need for a summary variable:

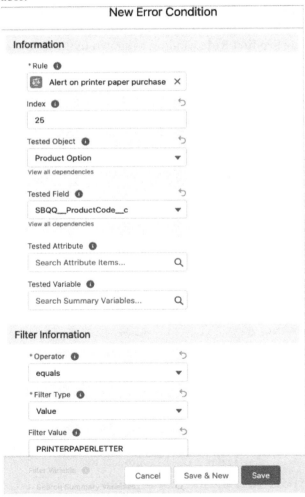

Figure 3.18 – Product rule error condition

Update the mandatory fields in the error condition as shown in the preceding figure. There is more than one way an error condition can be configured for a product rule. Let's learn more about the important fields that can be used to configure these error conditions:

- **Tested Object** and **Tested Field**: The object/field for which this condition should be evaluated. This should not be used if the tested variable is populated.

- **Tested Object**: For this example, we want to verify the product option.

- **Tested Field**: In the product option, we want to alert the user if printer paper needs to be added. The product code for printer paper is PRINTERPAPERLETTER, as shown in the test instance where this product rule is being created.

Associate the product rule to the bundle using the configuration rule for which the product rule should trigger.

Testing the validation product rule in the QLE

Now, let's see the end user experience with this product rule. Navigate to any opportunity → **Quote** → **Edit Lines**. This takes you to the QLE. Click **Add Products** → **Search Products**, search the **Laser Printer** bundle, and then click **Select**.

When the rep saves the production configuration, the alert will be displayed as shown here:

Figure 3.19 – Product rule alert message on the QLE

The user can continue and add the printer paper or cancel the alert as required.

Creating a selection product rule

Until now, we have seen how admins can help reps with the validation and alert product rules, where the system can guide them to add the correct products. Here, we see a product rule that will automatically add products to avoid issues and create the right configuration. This can be built using the selection product rules.

Let's consider an example where your company is selling products in multiple countries. Based on the location, you want to show US products or UK products to your reps. For instance, look at the example given in *Figure 3.20*; when the rep chooses the location in the QLE as the US, we want to show US products and hide or disable UK products:

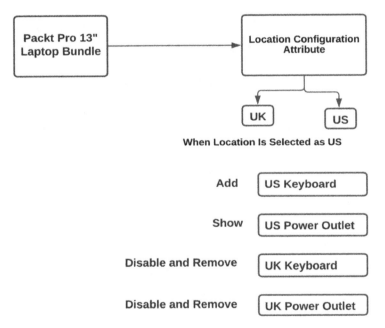

Figure 3.20 – Selection product rule use case

We can create a location field as a configuration attribute that is visible to the rep when configuring the bundles. First, let's create this *custom field* called location:

1. To create the location picklist field in the product option object, navigate to **Setup → Object Manager → Product Option → Fields & Relationships → New**. Select **Picklist → Next → Field Label** (*Location*) **→ Values** (enter the values United States and United Kingdom, with each value separated by a new line) **→ Field Name** (*Location*) **→ Next → Save Important** .

2. Update the target field picklist on the configuration attribute object to include the API name of the location field. Navigate to **Setup → Object Manager → Configuration Attribute → Fields & Relationships → Target Field → New** and type `Location__c` in the text box. Then, check **Configuration Attribute** and select **Save**.

3. Create the configuration attribute on the *Packt Pro 13" Laptop* bundle. Navigate to **App Launcher → Salesforce → Product Bundles** (Packt Pro 13" Laptop) → the **Related** tab. In the **Configuration Attributes** related list, click **New**. This will take you to the configuration attribute screen shown here:

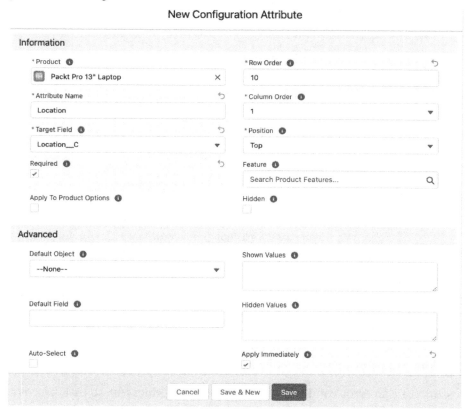

Figure 3.21 – Product rule configuration attribute

Update the mandatory fields as shown in *Figure 3.21*.

4. Next, the admin needs to create a **twin field** for the location in the quote line object. To do this, navigate to **Setup → Object Manager → Quote Line → Fields & Relationships → New**. Select **Picklist → Next → Field Label** (*Location*) **→ Values** (enter the values United States and United Kingdom, with each value separated by a new line) **→ Field Name** (*Location*) **→ Next → Save**.

When the rep selects the location as **United States**, a US keyboard and US power outlet should be added and displayed. To create a selection product rule, navigate to **App Launcher → Salesforce CPQ → Product Rules → New**. This will take you to the new product rule window, as shown next:

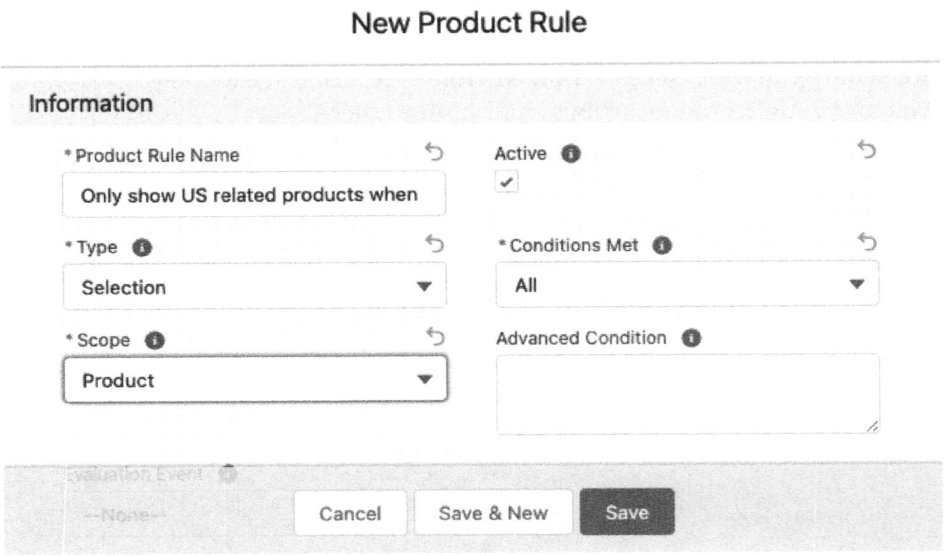

New Product Rule

Information

* Product Rule Name	Active ⓘ
Only show US related products when	✔

* Type ⓘ	* Conditions Met ⓘ
Selection	All

* Scope ⓘ	Advanced Condition ⓘ
Product	

Evaluation Event ⓘ

--None--   Cancel   Save & New   Save

Figure 3.22 – Selection product rule

Update the mandatory fields as shown in the preceding figure.

5. Because *Location* is a custom field, before we can use this field in the error condition, we need to update the **Tested Field** picklist. To do this, navigate to **Setup → Object Manager → Error Condition → Fields & Relationships → Tested Field → Values → New**, type Location__C, then click **Save** under **Picklist Options**. Click **Change** next to the controlling field of **Tested Object**. Click **Location__C** in the **Configuration Attributes** column and select **Include Values → Save**.

Now we can create an error condition for the selection product rule so that, based on the filter criteria, the rule gets triggered.

Creating a selection product rule error condition

To create an error condition for this alert, navigate to the selection product rule (**Only show US related products when location is US**) → **Error Condition** → **New**. This will take to the new error condition screen, as shown here:

Figure 3.23 – Selection product rule error condition

Update the filter condition for **United States**. Here, unlike the validation and alert product rules, where we displayed an error message to the user, we want to show the relevant products and select them automatically. This can be done by creating a product rule action.

Creating an alert product rule action

Salesforce CPQ provides several actions out of the box, such as **Enable, Disable, Add, Remove, Show,** and **Hide**. Based on the requirements, these actions can be selected in the **Type** field.

> **Important Note**
>
> Selecting **Remove** will deselect the **Product Options Selected** checkbox. If the product option is hidden, this action won't show in the configurator. You can still use other product rules to select or deselect the **Product Options Selected** checkbox. Selecting **Disable** will prevent users from selecting the **Product Options Selected** checkbox. Product rules let you adjust product options in a bundle on your quote.

In this example for a location-based selection product rule, let's create a sample action to hide the UK products. To do this, navigate to the **Only show US related products when location is US** selection product rule → **Actions** → **New** → **Type Hide & Remove** → **Product Keyboard UK Layout** and click **Save**. This will take you to the **New Product Action** screen, as shown here:

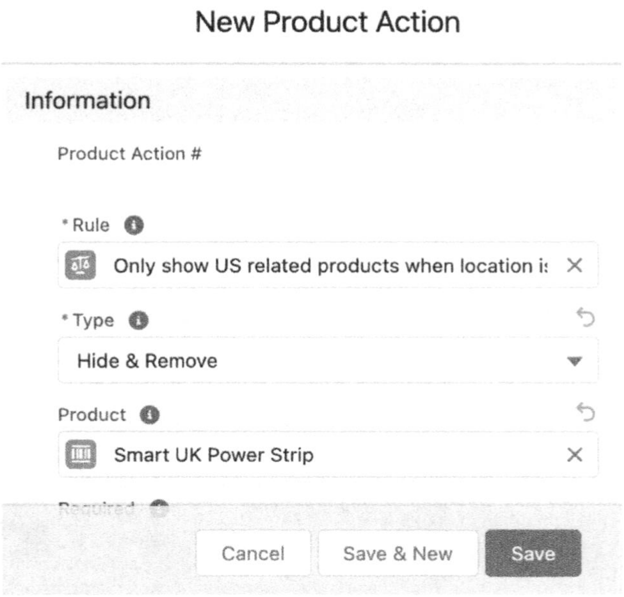

New Product Action

Information

Product Action #

* Rule ⓘ

| ⚖ Only show US related products when location is | ✕ |

* Type ⓘ   ↺

| Hide & Remove | ▼ |

Product ⓘ   ↺

| ▥ Smart UK Power Strip | ✕ |

Required ⓘ

Cancel   Save & New   Save

Figure 3.24 – Product action

For the example shown in the preceding figure, we have selected the type as **Hide & Remove** as we wanted to hide the UK products when the location is selected as **United States**.

> **Important Note**
>
> The **Required** checkbox needs to be selected for the add action product rule otherwise the rule will not work. Similarly, if the **Required** checkbox is checked for any other types, such as Hide, Disable, and Remove, the product rule will not work.

Similarly, create another **product action** to hide the UK products. Follow the same steps and create a product option for each UK product. After that, link the product rule with the bundle using a configuration rule (you can refer to the *Creating a validation product rule* section to see how to create a configuration rule).

Testing the validation product rule in the QLE

Verify the end user experience by opening any opportunity → **Quote** → **Edit Lines**. This takes you to the QLE. Click **Add Products** → **Search Products**, search the **Packt Pro 13" Laptop** bundle, and click **Select**. This will take you to the **Configure Products** page, where the rep can select the location. Before selecting the location, you can see that all the options are enabled, as shown in the following figure:

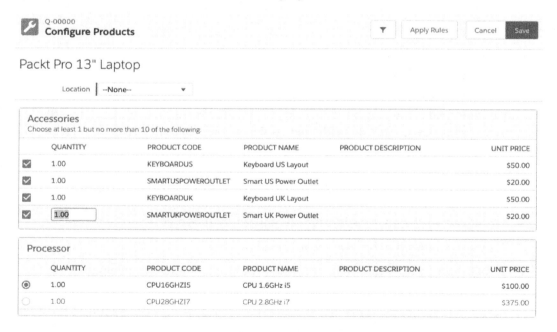

Figure 3.25 – Selection product rule in the QLE

As soon as the rep selects the location as **United States**, the UK accessories will be removed and disabled.

Creating a filter product rule

A filter product rule will dynamically add products to a bundle. The product feature option selection method needs to be dynamic for filter products to work. This will be helpful for use cases where there are new products added frequently. Instead of the rep modifying the options manually, we can use a filter product rule to automatically add them to the bundle.

We need to ensure that the option selection method for the product features is dynamic. This is very important for dynamic bundle creation. In addition, we should make sure that the filter field is available for products and product options so that we can compare both values and create the bundle automatically.

Let's create a product rule of the filter type and associate an *action* with it. Follow the steps provided in the previous product rule sections for the syntax. We will be able to automatically add options to the product bundle using a filter field. For example, you can filter all the products by *product family*, dynamically adding all products of the **promo** type. This product family picklist needs to be added to both products and product options. Based on this, the product rule filter condition can be created.

In the next section, we will learn about an out-of-the-box CPQ mapping that can help admins with CPQ configuration.

Creating twin fields

Salesforce CPQ can mirror custom field values from one object to the other. These fields are called **twin fields**. The values will be passed from one object to the other only if the fields are editable, have matching field types, and have the exact same API names (case-sensitive and even considering space).

Twin fields can replace the creation of formula fields, workflow rules, process builders, or other automation. There are a few points to remember when creating twin fields:

- Twin fields work only for custom fields and not standard fields.
- They are populated only upon record creation.
- Twin fielding is not a good solution when you need the value of a field to be maintained on two records throughout their life.
- Even though a bundle is defined as a favorite, adding the favorite bundle to the QLE will not capture the twin field values.
- Twin fields only map between specific objects.

For example, you want to have an attribute of your product that is defined in a field in the product record. This can be automatically populated in a quote line by using twin fields.

Please refer to the following Salesforce help link for a complete twin field mapping that is available out of the box:

```
https://help.salesforce.com/s/articleView?id=sf.cpq_twin_
fields.htm&type=5
```

Summary

In this chapter, you have learned how to configure products and guide sales reps in automating different business processes for adding products to quotes. Now that we have learned how to use CPQ product configurations out of the box, your reps can sell complex product configurations easily and accurately. These configurations are one-time activities that an admin can create as per the company's business requirements.

In the next chapter, you will learn how to price these products and learn more about CPQ pricing.

4

Configuring CPQ Pricing

In the previous chapter, we discussed how product configuration and CPQ automation help reps sell the right products at accurate prices. Adding the correct combination of products to a customer's quote is crucial for all businesses. It is equally important to sell products at the right price. For example, you may have a few customers who are eligible for special pricing and additional discounts. The same pricing structure may not be applicable for all your other customers. Also, you may be using different currencies in various countries. In addition, you may be selling products at a different price to your retail customers, compared to your wholesale customers. In these cases, how do you make sure the rep is always able to add the right pricing? Salesforce CPQ provides a lot of out-of-the-box functionalities that allow administrators to configure and tailor prices as per their needs. This helps reps automatically price products and add appropriate discounts. In this chapter, you will learn about the important pricing functionalities that CPQ offers.

In this chapter, we will be covering the following topics:

- CPQ pricing
- Learning about pricing methods
- Creating **Multi-Dimensional Quoting (MDQ)**
- Understanding the pricing structure

- Discounting in CPQ
- Creating price rules

CPQ pricing

We know that Salesforce provides **price books** to maintain the list prices of products. A price book is a standard object, which is also available for non-CPQ users. When a rep is working on an opportunity, they can choose the price book from which the products and pricing data will be pulled. Most businesses have different pricing requirements based on the customer to whom they are selling – retail, wholesale, government, commercial, and so on. These requirements can be handled by creating different price books but maintaining this data takes more work. For instance, you may need to change a price book entry only for a specific customer, or price a product based on the volume the customer is buying. Businesses too typically need to adjust pricing year on year. In these and many more such complex scenarios, CPQ pricing helps rather than creating new price books for these scenarios.

When your reps create a quote from an opportunity, it uses the standard selected price book. However, pricing exceptions can be added automatically when needed using CPQ configuration. The same product from the same price book can show two different prices when added to a quote based on the business requirements. The same product can also be added at zero-dollar cost when sold in a bundle and can be changed when sold separately. This configuration could be used in a scenario where you are selling laptops. You don't want your rep to add a price for a charger when sold with the laptop. But you want to charge your customer for the same product when sold outside the bundle. CPQ can help configure these use cases using price rules and other automations.

Price books are mandatory for all products. Make sure the products are active and have been assigned to a price book. If a **product entry** is missing from your price book and a rep creates a quote using that price book, then that product won't be available until you add it to the price book.

Salesforce CPQ provides several pricing methods. A product's price is defined using the associated price method. Based on your business process, admins can decide which pricing method is appropriate. In the next section, let's learn about pricing methods in detail.

Quote the Price Book

At any point, a quote can be associated with only one price book and one currency. Only active price book entries can be added to quotes. A quote should have the same price book as the related opportunity. Incongruous price books will cause syncing from quote lines back to opportunity products to fail.

Learning about pricing methods

CPQ can adjust and modify the price of a product that is derived from the price book. **Pricing methods** can be used to perform price changes when a rep adds a product to a quote. In the previous chapter, while creating products, we saw that we had a section related to pricing, where we can define product pricing attributes. A pricing method is a standard field in the product object. Salesforce CPQ offers the following four pricing methods out of the box:

- List price

- Cost

- Block

- Percent of total

Let's learn more about each of these pricing methods and how an admin can configure them in CPQ. Each pricing method is a picklist value in the product object.

Setting a list price

For the list price value, the price is retrieved from the price book entry of a product. This leverages the native price book and multi-currency features.

To set up the list price for a product, navigate to **App launcher** → **Products** (select any product from your org). In this example, we are setting the price of the product Packt Pro 13 Laptop by navigating to **Packt Pro 13" Laptop** → **Edit** → **Details** → **Salesforce CPQ Pricing** → **List**.

Creating the cost price

The **cost price** is the cost of a product plus the markup. Unlike the list price, the cost price starts with a base price and the rep can adjust this price by an amount or a percentage. For example, when customers have raw materials like wood, metal, and gas, the pricing may often change but not the markup that reps have agreed with the customer. So, the cost plus markup allows an organization to control raw material pricing outside of a price book (which is unfortunately challenging) and into cost records, which allows for the integration of an admin process to keep them up to date.

In CPQ, the cost is a child object of the product object and is very similar to a price book entry as there can be only one cost per product per currency. CPQ selects the cost based on the currency of the quote. Even though there is no price book associated with the cost price, we still need price book entries for these products. Without the price book entries, these products won't be available for selection while adding to a quote. As an admin, let's create a product with the cost price. In this example, let's create a sample product *Cost Price*. To do this, first, we will create the product by navigating to **App Launcher** → **Products** → **New** → **Product Name**. Enter Cost Price in the **Product Name** field and click **Save**.

Once the product is created, we can set the cost price by navigating to the product: **Cost Price** → **Salesforce CPQ Pricing** → **Pricing method** → **Cost** → **Save**.

Once you save the record, the product gets created, as shown here:

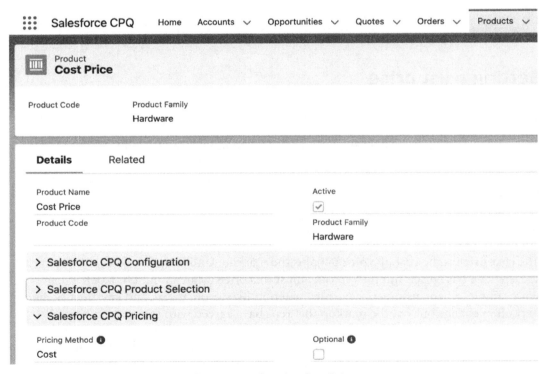

Figure 4.1 – Creating Cost Price

To add the product to the price book, click on the **Related** section of this product and then click on the button **Add to Price Book**. To define the cost for this product, create a cost record by clicking the **New** button. The following screenshot shows the price book entry and the cost record for our sample product, **Cost Price**:

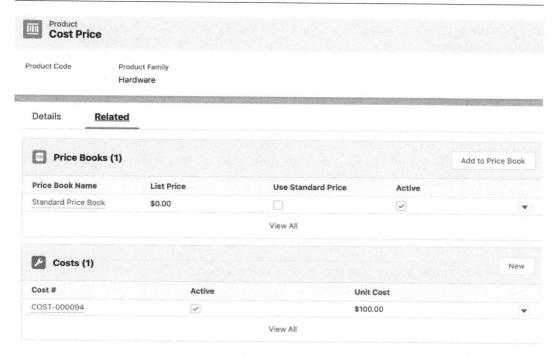

Figure 4.2 – Creating Cost Price

When the cost price is configured for a product, the list price in the price book is set to zero.

Now, this product is ready to be added to a quote. A rep can add this product to a quote by navigating to any sample quote using the path **Quote → Edit lines → Add Products → Search → Cost Price → Select**. This will take you to the **Quote Line Editor (QLE)** page, as shown in *Figure 4.3*. If the **UNIT COST** and **MARKUP** fields are not available in the QLE field set in the Salesforce org that you are working on, make sure your admin adds these fields to the field set.

☐. #	PRODUCT CODE	PRODUCT NAME	QUAN... ↑	UNIT COST	MARKUP	LIST UNIT PRICE	ADDI...	NET UNIT PRICE	NET TOTAL	>
☐ 1	Test CP	Cost Price Product	1.00	$100.00	15.00 %	$0.00		$115.00	$115.00	☆ 🗎 📋 ∿ >

SUBTOTAL: $115.00

QUOTE TOTAL: $115.00

Figure 4.3 – Cost Price QLE

As you can see in the preceding figure, the **UNIT COST** for our sample product, **Cost Price**, is **$100.00**, and when a rep adds a **MARKUP** of 15%, the **NET UNIT PRICE** is calculated automatically. The rep can also edit the **MARKUP** field in the QLE as needed.

Creating the block price

The block price is tier-based pricing. Tier-based pricing means that the price of the product depends on the quantity that a customer is purchasing. The price is also based on the range of the quantity and not the individual product. This is similar to applying volume-based discounts. Let's consider an example where your company is selling printer paper and you want to set a block price for this product. To configure block pricing, let's define the size of the range and prices for the printer paper as per the range. An admin can set up block pricing as shown here:

Printer paper (Quantity)	Price in $
1 to 100	25
101 to 200	50
201 to 300	75

Figure 4.4 – Block price example

Salesforce provides out-of-the-box functionality for block price configuration, which can be defined in the **block price** object. We are using the example shown in *Figure 4.4* to configure the block price of our Salesforce instance. For this example, we are selecting **Printer Paper A4**, which is a sample product in the Salesforce org. To set up block pricing for this product, navigate to **App Launcher → Salesforce CPQ → Products → Related list → Block Price → New**. This will open the screen shown here:

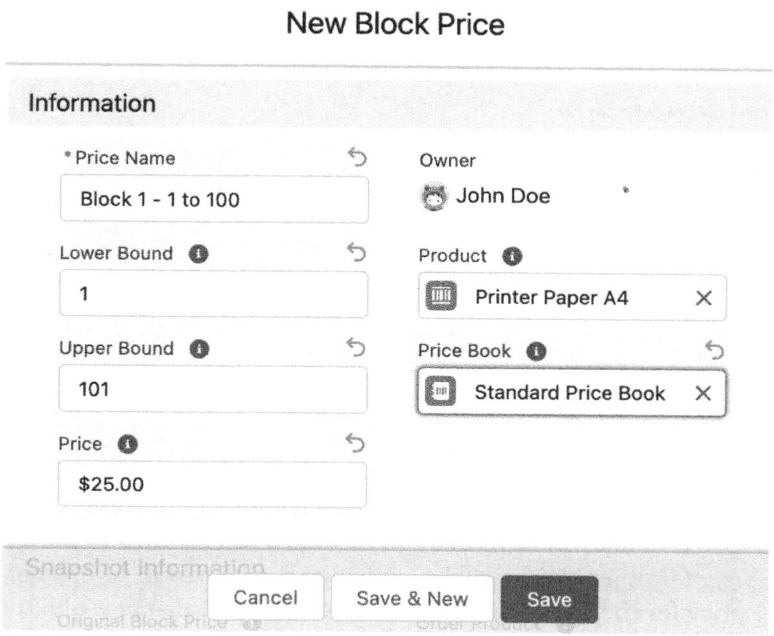

New Block Price

Information

* Price Name ↺

Block 1 - 1 to 100

Owner

🐱 John Doe

Lower Bound ⓘ ↺

1

Product ⓘ

▯ Printer Paper A4   ✕

Upper Bound ⓘ ↺

101

Price Book ⓘ ↺

▯ Standard Price Book   ✕

Price ⓘ ↺

$25.00

Snapshot Information

Original Block Price

Order Product

Cancel   Save & New   Save

Figure 4.5 – Create a block price

Following are a few important fields included in the block price configuration:

- **Price Name**: The name of the tiered pricing.

- **Lower Bound** and **Upper Bound** are the tier ranges. We cannot have any gaps between the lower bound and the upper bound values while defining the block price. The upper bound is excluded and the lower bound is included in the price calculation. When the final tier's upper bound is left blank, it is treated as infinite. It is a common practice when defining price tiers to leave the final tier's upper bound blank so that block pricing scales to any quantity.

- **Price**: The price for each block. For example, any quantity from 1 to 100 will cost $25.

- **Multi-Currency**: When this field is enabled, you will see additional columns for block pricing in each currency when configuring the price.

Similarly, we can create the other blocks and save the record. The following screenshot shows all three blocks in our example:

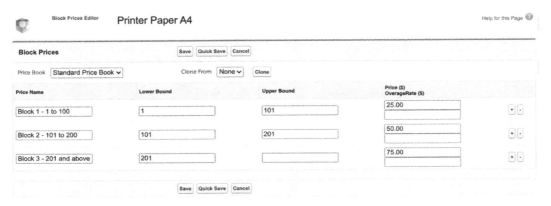

Figure 4.6 – Block price example

Any quantity between 1 and 100 will have a price of $25 when added to the QLE. Similarly, the price for other blocks will be applied as configured in *Figure 4.6*. Block price is the absolute price for the quote line and *NOT* the unit price that gets multiplied by quantity to arrive at the final price.

Adding a block price product to a quote

Let's see how the pricing is displayed when a rep adds a product to the QLE. For this, navigate to any sample quote and search the product you want to add to this quote. In this example, let's choose **Printer Paper A4** by navigating to **Quote → Edit Lines → Add Products → Search → Printer Paper A4 → select**.

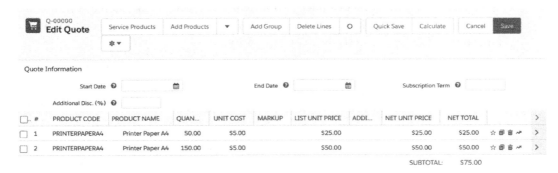

Figure 4.7 – Block Price in QLE

We have added the same product two times, as shown in the preceding figure, to show the block price. For the first line, the quantity is **50** and it falls into tier 1, hence the list price is $25. For the second line, the quantity is **150**, which falls into tier 2, and the price is $50.

What if your customer wants to buy just a few more additional units than the last block? In this example, let's say tier 3 ends at 300 and the customer wants to buy 305 units of paper. To help with this, CPQ provides another feature called **OverageRate** pricing. This is a CPQ **special field**. This feature allows us to define the per-unit price for any quantity above our highest tier.

The block price is the price for the applicable block + (additional units *overage rate).

In our example, let's set the **OverageRate** price as a dollar for each additional unit. The price for 305 units of paper will be the tier 1 block price ($75) + OverageRate per unit ($5).

To configure the OverageRate, admins need to create a special custom currency field in the block price object. To do this, navigate to **App Launcher → Object Manager → Block Price → Fields & Relationship → New → Currency → Next → Field Name → OverageRate** (API name `OverageRate__c`) **→ Next → Save**. This is a one-time setup.

In this field, admins can define the additional per unit price beyond the final block. For this example, we are creating an Overage Rate for **Printer Paper A4**. To do this, navigate to **App Launcher → Salesforce CPQ → Products → Related list → Block Price → Edit** and update **OverageRate**. The following figure shows the **OverageRate** configuration:

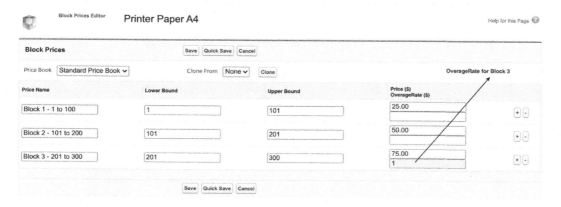

Figure 4.8 – Block Prices OverageRate

In this example, we have added an **OverageRate** of **$1** for the final block.

Creating a percentage of the total price

In this pricing method, the price is calculated as a percentage of its parent quote, quote line group, or bundle total price. For example, when you go to a restaurant, you calculate the tip as a percentage of your total bill amount. A **percent of total** (**PoT**) method is generally used for the subscription product sales process. When the pricing method for a product is set as a percentage of the total, Salesforce CPQ automatically calculates the price.

For example, your company is selling electrical equipment, and **Electrical Installation** is a product in your Salesforce org. The cost of the installation will be a percentage of the total cost of the electrical equipment. Admins can configure this by navigating to **App Launcher → Products → Electrical installation → Edit**. This will take you to the following screen:

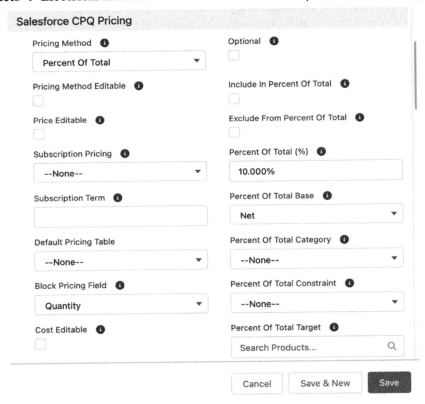

Figure 4.9 – PoT pricing method

On the preceding screen, let's learn about a few important fields related to PoT calculations:

- **Include In Percent Of Total**: This checkbox needs to be selected for fixed-price subscription products so that they are included in the PoT price calculations. This field does not affect non-subscription products.

- **Exclude From Percent Of Total**: When you select this checkbox, CPQ does not use the product (**Electrical Installation** in our example) for calculating the price of the PoT product.

- **Percent Of Total (%)**: This is the percentage that will be used based on the **Percent of Total Base** field. In this example, this field is set to 10 percent (you can set it to any value, as per your business requirements).

- **Percent Of Total Base**: If this field is set to **Net**, then the percentage of the total will be calculated based on the net price, and if it is set to **List**, then the percentage of the total will be calculated based on the list price. In this case, let's calculate it based on the net price. These fields can be set as per the company's price calculation requirements.

- **Percent Of Total Category**: PoT with a category calculates the price based on only the products of this specific category. For example, if you want a hardware maintenance PoT product to cover only hardware products, then this value can be set to **Hardware**.

Let's see how the price gets calculated when the rep adds the example product **Electric Installation** to a quote. To do this, navigate to any quote in your organization: then go to **Edit Lines → Add Products → Search → Electrical Installation → Select**.

When you add only **Electrical Installation** (a product in the Salesforce org) to the QLE without any other products, the price will be zero as there is no base price to calculate the percentage of the total. Now, let's add another product, **Electric Door lock** (this product has a pricing method of **List**). When you are implementing this in your org, you can add the product as required for your implementation. As shown in the following figure, the price of the product **Electrical Installation** is calculated as 10% of the net price of the other products (in this example, **Electric Door lock**):

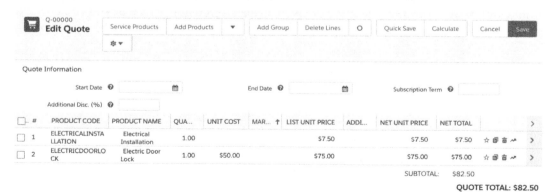

Figure 4.10 – PoT in QLE

The pricing methods that we have seen so far are configured by the Salesforce admin and a rep can use the automated calculations. CPQ also allows reps to manually override price settings. In this scenario, the rep can adjust the prices in the QLE. If your business process needs this functionality, admins can select the field **Price Editable** in the product record. Use this setting with caution as all reps may not be aware of the implications of incorrect pricing. Price editable is often used in negotiated selling environments and paired with appropriate approval rules. This allows sales reps to modify pricing as a negotiation tactic while ensuring all sales are financially sound by requiring appropriate approvals.

We now have learned how to customize the different out-of-the-box CPQ pricing methods. In the next section, we will learn about another pricing functionality that is specific to subscription products and the associated pricing.

Creating Multi-Dimensional Quoting (MDQ)

MDQ allows you to break a long subscription into smaller blocks. This will be useful for scenarios where you have a subscription for 2 years and you want to provide a special discount only for the first year. This flexibility in special-term pricing will help reps to negotiate and close deals faster. Ramp billing and milestone billing contracts are common use cases for MDQ.

MDQ allows you to segment a subscription product multiple times within a single quote in the QLE. Each segment will have its own quantity and discount. For each segment, a separate quote line will be created. Admin can define the segment duration, for example, as either monthly, quarterly, or yearly.

Let's see how an admin can set up a product as an MDQ product. Navigate to the product for which you want to set up an MDQ using the path **App Launcher → Product → Related → Price Dimension → New**. In this example, we are selecting the sample product **VPN License**. This will open the **New Price Dimension** screen as shown here:

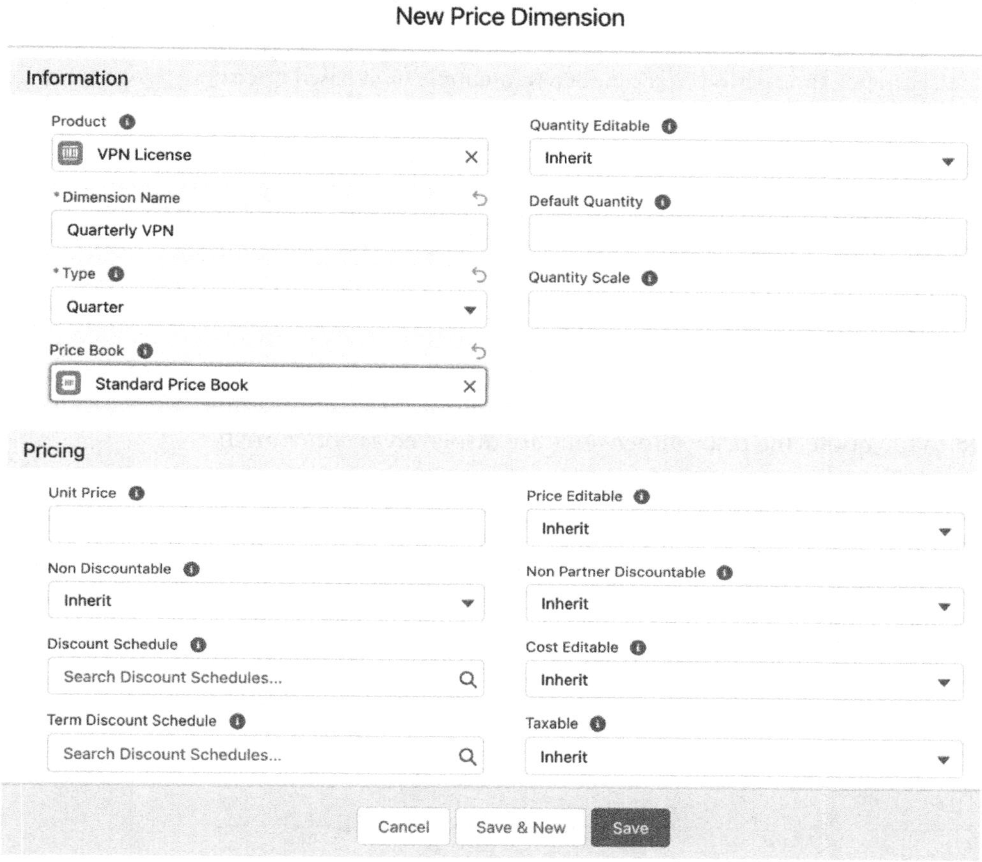

New Price Dimension

Information

Product ⓘ
| 🎬 VPN License | ✕ |

*Dimension Name ↺

Quarterly VPN

*Type ⓘ ↺

Quarter ▾

Price Book ⓘ ↺
| 🗐 Standard Price Book | ✕ |

Quantity Editable ⓘ

Inherit ▾

Default Quantity ⓘ

Quantity Scale ⓘ

Pricing

Unit Price ⓘ

Non Discountable ⓘ

Inherit ▾

Discount Schedule ⓘ

Search Discount Schedules... 🔍

Term Discount Schedule ⓘ

Search Discount Schedules... 🔍

Price Editable ⓘ

Inherit ▾

Non Partner Discountable ⓘ

Inherit ▾

Cost Editable ⓘ

Inherit ▾

Taxable ⓘ

Inherit ▾

Cancel   Save & New   **Save**

Figure 4.11 – New Price Dimension

Let's learn how to configure a few important fields during price dimension creation:

- **Dimension Name**: This field provides a meaningful name.

- **Type**: This field is used to select the time segment. It defines how the quote line can be segmented and can have the values **Year**, **Quarter**, **Month**, **Custom**, or **One Time**. When you select **Custom**, your sales rep gets to select the segments in the QLE. In this example, we selected **Quarter**. For **subscription** billing, we can only have one type of price dimension for a product. There is only one way you can segment a product. For **one-time** billing, you can have multiple dimensions.

- **Price Book**: This field is used to associate a price book and a currency.

> **Important Note**
> There must be a dimension created for each combination of price book/
> currency/time period. You cannot have multiple time-based price dimensions
> for the same currency.

For most of the fields under the **Pricing** section, as shown in *Figure 4.11*, you can inherit
the values from the product. However, these values can be overridden when needed. If
you set the field **Unit Price**, then this price will override the price inherited from the
price book.

Let's see the end user experience for MDQ. To do this, navigate to any quote, then **Edit
Lines → Add Products** and add the MDQ product that your admin has configured. As
shown in the following figure, when an MDQ product (in this example, **VPN License**) is
added to the quote, the price dimensions are displayed as configured:

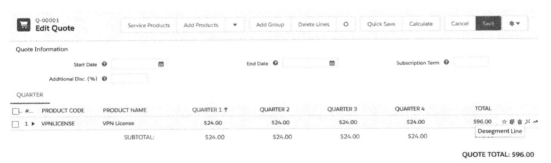

Figure 4.12 – MDQ in the QLE

In this example, the price for each quarter is displayed. Clicking the desegment icon
shown in *Figure 4.12* will hide these segments in the QLE. When we click the same
icon again, the segments reappear. A rep can display the segments as needed. CPQ
creates a quote line for each segment. So, for the aforementioned example, this would be
represented as four quote lines. This can have implications downstream with reporting
and should be taken into consideration. We will learn more about subscriptions in
Chapter 7, Creating Contracts, Amendments, and Renewals.

Before we learn about discounting, it's important to understand how CPQ calculates
the net price from the original price. There is a specific order in which the CPQ pricing
engine calculates net prices. Let's learn about the pricing structure in the next section.

Understanding the pricing structure

This pricing structure describes how Salesforce CPQ applies different prices and discounts to calculate the net price from a list price. The prices defined in each box, such as the original price, list price, and so on, are out-of-the-box features provided by CPQ. This model follows the top-down approach for calculating prices and is also called the **price waterfall**.

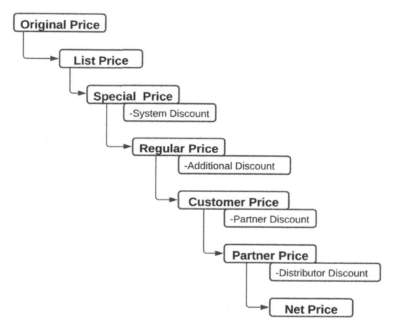

Figure 4.13 – CPQ price waterfall

As shown in the preceding figure, let's learn what each of these prices refers to:

1. **Original Price**: A copy of the price of a product from the price book.

2. **List Price**: This is also a copy of the price, but it can be updated with a price rule or other automation.

3. **Special Price**: This is used for specific situations. The contracted pricing approach described earlier can be used to set a special price. Special prices can also be used in price rules.

4. **System Discount**: When someone purchases a bulk quantity or configures a bundle and so on, then system discounts are applied to the special price. This gives the regular price of the product.

5. **Regular Price**: The special price minus the system discount.

6. **Customer Price**: A sales rep may apply a discretionary discount using a percentage value or an amount. This will be taken off the regular price and the difference is the customer price.

7. **Partner Discount**: Partners may have specific discounts that are applied as needed.

8. **Partner Price**: Calculated by subtracting the partner discount from the customer price.

9. **Distributor Discount**: Applied to the partner price, which gives a final net price.

Out of the box, waterfall prices will be calculated as applicable. If we need to switch the waterfall order, it's not a standard process – admins need to use special fields and customization. **Special Fields** are a specific CPQ feature and admins need to consult Salesforce Help (`https://help.salesforce.com/s/articleView?id=000312751&type=1`) to access the details to use this functionality.

We have just learned how admins can set different pricing methods at the product level and how the price waterfall applies these prices. Let's learn about CPQ discounting and how it can be configured and customized for various business scenarios.

Discounting in CPQ

When a rep is adding products to a quote, most business scenarios will need discounting. These discounting requirements may be specific to a product, customer, partner, quote, or the quantity of the products. CPQ provides several out-of-the-box features for configuring discounts. Let's look at some of the main configurations in the following subsections.

Discount schedules

Discount schedules are system discounts based on the following:

- **Volume**: CPQ can apply discounts based on the volume of products a customer buys.

- **Term**: CPQ provides discounts based on the term length of a subscription product.

- **Cost**: Discounts can be applied directly to a product's cost instead of the list price.

While configuring discount schedules, the upper bound is excluded, and the lower bound is included in the discount tiers, like block pricing. A discount schedule must be assigned to a product's **Term Discount Schedule** field for it to be based on subscription term. Salesforce CPQ evaluates the schedule's discount tiers by subscription term length instead of quantity. To create a discount schedule, navigate to **App Launcher → Discount Schedule Object → New**. This will open the **New Discount Schedule** screen, as shown here:

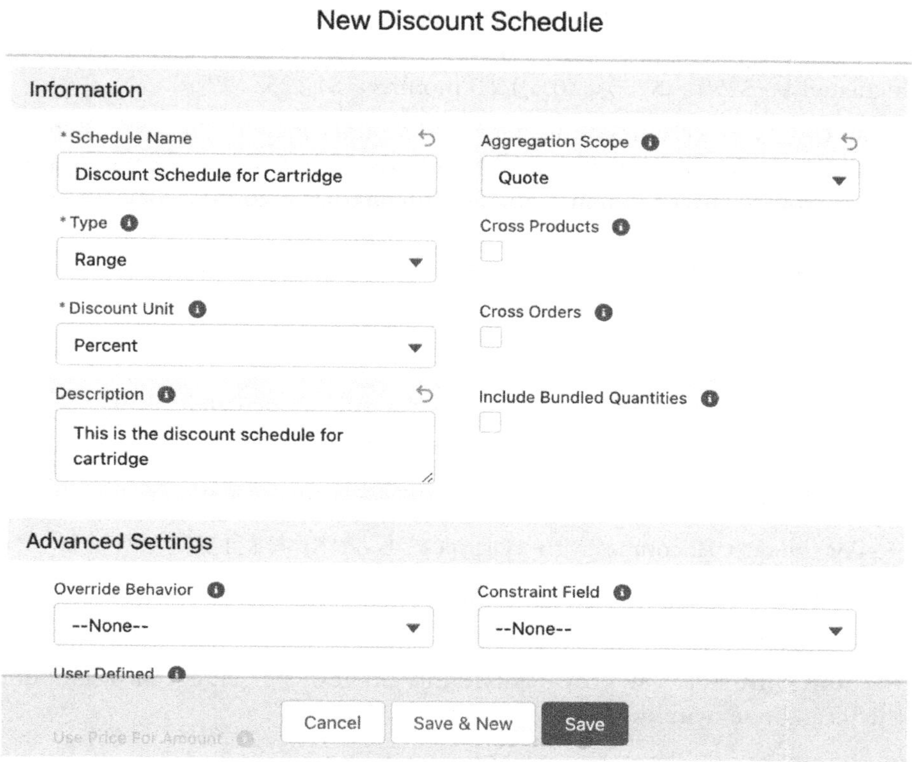

New Discount Schedule

Information

* Schedule Name
Discount Schedule for Cartridge

* Type
Range

* Discount Unit
Percent

Description
This is the discount schedule for cartridge

Aggregation Scope
Quote

Cross Products

Cross Orders

Include Bundled Quantities

Advanced Settings

Override Behavior
--None--

Constraint Field
--None--

User Defined

Use Price For Amount

Cancel   Save & New   Save

Figure 4.14 – New Discount Schedule

Following are a few important fields in discount schedule creation:

- **Schedule Name**: This field provides a descriptive name for the discount schedule that you are creating so that you are aware of its purpose.

- **Type**: CPQ provides two values for this field. These two values determine how discounting calculations are applied:

  - **Range**: Based on the range in which the product quantity falls, a corresponding percentage discount will be applied. For example, let's assume there is a product called *Packt Subscription* and the monthly subscription costs $250. The discount for this product is set to **Range**. The discount schedule is as follows:

    - 1 to 5 Months – 10%

    - 6 to 10 Months – 15%

    - 11 to 15 Months – 20%

If the buyer purchases a 5-month subscription, then a 10% discount will be applied to the list price. In this example, if there are no additional discounts, the net price is calculated as ($250 - ($250 x 10%)) x 5 months = $1,125.

- **Slab**: Units with certain bounds receive discounts equal to the tiers' discount value. Let's take the example of the *Packt Subscription* product whose list price is $15. A volume-based slab discount is configured as follows:

  - 1 to 25 courses – 10%

  - 26 to 50 courses – 20%

  - 51 to 75 Courses – 25%

If the buyer purchases 60 courses, the pricing will be calculated as follows:

  - For 25 courses – 25 * [15 – (10 % of 15)} = $337.5

  - For the next 25 courses – 25 * [15 – (20 % of 15)] = $300

  - For the next 10 courses – 10 * [15 - (25 % of 15)] = $112.5

If there are no additional discounts, the net price amounts to $337.5 + $300 + $112.5 = $750.

- **Discount Unit**: Reps can provide discounts either by percentage or by amount, which can be set with this field.

- **Aggregation Scope**: Discount schedules work on a single quote line. If the same product is added across multiple quote lines in the same quote, this field allows us to aggregate the discounts across a quote or a group within the quote.

- **Cross Products**: When this checkbox is selected, CPQ combines the quantities of all products on the quote for calculating the line quantity against the volume discount tiers. All the products need to share the same **Discount Schedule**. This checkbox can only be set for the **Type** range and not for **Slab**.

- **Cross Orders**: If you want to extend discounts by considering past orders, we can use this checkbox. We will learn more about this in *Chapter 7, Creating Contracts, Amendments, and Renewals*.

- **Include Bundled Quantities**: Selecting this checkbox will take into consideration bundle options. Sometimes, bundled products are included free of charge when the **Bundled** checkbox is enabled on the product options. For example, a keyboard may be free when included in the laptop bundle. By default, the quantities for these free products are not included in the discount schedule calculations. The **Include Bundled Quantities** checkbox can be selected to include these free products in discount calculations.

- **Override Behavior**: This field has two values:

  - **All**: This allows reps to update all tiers.

  - **Current Tier**: This allows reps to update only that specific line.

By default, the discount schedule is based on quantity fields, which can be changed to custom fields as per the business needs. After saving the discount schedule, you can define the tiers. Navigate to **Discount Schedule → Edit Tiers**. In this example, we schedule a discount schedule for **Cartridge**, a sample product in the Salesforce org. This will open the **Edit Tiers** screen as shown here:

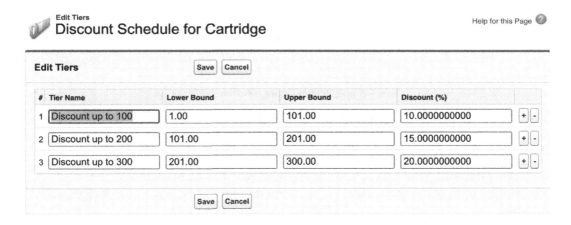

Figure 4.15 – Edit discount tiers

The admin has defined three sample tiers, as shown in the preceding figure. Since the admin selected **Discount Unit** as **Percent**, we see the **Discount (%)** column. If we select **Discount Unit** as **Amount**, then we see the corresponding field. Also, if we have multi-currency enabled at the Salesforce org level, additional fields will be displayed.

Associating the discount schedule with a product

Now that we have created the discount schedule, let's see how an admin can link this to a specific product. To do this, navigate to **App Launcher** → **Product**. For this example, search and select **Cartridge** and then click **Edit**. This will open the screen shown here:

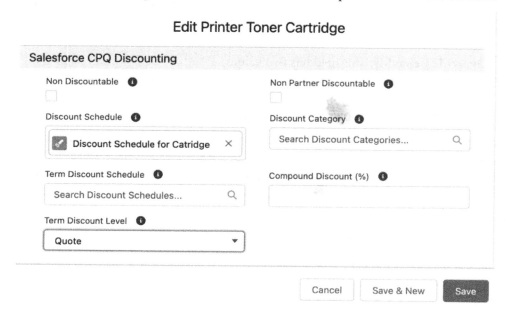

Figure 4.16 – Associate a discount schedule with a product

As shown in the preceding figure, the **Discount Schedule** field is used to apply the volume-based schedule to a product. It is applied based on the quantity. In this example, we linked it to the **Printer Toner Cartridge** product.

The **Term Discount Schedule** field is the discount schedule associated with the subscription term of the **quote line**. For the term discount, we can use only **Range** and not **Slab**.

Discount schedules can also be applied to a product **feature** or an **option** level (we discussed features and option levels in *Chapter 3, Configuring CPQ Products*). The one that is most specific takes precedence. For example, the discount schedule at the option level overrides the discount schedule at the feature level. The discount schedule hierarchy from highest to least priority is as follows:

- Contracted price
- Price dimension
- Product option

- Feature

- Product

Let's view the sample discount schedule in the QLE, shown in *Figure 4.17*. To demonstrate the discount, schedule calculations for two lines have been added. The first line has a quantity of 200 units, which is eligible for a 15% discount as per the discount tier set up. So, the net price is 15% of the list price ($125). For the second line, the quantity has been updated to 50 units, which is eligible for the 10% discount. The net price for line two is 10% of the list price ($125).

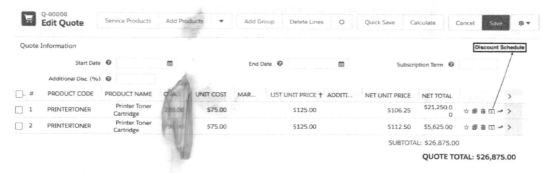

Figure 4.17 – Discount schedule in the QLE

In most business scenarios, a fixed price per unit will be adequate. In addition, pricing methods, discounting tools, and subscription pricing will suffice. For complex pricing requirements, Salesforce CPQ provides a powerful configuration – **price rules**, which can be customized. Let's learn about price rules in the next section.

Creating price rules

Price rules are used to update a product's price in quote lines and automate price calculations in CPQ. They are an extension of out-of-the-box CPQ functionality. These rules are helpful for your business when you have products that change in response to the presence of other products in a quote. Price rules allow admins to conditionally update the value of any field (not only the price) in the quote, quote line, or quote line group. Price rules are useful if you need product values to dynamically change based on other products in the quote. For example, if your rep wants to sell two ink cartridges and one printer paper whenever a printer is sold, then a price rule could be created to automatically add two cartridges and one printer paper when a printer is added to the quote. Price rules also can handle dynamically changing data for subscriptions by utilizing MDQ (multi-dimensional quoting). Price rules can also be used in quote templates, which we will learn about in *Chapter 5, Generating and Configuring Quote Template*.

Like product rules, price rules also follow the `if`/`then` structure. Price rules have a **price condition**, **scope**, and **action**. In the previous chapter, we saw that product rules mainly control the user interface of a QLE or a configurator. You can hide/show/enable/disable products. Product rules restrict the visibility of products based on conditions. They also provide alerts and validations to control product additions to a quote. Price rules are different and much more powerful, and they can replace standard Salesforce configurations such as **Workflow**, **Flow**, or **Apex** logic.

> **Important Note**
> Salesforce CPQ does *not* recommend that any of this logic should be used with quote lines or subscriptions.

Price rules inject value into a quote or quote line object field.

Enabling the advanced calculator

Price rules will not work with the CPQ **Legacy Calculator**. As a prerequisite, we need to enable the advanced calculator in the CPQ package settings. To do this, navigate to **Setup → Installed Packages → CPQ → Pricing and Calculation → Use Legacy Calculator**, uncheck the **Legacy Calculator** checkbox, and click **Save**. This action will display the message shown here:

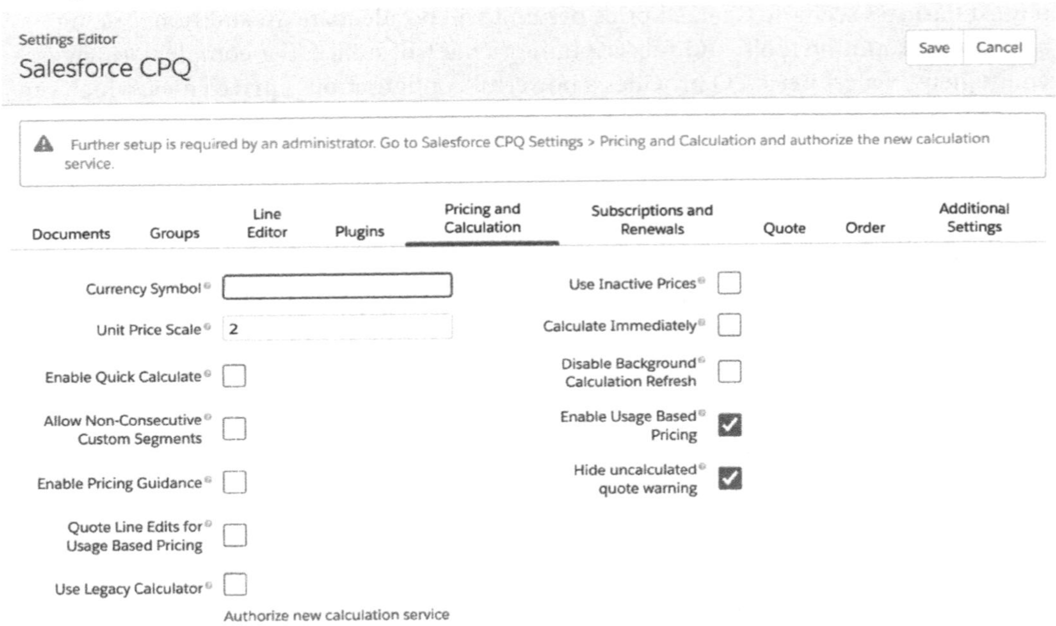

Figure 4.18 – Enable the advanced calculator

Click on **Authorize new calculation service** and then click **Allow**. Once you refresh the screen, the popup (warning) shown in the preceding figure will be disabled.

Creating a sample price rule

Let's create a price rule to understand the concept. This price rule can be extended to build complex rules with multiple conditions. For instance, *Packt Corp* is selling laptops to multiple customers. An **account** object has the field **Account Type**, which captures the type of the customer. There will be different types of customers in the Packt Salesforce org, including direct customers, channel partners, technology partners, and many more. For example, we want Salesforce CPQ to automatically calculate and apply discounts based on the account type. When a laptop is sold to a direct customer, we would like the discount to be 10%; for channel partners, 15%; and for technology partners, 25%. For accounts where the tier is blank, no discounts should be applied. We need to create the *account type* in the quote object with the same picklist values as we have in an account object.

Let's learn how admins can configure this scenario using price rules. To create a price rule, navigate to **App Launcher → Price Rules → New**. This will open the **New Price Rule** window as shown here:

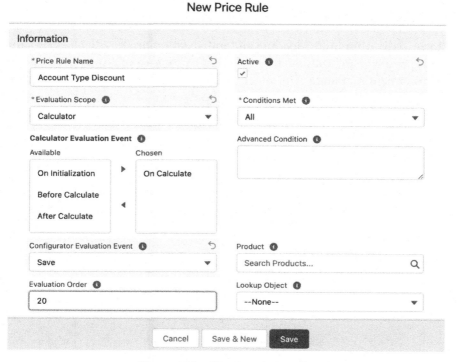

Figure 4.19 – Creating a price rule

Price rules can be created to target either the **configurator** or the **calculator**. In the preceding figure, we can view a few important fields involved in price rule creation, which include the following:

- **Price Rule Name**: This provides a descriptive name to identify the price rule.

- **Active**: This field indicates whether the price rule is active or not. This checkbox can be deselected in the process of testing and reselected for the implementation of Salesforce CPQ.

- **Evaluation Scope**: This defines where the price rule will be evaluated. Set this value to **Configurator** when you want the price rule to be triggered when your rep is configuring the products. If you want this rule to fire when a user is adjusting price in the QLE, select **Calculator**. For this example, let's select **Calculator** as we want the rule to fire in the QLE.

- **Conditions Met**: We will be adding one or more conditions to the price rule. We can select **Any**, **All**, or **Custom**, based on the criteria that trigger this price rule. For this example, let's select **All** for this field, as we want to fire the rule when all the conditions are met. When you select **Custom**, you can provide the logical conditions in the **Advanced Condition** field (for example, 1 AND (2 OR 3)).

- **Calculator Evaluation Event**: This field will have the following picklist values:

  - **On Initialization**: In the loading and initialization process, the CPQ engine loads **products** and **options** first, followed by **lookup relationships**, and then the **formula field metadata**. The system then evaluates the price rules if this **option** is selected. **On initialization** is executed only once when you edit lines and enter CPQ Visualforce pages.

  - **On Calculate**: When this value is chosen, then the price rules are evaluated while CPQ calculates the quote's price.

- **Before Calculate**: When this value is chosen, then price rules are evaluated before CPQ calculates the quote's price.

- **After Calculate**: Price rules are evaluated after CPQ calculates the quote's price.

For this example, let's choose **On Calculate**.

- **Configurator Evaluation Event**: This field can have two values, **Save** or **Edit**. Selecting **Save** will fire the rule when the record is being saved and **Edit** will fire the rule in real time. Unless you really need to see the calculations in real time, it is not advisable to select **Edit** as this will impact performance.

- **Evaluation Order**: When your Salesforce organization has multiple price rules, this field determines the order in which the price rules will be triggered. Higher-order rules are evaluated last. CPQ evaluates price rules in order from lowest to highest. For example, a price rule with **Evaluation Order** set to 10 is evaluated before a price rule with **Evaluation Order** set to 20. Therefore, if multiple price rules act on the same product, the price rule with the lowest evaluation order takes precedence. Numbering is within the evaluation event. While creating the rule, leave some gaps in the evaluation order numbering, so that when there is a new requirement, you can easily add that. Please refer to Salesforce help at `https://help.salesforce.com/s/articleView?id=sf.cpq_price_rule_considerations.htm&type=5` to understand how price rules operate.

- **Lookup Object**: Let's learn about this in the *Creating a price rule using a lookup object section*. You can leave this field blank for this example.

Creating a price condition

Now let's create a price condition for an example product where we want to provide different discounts based on the account type. The price condition determines when the rule should trigger. To create a price condition, navigate to **App Launcher → Price rules**. Select the example product account type discount for which you want to create the rule by navigating to **Account Type Discount → Price Conditions → New**. This will open the screen shown here:

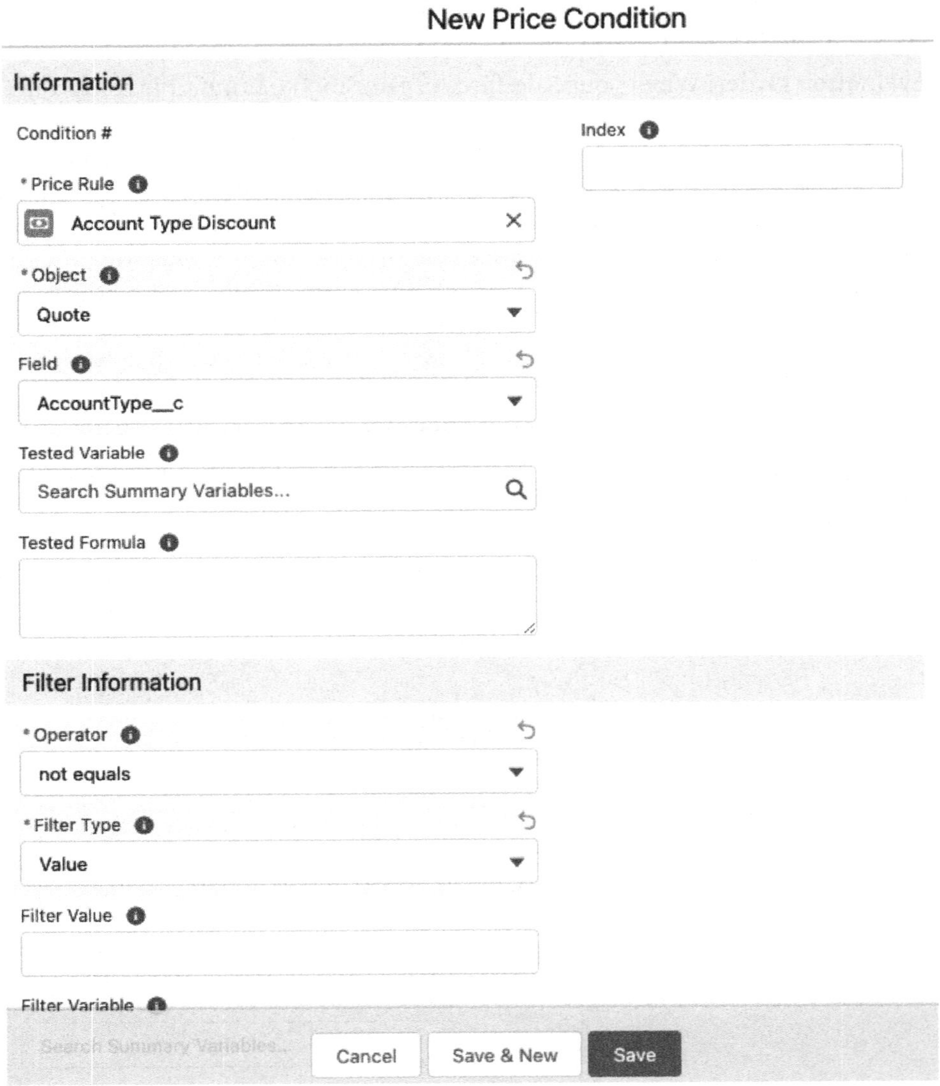

Figure 4.20 – Creating a price condition

Price conditions are like the product rule conditions that you learned about in the previous chapter. As shown in *Figure 4.20*, a few important fields in price conditions include the following:

- **Price Rule**: The name of the price rule for which you are creating this condition. A price condition is evaluated based on the fields **Object** and **Field**. In this example, we want to verify the **Account Type** field in the quote. When it is not blank, we want to assign different levels of discounts that we can configure in price actions.

- **Tested Variable**: A summary variable can be created and used in the tested variable to evaluate the price condition. For this example, we can leave this blank. We have already covered summary variable creation details in the previous chapter. You can use it if your requirements need this condition to be evaluated using a summary variable.

- **Tested Formula**: You can add any cross-object formula to evaluate the tested formula value. For this example, we can leave this blank.

- **Filter Type**: This field determines how the filter can be evaluated. It can have the following options:

  - **Value**: When you choose this option, the filter condition will be evaluated based on this value.

  - **Variable**: When you choose a variable for the type, you can use a summary variable to assess the filter condition.

  - **Formula**: When you choose a formula for the type, you can create a cross-object formula to evaluate the filter condition.

For this example, we are setting **Filter Type** to **Value**.

Based on your business requirements, other configurations can also be used to define price conditions. For using formulas, the standard Salesforce formula syntax can be followed. A price condition record is unnecessary if you want your price action to execute irrespective of any condition.

Let's create a price action to update the field values – in this case, *discount*.

Creating a price action

A price action describes what the price rule should do, and which value it should update.

We have created a price rule and a price condition to apply the account type discount. In this section, we will define the price actions, which are the actions that the rule will perform once the conditions are met. First, navigate to **App Launcher** → **Price Rules**. In this example, we select the price rule **Account Type Discount**. Then, create a price action by navigating to **Price Action** → **New**. This will open the screen shown here:

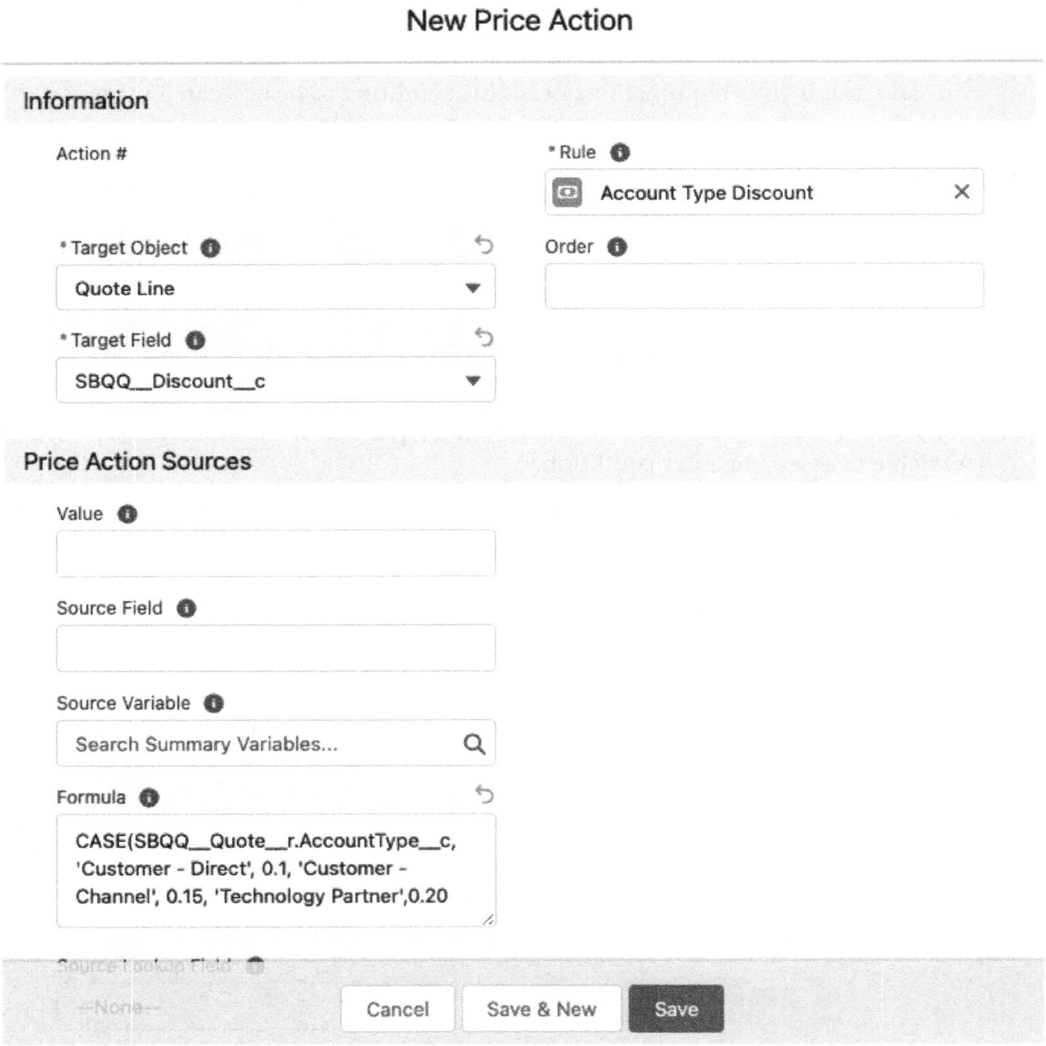

New Price Action

Information

Action #		* Rule ℹ
		🔳 Account Type Discount ✕

* Target Object ℹ ↺	Order ℹ
Quote Line ▼	

* Target Field ℹ ↺

SBQQ__Discount__c ▼

Price Action Sources

Value ℹ

Source Field ℹ

Source Variable ℹ

Search Summary Variables... 🔍

Formula ℹ ↺

CASE(SBQQ__Quote__r.AccountType__c,
'Customer - Direct', 0.1, 'Customer -
Channel', 0.15, 'Technology Partner',0.20

Source Lookup Field ℹ

--None--   Cancel   Save & New   Save

Figure 4.21 – Creating a price action

A few important fields while creating a price action include the following:

- **Target Object** and **Target Field**: They determine the field that needs to be updated for a specific object. The API name of the field should be added to the picklist **Target Field**. In this example, when the price conditions are met, we want to update the discount field (**SBQQ__Discount__C**) in the **Quote Line** object.

- **Price Action Sources**: This determines the source for the value to be updated in the target field. CPQ provides five different sources:

  - **Value**: You can directly provide a value that you want to update the target field with. For this example, we are leaving it blank.

  - **Source Field**: If you want to update this source from another quote line field, you can provide the field reference here.

  - **Source Variable**: Use a summary variable as required. For this example, we are leaving this blank.

  - **Formula**: Provide a formula if you want to use the formula result field to update the target field. For this example, we want direct customers to have 10%, channel customers to have 15%, and technology partners to have a 20% discount. We are using the formula using case statements, as shown in *Figure 4.21* to calculate the discount value.

  - **Source Lookup Field**: The API name of the field from the lookup object record that matches the price condition. Lookup queries are covered in the *Creating a lookup query for the price rule* section of this chapter.

Testing a price rule in the QLE

Let's verify the end user experience for this sample price rule. Verify that the account type related to a sample quote is set to one of the three values **Customer - Direct**, **Customer - Channel**, or **Technology Partner** (these are sample account types in our Salesforce instance). For this example, let's choose **Technology Partner**. To verify the discount price rule, navigate to **Quote → Edit Lines**. Add any product and the corresponding discount will be applied automatically in the quote line **Additional Discount** field. This works for any product because the **Product** lookup was left blank in the initial rule configuration.

Creating a price rule using a lookup object

In the *Creating a price action* section, we saw that there are five sources where we can provide the source field to update the target field. One of the price action sources is the lookup object. In this section, we will see how a price rule can be created using a lookup object. In the previous example, we created a price rule to apply discounts based on the account type field. This use case may also have additional requirements such as applying these discounts only for hardware products. We need to verify the product family (this is a standard field for the product object) along with the customer type.

We can create multiple price rules for this scenario but as the attributes increase, the logic becomes complex. We can use a lookup object to store this custom data. Using this lookup object, we can define a single price rule that will automatically apply a discount.

As shown in *Figure 4.22*, a custom object is created where you list all the attributes that need to be stored and use the fields of that custom object in the price action source. To demonstrate this, we have created a custom object called **Account Type Discounts Name** and added test data.

	Account Type Discounts Na... ↑ ∨	Account Type ∨	Product Family ∨	Discount ∨
1	Discount001	Customer - Direct	Service	5%
2	Discount002	Customer - Direct	Hardware	8%
3	Discount003	Customer - Channel	Hardware	9%
4	Discount004	Customer - Channel	Service	10%
5	Discount005	Installation Partner	Hardware	10%
6	Discount006	Installation Partner	Service	12%

Account Type Discounts
Recently Viewed ▼
6 items · Sorted by Account Type Discounts Name · Updated 2 minutes ago

Figure 4.22 – Lookup object example

The preceding figure shows the sample data for applying discounts. When the rep selects an account, **Customer - Channel**, and adds a product belonging to the product family **Service**, then a 10% discount should be applied automatically. Additional attributes can be added to this custom object as required. Now, let's create a price rule using the lookup object. Navigate to **App Launcher → Price Rules → New**. This will open a **New Price Rule** window as shown here:

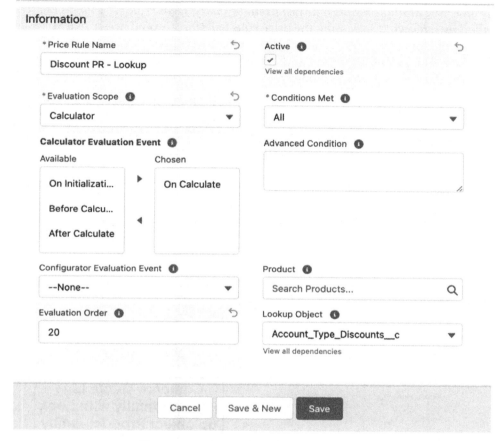

Figure 4.23 – Price rule with a lookup object

Compared to the previous price rule in *Figure 4.19*, where **Lookup Object** was blank, in this price rule, we update **Lookup Object** with the custom object value **Account_Type_ Discounts__c** and then click **Save**. CPQ knows that this custom object holds the data to configure the price rule.

Creating a lookup query for the price rule

Now let's add price conditions as required. Refer to the previous price condition for the navigation path and syntax.

Next, create a lookup query associated with the price rule. The lookup query *must* return exactly one result. When the lookup query returns multiple records (rows), CPQ will display an error: *Multiple results returned from the query. Please contact your Salesforce CPQ administrator* while executing the price rule. Salesforce would prefer that you keep the number of lookup queries in your org at less than 10. Also, the same custom object can support multiple queries as long as the query returns a single result. Lookup queries will filter the data from the lookup object.

A user can select the attributes for the quote. In this example, the user selects a product family – **Service**, and account type – **Customer - Direct**. To create a lookup query, navigate to **App Launcher → Price Rules**. In this instance, select the price rule **Discount PR - Lookup → Related → Lookup Queries → New**. This will open the **New Lookup Query** screen as shown here:

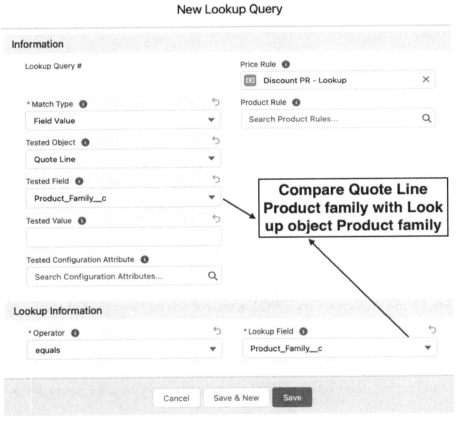

Figure 4.24 – New lookup query

Let's learn about some of the important fields for configuring the price rule lookup query:

- **Match Type**: Using this field, the target data for the lookup query will be evaluated. This can have three values:

    - **Field Value**: When you choose this value, select an option from the **Tested Object** drop-down field and an option from the **Tested Field** dropdown.

    - **Static Value**: If you select this picklist option, then enter the user-defined value in **Tested Value**.

    - **Configuration Attribute**: If we choose this value, then we need to select the configuration attribute from the dropdown **Tested Configuration Attribute**.

- **Tested Object** and **Tested Field** names are compared against the lookup values. In this example, we are going to check the field value **Service (Tested Field)** in the **Quote Line (Tested Object)** object. **Service** is the picklist attribute of the **Product Family** field that we created. This picklist value will not be available in the lookup query object, and you need to add this picklist value (**API** value). You will be comparing this value against an **Operator** in the **Lookup** field. In this example, we are using the *equals* operator and the **Lookup** field product family (**Service**). Again, this lookup field's picklist value needs to be updated (**API** name). In the lookup query, we are only specifying the **Lookup** field name. The lookup object is linked at the time of creating the price rule header.

Multiple lookup queries can be created as required. To satisfy the use case of providing a discount based on product family and service, another lookup query is needed for this rule. Once the lookup queries are configured, we are ready to create a price action.

Creating a price action for the lookup query price rule

To create a price action, navigate to **App Launcher** → **Price Rules**. In this instance, select the price rule **Discount PR Lookup** → **Price Action** → **New**. This will open the screen shown here:

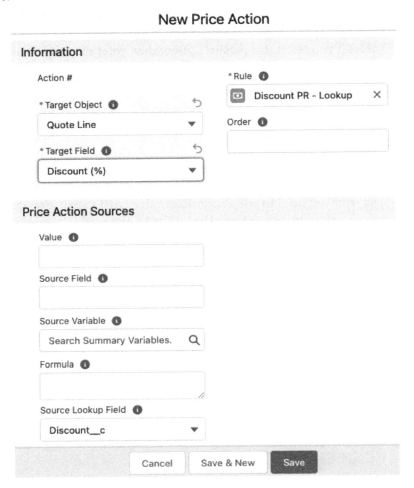

Figure 4.25 – Lookup query price rule – New Price Action

As shown in *Figure 4.25*, **Target Field** – in this example **Discount (%)** in the quote line – is updated by **Source Lookup Field** (the discount from the lookup object).

You can verify the end user experience by adding this sample product to the QLE. Based on the lookup object data, the corresponding discounts will be applied automatically. Salesforce debug log will create a log entry for the actual query and results (if any). This is quite useful during troubleshooting.

Summary

In this chapter, you learned how pricing and discounting can be automated using CPQ. We also discussed the creation of price rules, which help control quoting and optimize sales. These CPQ pricing concepts can help customize use cases as per company-specific business processes. In addition, we learned about out-of-the-box CPQ pricing methods: list prices sourced from price book entries, cost prices sourced from costs, block prices featuring tiered pricing, and PoT where the price can be calculated based on other line items.

We looked at MDQ basics, which helps break a long subscription into smaller pieces to treat each piece differently. We also covered how discount schedules can be used to create volume-based discounts considering the quantity or terms of quote lines. This pricing automation can help reps accurately create quotes for customers and close deals more quickly, which helps increase revenue. In the next chapter, we will learn how we can configure quote templates, generate quotes, and send them to customers using CPQ.

5
Generating and Configuring Quote Templates

So far, we have learned how to create **opportunities**, associate them with **quotes**, and add **product configurations**. We also learned how we can automate pricing and provide accurate discounts to customers. The next step is to finalize the quote, which is then sent to customers for approval and to have their signatures added. Quotes contain information about products and pricing. Reps can generate multiple quotes as per customer requirements and easily share them.

In this chapter, we will learn about generating CPQ documents. **Salesforce CPQ** provides out-of-the-box features to customize quote documents. Reps can send quotes to customers in an email, and we can also have third-party integrations for eSignatures.

In particular, we will be covering the following topics:

- Generating PDF quotes using quote templates
- Creating quote templates and template content
- Creating template content and linking quote templates
- Integrating **DocuSign** for eSignatures

Generating PDF quotes using quote templates

The formatting and the content of a quote document are controlled by the **Quote Template**. Templates contain different sections, and both the template and sections can be customized to configure which line items are displayed, what fields and signature fields can be added, what terms and conditions can be added, and so on. Templates can contain any number of sections, and we can reuse sections between multiple templates. Quote templates contain information about quotes, quote lines, products, pricing, discounts, and much more. These quote templates can be customized and used to present this information in a professional-looking document, which can be in the form of a **PDF** or Microsoft Word document.

In the next subsection, let's learn how an administrator can generate quote documents in Salesforce CPQ.

Generating a quote document

To generate a quote document, navigate to any quote that you have created in your Salesforce org. Navigate to **App Launcher → Salesforce CPQ → Quote**. Then, select any quote that you have created previously. On the quote page layout, you will find two buttons: **Preview Document** and **Generate Document**.

In this example, we will select the **Preview Document** button. Once the user selects this button, it opens the following screen:

Figure 5.1 – The quote Preview Document dialog in Salesforce CPQ

Reps can select the template name and the paper on which the quote PDF needs to be printed. For this example, we are selecting **Training Sample** for the template and **Default** for the paper size.

When you click on the **Preview** button, the preview document opens, as shown here:

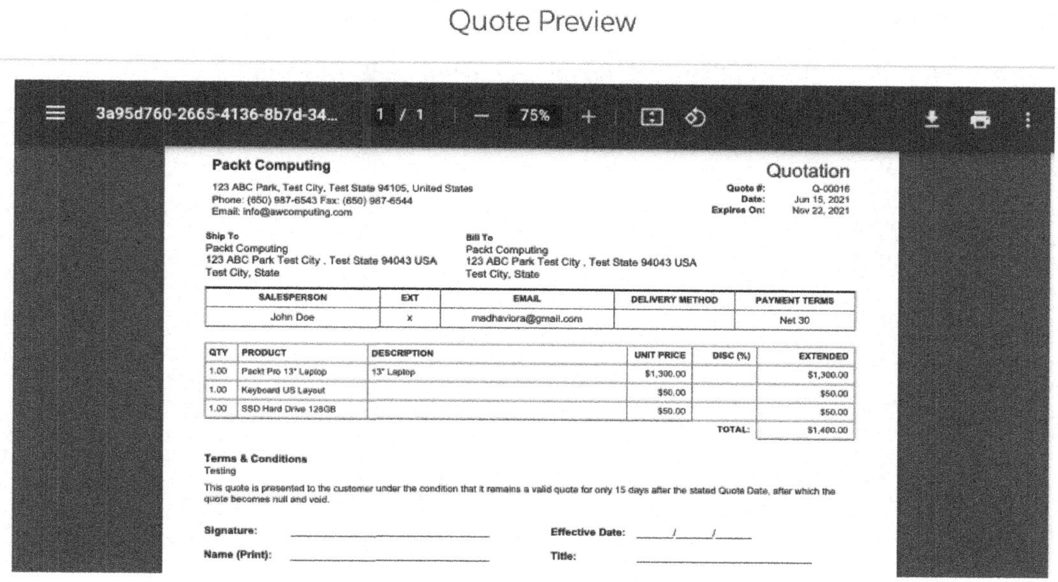

Quote Preview

Figure 5.2 – The Quote Preview document

Here, you can see the header, company logo, shipping and billing addresses, and much more. You can see the quote line items, terms and conditions, and signature fields. The quote preview mode helps reps to validate all of this information. They can ensure that all details are accurate, or they can make changes before generating the actual quote. Once the rep validates everything, the quote document can be generated by using the **Generate Document** button on the **Quote** page layout.

Salesforce CPQ provides a sample template that can be either used as it is or customized as per your business needs. The template that we used to print the quote in *Figure 5.2* is a sample out-of-the-box template that Salesforce CPQ provides. Administrators can create different templates and add content as required.

In the next section, let's learn how administrators create new templates.

Creating quote templates and template content

A quote template controls the format of your company's quotes. Templates can be created as per your company's quote generation requirements. They contain different sections, which can be customized. You can create multiple quote templates as per your business requirements and set one as the default.

To create a new template, navigate to **App Launcher → Quote Template → New**. This will open the following screen:

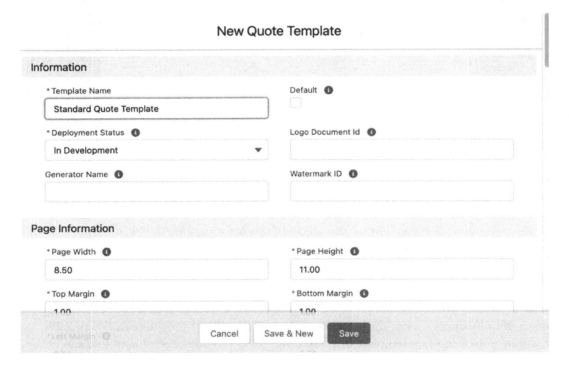

Figure 5.3 – The New Quote Template form

As shown in *Figure 5.3*, there are a few important fields in the **New Quote Template** form:

- **Template Name**: This field is used to provide a meaningful name for your quote template.

- **Default**: You can select this checkbox if you want to set this template as the default template for reps when they are creating new quote documents.

- **Deployment Status**: While your administrator is working on building the template, this status can be set to **In Development**, and once the template is built, this status can be set to **Deployed**.

- **Logo Document Id**: If you want to add a company logo, then you can add the record ID corresponding to the logo stored in Salesforce **documents** in this field.

- **Watermark ID**: Here, you can provide the record ID of the watermark image that you want to use in your PDF. The watermark can be conditionally displayed for specific quotes. You have a **Watermark Shown** checkbox on the quote that needs to be selected for the watermark to get printed on the quote template. You can upload the watermark image in **Salesforce Files** to get the record ID. This checkbox can also be updated using a salesforce **flow** or **apex** that is based on business requirements, rather than reps updating it manually for every quote. For example, whenever the quote status is approved, this field can be automatically updated using apex code logic in the backend.

- **Page Information**: This section contains many formatting options, such as height, width, margins, and much more.

The rest of the quote template contains the sections **Header/Footer Information** and **Corporate Information** for the company details. It also includes a section to define the font and styling, including group styling, section titles, and print options. Most of these details are for formatting the template. You can fill in these details as required and save the template.

Attaching additional documents

Apart from sending a quote to customers, we can send them additional documents. For example, if you have product specifications, installation instructions, special instructions, a company overview, and anything else that you would like to send to your customers, you can upload those documents to Salesforce Files and capture the record ID, which will be later used to attach the documents. Additional documents can be attached to a quote in three different ways:

- We can attach additional documents to the quote template. To link the additional documents to the quote template, navigate to any **Quote Template → Related → Additional Documents → Reference** to add the record ID in the **External Id** field and enter details into the **Document Name** and **Display Order** fields, as shown here:

Figure 5.4 – Attaching an additional document to a quote template

- Instead of attaching the additional documents to the quote template, you can also attach them directly to the quote. To do this, navigate to any **Quote → Related → Additional Documents → New**. The record ID of the additional document can be updated here. This will be useful if you want to send a specific document or any promotional info to your customers.

- Additional documents on a quote can be associated with the **Product**, **Opportunity**, or **Quote** fields. Attaching it to the **Product** field provides dynamic behavior. For example, based on the specific product, a related document can be attached. Quote templates and additional documents can be selected by the rep while previewing or generating the quote documents.

In the next section, let's learn how quote templates can be customized in the backend by administrators. Template content can be created in a **Template Content** object in Salesforce.

Creating template content and linking quote templates

First, we need to build the content and then link the content to create the quote template. The created content, such as the cover page, customer information, signature blocks, and much more, can be reused in multiple templates. A template's content can be adjusted and displayed in a quote template, and the same content can be displayed in a completely different order in another template. Based on the content, templates are formed and template sections are how content is added:

- Quote templates define the layout of the documents that your reps generate from a quote.

- Template content is created to store specific data in the quote sections.

- Template sections are used to position and style the template content in the quote document.

The types of content

Six types of content can be generated in Salesforce CPQ:

- **HTML**: This is static text, with or without merge fields. This type of content is mainly used for the cover letter, cover page, customer information, company information, signature block, and much more.

- **Line items**: These display details about the quote line fields such as products, quantities, discounts, and so on. Line items can be displayed in a tabular format. We can also group them by a field or display them in separate blocks and display columns dynamically. The quote template should be a representation of the products purchased without changing the product catalog to meet the needs of the template.

- **Quote terms**: These contain the terms and conditions for the quote. This can also be dynamic and based on the quote type. The quote terms can also be stored and presented using product records.

- **Custom**: Custom content allows us to display a **Visualforce page** within the section of our quote template.

- **Template top**: The template top and bottom can be used in a similar way to a header and footer in any document. The template top can contain the company logo, the billing and shipping addresses, and so on.

- **Template bottom**: The template bottom can include notes, signatures, dates, and much more.

Now, let's learn how to create each of these types of content in the Salesforce instance.

Creating HTML content

We can create HTML content as per the company's requirements and add it to the relevant section of the template. Let's learn how an administrator can create HTML content. In this example, we want to create template content named `Prepared For`. To build the template content, navigate to **App Launcher** → **Template Content** → **New** → **HTML** → **Continue**. This will open the following screen:

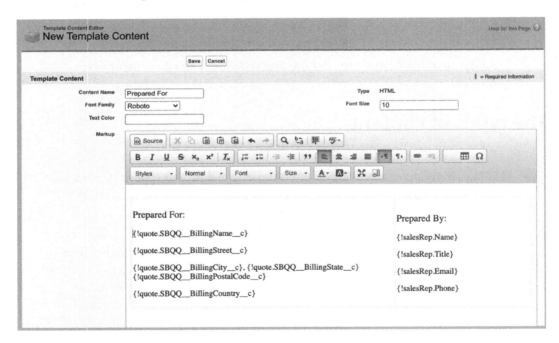

Figure 5.5 – Creating HTML content in Salesforce CPQ

Let's learn about a few important fields in the **New Template Content** form:

- **Content Name**: This field allows us to enter a meaningful name for the template content.

- **Type**: This field indicates the type of content you choose to create. In this example, we are creating HTML content.

- **Font Family**, **Font Size**, and **Text Color**: These controls are for formatting options that can be chosen as per your requirements.

- **Markup**: This field is where we will create and customize the content. We have a lot of formatting options here. This field can contain static and dynamic content. Merge fields can be used to create dynamic content. Merge fields are automatically updated in your content when the referenced field is updated on the object.

  The syntax for a merge field is `{!objectName. FieldName }`. For example, if you want to reference the **Billing Name** field on the quote object, then the merge field syntax would be `{!quote.SBQQ__BillingName__C}`.

  The data in the HTML section can be sourced from the Salesforce objects, as shown in the following table:

Object Name	Merge Field
All fields in CPQ Quote	`!template`
All fields in Quote Template	`!quote`
All fields related to Primary contact on CPQ Quote	`!primaryContact`
All fields related to Salesrep on CPQ Quote	`!SalesRep`

Table 5.1 – Merge field objects

It is important to note that for a field to be available as a merge field, it must exist on the quote. If you need to reference fields from other objects, such as **opportunities** or **accounts,** you can create a **formula** field or use any other automation to move the related field to the quote. We cannot reference quote line data in the HTML section. Instead, it's always going to be referenced in the quote line section.

- **Source**: We can use this button if the administrator wants to work directly in CSS and HTML to perform the edits.

Linking the HTML content to a quote template

The content that you have created can be linked to a quote template. Content can be reused in multiple templates in the order and format that you need. To link the HTML content, open the quote template that you want to customize. In this example, let's use the template named Standard Quote Template that we created in *Figure 5.3*. To do this, navigate to **Quote Template**. Click on the **Related** tab. Select **Sections** → **New**. This will open the following screen:

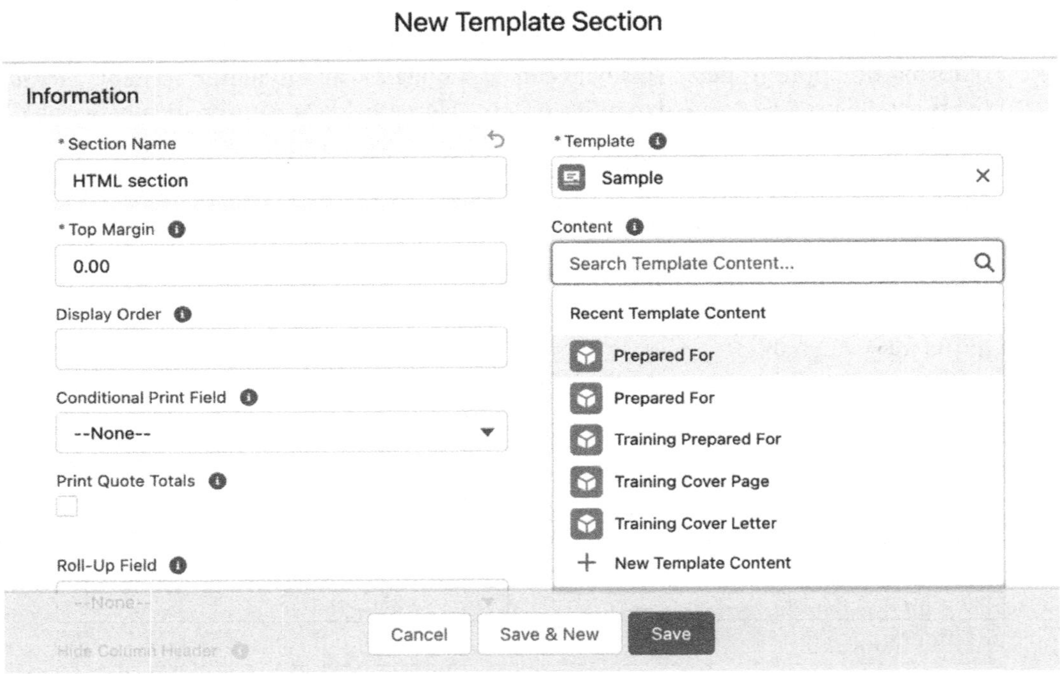

Figure 5.6 – The New Template Section dialog

Template sections are the links between the template content and the quote template itself. They contain the **Section Name** and **Template** fields. The **Display Order** field shows the order in which this section is rendered, related to other sections. As a best practice, leave enough gaps (for example, 10, 20, and so on) so that additional template sections can be rendered in between, as required. The **Content** field is where we link the HTML content to the template. When we click this dropdown, it displays all of the template content that we have created in our Salesforce instance. In this example, we can see the **Prepared For** HTML content that we created in *Figure 5.4*. There are a lot of other display and formatting fields that can be filled as required. Template sections also include page breaks and filtering information that determine the formatting when we print the quote.

Creating line item content

Line item content is used to display quote line data in tabular format. This shows the quote line product, discount, unit price, and much more.

We can use the **Quote Line Group** field in the line items to group fields and display the related subtotal. For example, we can group our quote lines based on the **Product Family** field (that is, hardware, software, service, and so on). Rather than creating multiple line item sections, we can group the line items in one line item section to display on the quote.

Conditional print fields can be used to dynamically show or hide fields – for example, if we want to show the discount only when applicable and not include a blank field in our quote template. We can create a checkbox and, based on the Boolean value, we can hide or show a field. Template sections can also be printed conditionally.

To create the piece of line item content, navigate to **App Launcher** → **Template Content** → **New** → **Line Items** → **Continue**. Fill in the **Content Name** field, the formatting options, and the **Table Style** field. Then, click **Save**, as shown here:

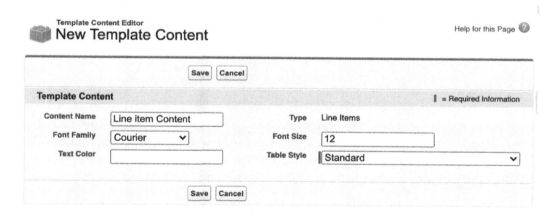

Figure 5.7 – Creating a New Template item content

The template content can be linked to one or more quote templates as required.

Linking the line item content to a quote template

Now, let's link the line item content created in *Figure 5.7* to a quote template. To do this, navigate to any **Quote Template**. Click on the **Related** tab. Select **Sections → New**. This will open the following screen:

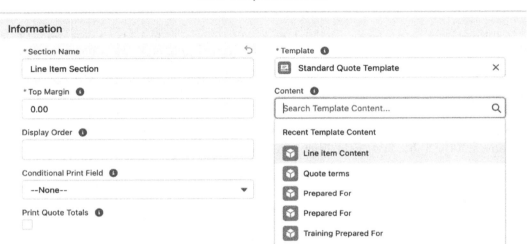

Figure 5.8 – Linking line item content to a quote template

As shown in *Figure 5.8*, using the **Content** dropdown, we select **Line item Content**, which we created previously. The other optional fields in the **New Template Section** dialog can be selected as per the business requirements. There are a lot of formatting fields that the administrator can use to create these template sections and adjust the formatting.

Once the section content is saved, go back to the **Related** section in the quote template. There is another related section in the quote template, which is called **Line Columns**. In the **Line Columns** section, we can define the columns we want to be displayed in the table.

We can create a new line column by navigating to **Quote Template → Related → Line Columns → New**. This will open the following screen:

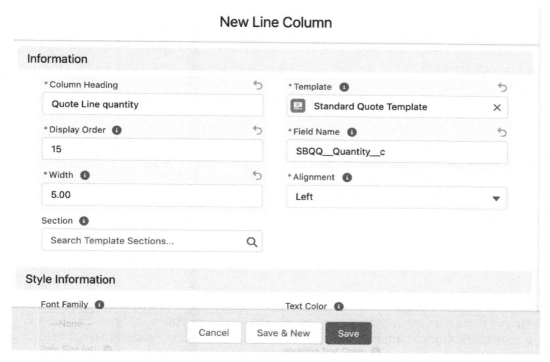

Figure 5.9 – Creating New Line Column

Let's learn about some of the mandatory fields that an administrator needs to update in the **New Line Column** dialog:

- **Column Heading**: This is the heading that will be displayed for the quote line table column field when you print the quote.

- **Display Order**: This is the order in which this field will be displayed on the quote. Add some gaps when creating display orders so that new fields can be inserted as needed.

- **Width**: This field describes the column width. The width of all the columns in the table should add up to `100`.

- **Template**: This is the name of the template for which you are creating the line item column.

- **Field Name**: This is the API name of the quote line object field.

- **Alignment**: This option lets you format the alignment for a specific field when you print the quote.

The rest of the fields are optional, and most of them are formatting fields. A few of them are useful for customizations, such as the **Conditional Print** field. This field can be used to conditionally render a field onto the quote template. For example, if we want to display the discount field only when the value is greater than zero, we can create a custom field checkbox – `Display_Discount__c` (API name) – and add the field to the quote page layout. We can also use CPQ price rules to automate this.

A sales rep can manually check this checkbox, or we can update this field automatically based on the condition we set for the discount to be greater than zero. This custom field can be used in the **Conditional Print** field. The column will be displayed only when the custom field checkbox is set to `true`. The **Conditional Print** field can also be used to show or hide template sections.

For example, when there are no discounts applied to a quote, we do not want to send the quote document with blank discount columns. This column can be conditionally rendered only when the discount values are present. For this example, let's use the additional discount field on the quote as a conditional field. Copy the API name of the field on the quote – in this example, that's the additional discount field API. Now, navigate to **Object Manager → Line Column → Fields & Relationships → Conditional Print → Values → New** and paste here the API name we copied from the quote object, and click **Save**. Next, navigate to the **Quote template → Related → Discount Percent → Conditional Print Field** and select the picklist value of the additional discount field API name. Now, when we print the quote document, the discount column can be controlled with the conditional print field.

To test the content, navigate to any quote in our Salesforce org and preview the quote template, as shown previously in *Figure 5.1*.

Creating quote terms content

Salesforce CPQ provides out-of-the-box functionalities to generate several **Term Conditions**. These can be displayed in all quotes, or they can be customized to only appear in specific quotes as per the business needs. For example, the terms and conditions for hardware products might be different from software products. The **Term Conditions** field on a quote determines when to display the terms and conditions. The **Condition Met** field is used to display the relevant terms only when the associated conditions are met. Using this feature, the quote terms can be dynamically displayed. When we have multiple terms, they are displayed in the template based on their print order values. For example, when our quote contains software products, we might want to display the terms and conditions for software purchases.

We can allow users to modify the quote terms by using the **Modified Terms** feature in a quote. This feature needs to be used with caution, depending on your company's business needs. Modified quote terms are only applicable to the specified quote and will not apply to other quotes. For reps to modify terms, they may require approval from their managers.

> **Important Note**
> Modified quote terms will not apply to **amendments** and **renewals**.

To create quote terms content, navigate to **App Launcher** → **Template Content** → **New** → **Quote Terms** → **Continue**. This will open the following screen:

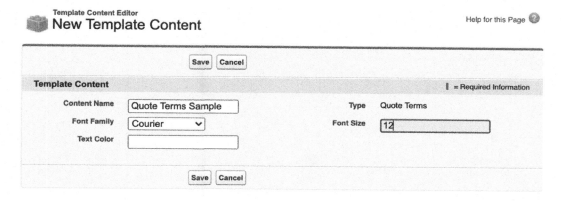

Figure 5.10 – Creating quote terms content

Enter a meaningful name in the **Content Name** field, set your preferred formatting options, and save the record.

Linking quote terms to a template

The quote terms content can be linked to a quote template using the **Sections** related list. To do this, navigate to **Quote Template** → **Related** → **Sections** → **New**. Let's use the Quote Terms Sample content created in *Figure 5.10* and link it to Standard Quote Template, which we created in *Figure 5.3*.

A quote term object can be used to create terms and conditions. To do this, navigate to **App Launcher → Quote Term → New**. This will open the following screen:

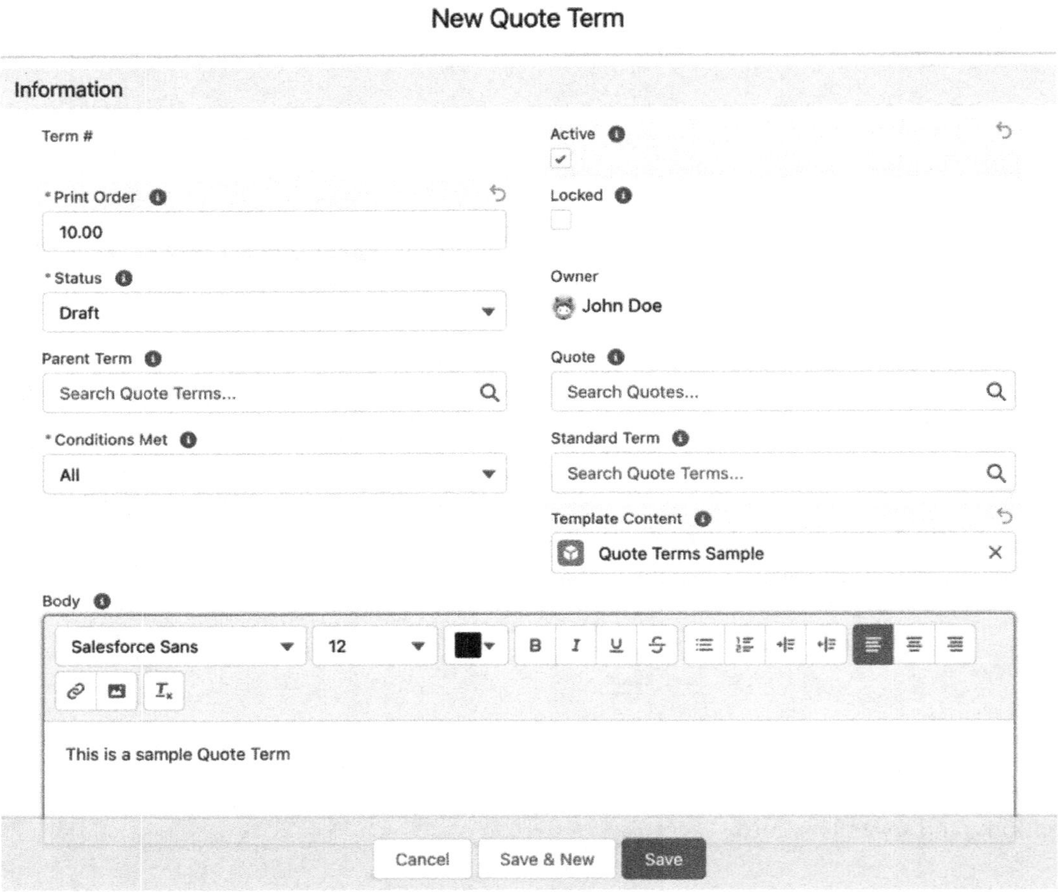

Figure 5.11 – Creating a quote term

Let's learn how to configure a few important fields here:

- **Term #**: This will be autogenerated once you save the new term record.

- **Print Order**: This specifies the order in which the terms are displayed when we preview or generate the quote document.

- **Status**: This determines the status of the quote term.

- **Parent Term**: If you have multiple terms, you can link all of the child terms to a parent.

- **Conditions Met**: This field is used when we have quote terms that need to be printed based on a condition. If we have more than one condition, we can specify whether we need all, any, or a custom number of conditions to be met.

- **Active**: This checkbox is used to activate a quote term.

- **Locked**: This checkbox is used to control the edit functionality for quote terms by end users. A best practice is to keep terms locked unless there is a very compelling reason not to.

- **Template Content**: This is used to link the content for which the term is applicable. We can define standard terms that apply to all templates and specific terms that apply to only some quotes.

- **Body**: This is where the actual terms and conditions text is updated.

Fill in all the required fields and save the quote term created in *Figure 5.11*. To dynamically display a quote term, navigate to the related section of the quote term and create a new term condition by clicking **Term Conditions**. Administrators can use a **tested variable** or a **summary variable** (that is, the configurations we learned about in previous chapters) to evaluate the term condition.

Now that we have learned how to create and customize quote templates, let's see how they can be sent to customers to be signed with eSignatures.

Integrating DocuSign for eSignatures

Prior to the development of eSignatures, a sales rep would email a quote template to customers, which would then be printed by the customer to sign before returning. Today, using eSignatures is becoming the standard way quotes are signed by customers. However, Salesforce CPQ allows automating this process by integrating with third-party tools such as **DocuSign**. These tools can be used to directly email the quote document to customers, which can then be signed electronically. Then, the documents can be saved in Salesforce objects. Both administrators and customers can save time by using these integrations. So, let's learn how DocuSign can be integrated with Salesforce CPQ.

Your administrator can create a case with Salesforce support for the installation of the DocuSign package. The **DocuSign** for Salesforce CPQ package uses the SBQQDS **namespace**. The DocuSign for Salesforce plugin requires the **DocuSign Business Pro** edition. To install DocuSign for Salesforce, you need to follow these steps:

1. Log in to your Salesforce org where you want to enable eSignatures using DocuSign.

Update the electronic signature field in the package settings to the DocuSign plugin. To do this, navigate to **Setup → Quick Find → Installed Packages → Salesforce CPQ → Configure → Plugins → Electronic Signature Plugin → SBQQDS. DocusignPlugin → Save**.

2. Now, Salesforce CPQ will add a **Send with DocuSign** button to your **Generate Document** page on the quote.

3. In the quote document page layout, create a DocuSign information section and add a **Notes & Attachments** related list.

4. In your **Quote Template** page layout, add a DocuSign recipients-related list.

5. Next, we need to configure the remote site settings for DocuSign. To do this, navigate to **Setup → Quick Find → Remote Site Settings → New**. Enter the name in the **Remote Site Name** field without spaces, and then navigate to **Remote Site URL**. For this example, it will be `https://app2.docusign.com`. Then, select **Active**.

6. The next step is to set up the DocuSign custom settings. We need a DocuSign account ID to configure these settings. The account ID can be found in your DocuSign user profile. Select the user profile in the drop-down menu located on the upper right-hand corner of your DocuSign home page. To update the custom settings, navigate to **Setup → Quick Find → Custom Settings → DocuSign for Salesforce CPQ Settings → Manage → New**. Enter the DocuSign account ID in the **Account ID** field, then, update the **Batch Size** field to 5 and update the **Endpoint** field from `https://docusign.net/` to `https://docusign. net/restapi/v2`.

7. Finally, click the **Save** button.

8. Next, set up the DocuSign user profiles. This can be done in two ways:

   - **Adding a custom links section**: Navigate to **Setup → Quick Find → Users → Edit Layout → Custom Links → Drag**. Here, drag the DocuSign for Salesforce CPQ object to the desired position in the **Custom Links** section, and then, click **Save**. This takes you back to the user detail record. Administrators can click the **DocuSign for Salesforce CPQ** setup link in the **Custom Links** section of the user profile and enter their DocuSign credentials.

   - **Adding a Visualforce page in the user profile**: Navigate to **Setup → Quick Find → Users → Edit Layout → Visualforce Pages**. Drag and drop the **SetUpUser** object to the desired position on your page layout, and then, click **Save**.

Users can go to their **profile** and enter their DocuSign credentials on the DocuSign for Salesforce CPQ setup **Visualforce** page.

9. Next, set up DocuSign recipients for CPQ quotes. To do this, navigate to **Quote Template → Related → DocuSign Recipients → New**. Update the recipient **Role Name** field, which is unique within the template, and match the appropriate recipient's name in your DocuSign template. Enter a value in the **Role Type** field and save the record.

10. Connecting DocuSign to Salesforce CPQ creates a relationship between the DocuSign account and your Salesforce CPQ DocuSign package. To define this connection, log in to DocuSign. Then, click the profile icon on the upper-right corner of the page, then, use the drop-down arrow to navigate to **My Preferences → Connected Apps → Connect Salesforce**, and then, provide the credentials of the Salesforce org that you want to connect with DocuSign.

11. For DocuSign to push updates from the signature process back to Salesforce CPQ in real time, we need to add a quote document object. To set this up, navigate to **DocuSign Account → User Profile**. Select **Go To Admin** in the **Integrations** sidebar. Next, click **Connect** in the **Salesforce Connection** sidebar, select **Actions → Edit** on the **Salesforce Object** page → **Connect Objects section → New Object → Salesforce Object →** update **Object** to **Active →** update the **Select Salesforce Object picklist** to **Quote Document →** Update **Object Name** to **Quote Document**.

12. When you install DocuSign for Salesforce CPQ, it creates a few fields in your **Quote Document** object:

    - **Envelope**
    - **ID**
    - **Error Message**
    - **Signed Date**
    - **Voided Reason**

By default, DocuSign links the **Envelope ID** field on the quote document with the DocuSign envelope ID field. You can also link additional fields as required, based on what additional fields you would like to see on the quote document object from DocuSign. You can find the complete details on the DocuSign documentation at this link: `https://support.docusign.com/en/guides/docusign-for-salesforce-cpq`.

Summary

In this chapter, we learned how to create and customize quote templates in Salesforce CPQ, and we explored the out-of-the-box features that administrators can apply to configure quote templates. Quote templates can be created, customized, and reused multiple times. Also, Salesforce CPQ allows us to create multiple templates, and reps can choose the right template based on their business requirements. We have also learned how third-party applications for eSignatures can be integrated with Salesforce CPQ. This helps reps to directly send quote documents using eSignature plugins, and this means they can avoid relying on manual emails for quote signatures. This improves the overall quote-to-cash process efficiency, as we can complete deals and receive signatures with no errors in minutes.

In the next chapter, we will learn about guided selling, which is another out-of-the-box feature that Salesforce CPQ provides for the sales process.

Section 2: The Next Stage of the CPQ Journey

With the basics of Salesforce CPQ knowledge out of the way, you are now ready to embark on the journey to learn some of the intermediate and advanced Salesforce CPQ concepts.

Because it's difficult for sales reps to sell and connect the right products to the right customers at the same time, you will learn how a guided selling feature helps you to quickly navigate through a complex product catalog and choose the right products.

This section also provides details on how amendments and renewals can be configured and customized in CPQ. You will then learn how CPQ package configurations can influence your business-specific customizations.

This section comprises the following chapters:

- *Chapter 6, Configuring Guided Selling*
- *Chapter 7, Creating Contracts, Amendments, and Renewals*
- *Chapter 8, Configuring CPQ Package Settings*

6
Configuring Guided Selling

In the previous chapter, we discussed how product configurations and CPQ automation help reps sell the right combination of products at accurate prices, which is crucial for all businesses. But most businesses have extensive product catalogs, which make it hard for reps to remember product details. **Guided selling** is a Salesforce CPQ out-of-the-box feature that helps reps to guide customers to buy products, based on a few simple and easy-to-understand questions.

In this chapter, we will be covering the following topics:

- Guided selling and its advantages
- Configuring guided selling in Salesforce CPQ

By the end of this chapter, you will learn how guided selling helps automate the sales process.

Guided selling and its advantages

Guided selling in Salesforce helps admins create a set of questions that can be used by reps in the **Quote Line Editor** (**QLE**) while adding products to a quote. For example, these questions collect relevant customer data, such as the type of products the customer wants to buy, customer size, customer type, whether they are a partner or an end customer, and volume. It can also include information such as location, industry, and other specifics depending on the nature of your business. When there are many products, guided selling is like an interview process that can help reps quickly and easily sort their products. This will help reps easily navigate through large product catalogs. At the beginning of the quote creation process, when the reps are ready to add products to the **Product Selection** screen, they will start with a **Guided selling** screen, which presents a series of questions.

To set this up, your business should have at least one question to identify the products to start with. The answers act as the conditional logic to determine the next set of questions to be displayed. In addition, the questions act as filters, and the answers drive which products need to be displayed. The rep can then click the **Suggest** button to display the corresponding products. Salesforce-guided selling filters the product in the backend and, therefore, only relevant products will be displayed on the **Add Products** page.

For example, imagine that *Packt Corporation* is a cell phone distributor operating in multiple regions, such as America, **Asia Pacific** (**APAC**), and **Europe, Middle East, and Africa** (**EMEA**). Packt has reps working across regions. The types of cell phones and accessories that Packt sells in the US might be different than the type of cellphones and accessories it sells in Asia. The first question in guided selling is to find the country name. In this case, if the country is the US, then the Apple iPhone bundle with a 110 V charger will be displayed along with other matches. When the country is India, the same product bundle will be displayed, but with a 220 V charger. The next set of questions, based on the country, can be refined further.

As you can see, guided selling can be customized for the products your company is selling and how your business operates. It is hard for the rep to scroll through thousands of products manually to find a match. Guided selling helps streamline the sales process and new reps can be onboarded quickly. It can also help reps win more deals, drive customer satisfaction, and, in some scenarios, allow customers to self-serve (customers can use guided selling in communities where they will be able to search and add relevant products to the quote without needing help from a sales rep).

Configuring guided selling in Salesforce CPQ

The guided selling process is like navigating a flowchart on the backend to display the right set of products. It's best practice to map out your entire guided selling process before beginning any configuration. Let's imagine *Packt Corporation* sells a large number of products. The following diagram shows the flowchart for the products sold by *Packt Corporation*:

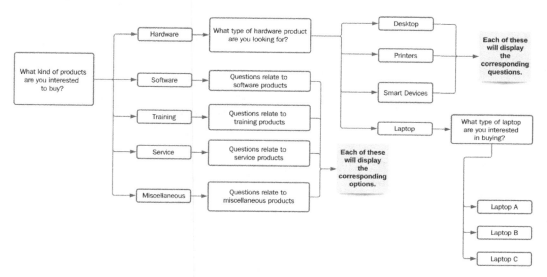

Figure 6.1 – Sample flowchart for laptop products

In the preceding diagram, in the quote that the rep created, the customer wanted to see all the available laptops and choose the right one from that list. So, we will configure the guided selling flow to display all the laptop models. First, we want to know what kind of products customers are interested in. Reps are already trained to know these high-level details about the products. When the rep chooses *Hardware,* then the questions related to hardware products will be displayed. If the customer wants to buy *Software* or *Training* products, we need to configure the corresponding questions.

For the sake of this example, we will only configure the questions that will lead the rep to the laptops. Based on your company's business process, create a flowchart for filtering products.

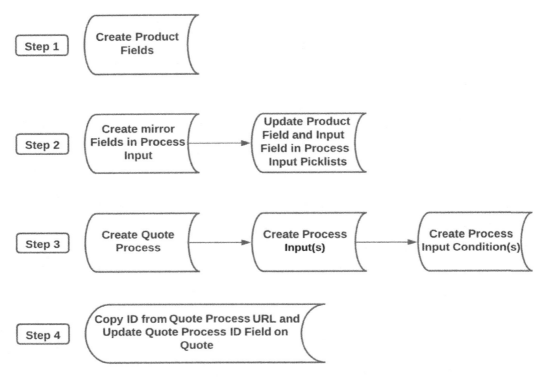

Figure 6.2 – Guided selling configuration

Once you have this kind of logical model of your products, your admins can configure guided selling in Salesforce. Guided selling can be set up in four steps:

1. Create product attributes that can be used by guided selling to filter products based on rep input.

2. Define process inputs, which are questions that select products based on rep feedback.

3. Create a quote process that orchestrates the user through a series of process inputs to reveal the most suitable products for the sale.

4. For testing purposes, admins can manually paste the process ID into the **SBQQ__ QuoteProcessId__c** field. However, in practice, populating this field must always be automated as a user would never populate this as part of the selling flow.

Let's use the flowchart shown in *Figure 6.1* to configure guided selling in CPQ. Guided selling matches the answers the rep provides to the questions displayed with the fields on the product object to filter the right products. Admins need to define fields on the product object that match new **Process Input** fields. It is recommended to use picklist and checkbox fields for the input method. We can use standard out-of-the-box product fields when the products can be identified using the standard fields. Alternatively, custom fields can be created as required. In this example, we will demonstrate creating a custom picklist:

1. First, we need to make sure products have fields that the guided selling prompt can filter through. Create picklist fields on the product to store the values of attributes you want to filter. In this example, you need to create a product type picklist field with the values **Hardware, Software, Training, Service**, and **Miscellaneous**, as shown in *Figure 6.2*. To do this, navigate to **Set up → Quick Find → Object Manager → Quick Find → Product → Field & Relationships → New → Picklist → Next → Field Label** and choose **Product Type**. Now, in the **Values** field, enter picklist values by selecting the **Enter values, with each value separated by a new line** radio button. Under **Field Name**, select **Product_Type**. Next, choose the field level access, add it to the required page layouts, and save.

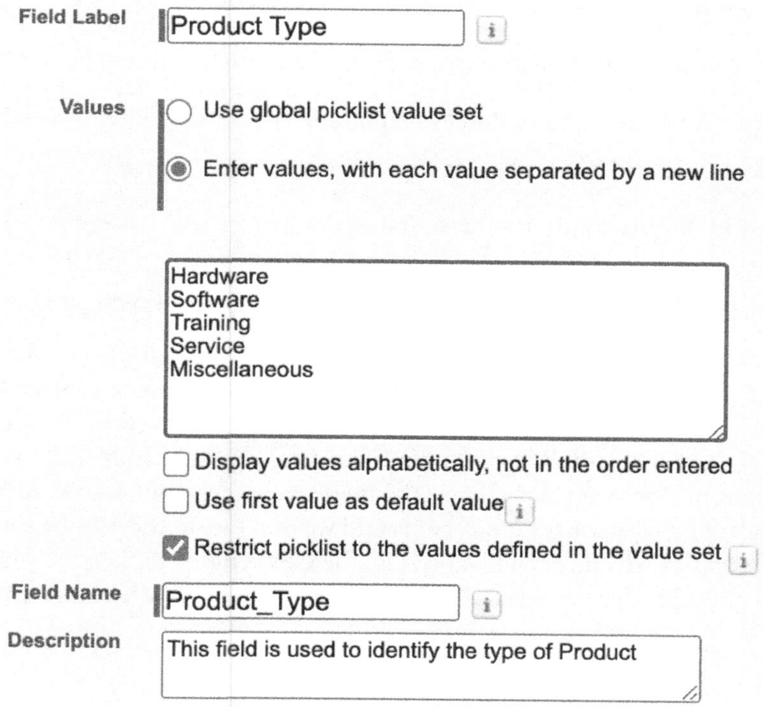

Field Label	Product Type	i

Values
○ Use global picklist value set

● Enter values, with each value separated by a new line

```
Hardware
Software
Training
Service
Miscellaneous
```

☐ Display values alphabetically, not in the order entered
☐ Use first value as default value i
☑ Restrict picklist to the values defined in the value set i

Field Name	Product_Type	i

Description | This field is used to identify the type of Product |

Figure 6.3 – Product object picklist

Similarly, create the other picklist values. As shown in *Figure 6.1*, we need to create two more picklist values. One is for Hardware with the values Desktop, Printer, Smart devices, and Laptop, and the other is for Laptop with the values Laptop A, Laptop B, and Laptop C.

Once the backend configuration is done, navigate to the **Product** tab and set up some products with these picklist values so that we can test them in the QLE. For the actual implementation, you may have to perform a one-time data load to update products with the defined picklist values.

2. The next step is to create the **Process Input** fields, which are the questions to be displayed while configuring products using guided selling. Each process input record defines a question. In our example, we want our first question to be *What kind of products are you interested in buying?* Your admins can create a picklist field called **Product Type**. Custom fields can be created on this object, which can be used for configuring the questions you want to ask your reps. The picklist values *hardware, software, training, service,* and *miscellaneous* need to exactly match the picklist values that were created in *step 1* on the **Product object**. As a best practice, a global picklist value set can also be used to keep the product and process input values in sync.

The setup of the process inputs requires two pieces of configuration to be in place:

- Create picklist values on the Process Input object.
- Link the API values to the Process Input object fields.

Let's learn how to do this configuration in the next sub-sections.

Creating picklist values on the Process Input object

Create these picklist values on the **Process Input** object, similar to the picklist values created in *Figure 6.3*. To do this, navigate to **Set up → Quick Find → Object Manager → Quick Find → Process Input → Fields & Relationships → New → Picklist → Next → Field Label**, choose **Product Type**, enter picklist values → **Field Name** Product__ Type, and then click on **Next** and choose the field level access, but do not add them to the **page layouts** as they are user input fields and we don't want them to be modified on the object. These picklist values will be used by the CPQ engine and compared with the product picklist values that we created in *step 1*. We'll display only those products that match.

Similarly, create the other picklist values on the **Process Input** object as required. For the example in *Figure 6.1*, we need to create two more picklist values. One is the `Hardware` type with the values `Desktop`, `Printer`, `Smart devices`, and `Laptop`, and the other is the `Laptop` type with the values `Laptop A`, `Laptop B`, and `Laptop C`.

Linking the API values to the Process Input object fields

After creating the necessary picklist values, we need to link the product field API values to the **Process Input** object fields. On the **Process Input** object, we have two out-of-the-box picklist fields that need to be updated:

- **Input Field**: This field needs to be updated with the Product Type API name that we created in *step 1*. To do this, navigate to **Set up → Quick Find → Object Manager → Quick Find → Process Input → Fields & Relationships → Input field → Values → New** and add the Product Type field API name. In this example, it will be `Product_Type__c`. Then, click on **Save**.

- **Product Field**: Navigate to **Setup → Quick Find → Object Manager → Quick Find → Process Input → Fields & Relationships → Product Field → Values → New** and add the Product Type field API name, in this example, `Product_Type__c`, and then save.

In this case, the field API names that have been created on the **Product** and **Process Input** objects are the same. These values can also be different.

Similarly, add the other product picklist API names (in this example, `Hardware type` and `Laptop type`) that you created in the product object. This is a prerequisite for the next step of the **quote process** creation.

Finally, we create a new quote process for guided selling. The quote process object stores all the parameters that you have created for the guided selling prompt. This object defines how the prompt appears and how it adds products based on user input. The quote process record contains a related list for process input. To create a quote process, navigate to **Setup → App Launcher → Quote Processes → New**.

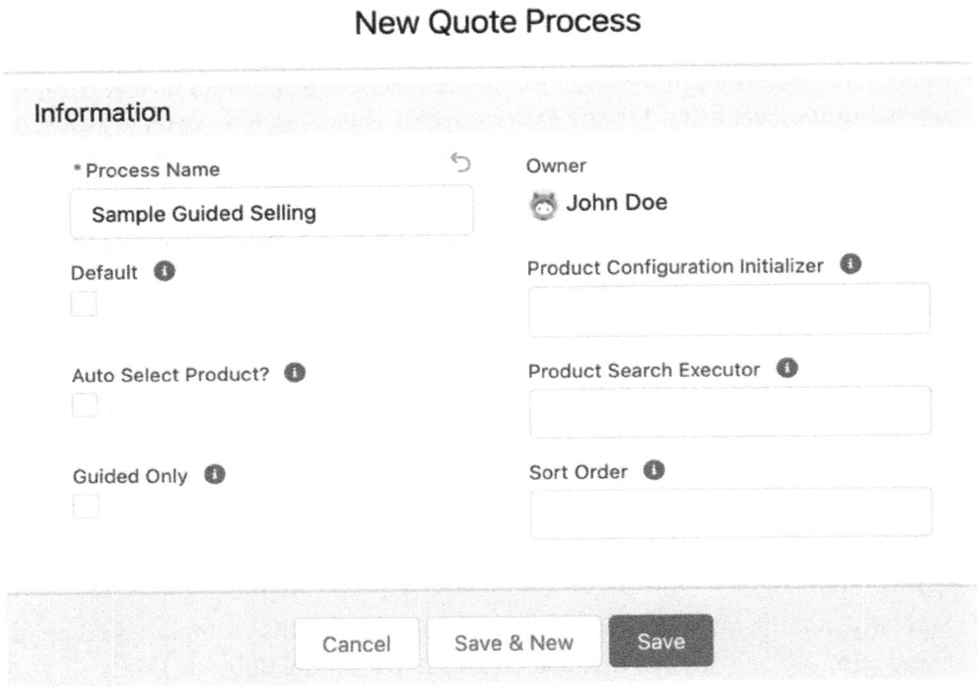

New Quote Process

Information

* Process Name   ↻   Owner

Sample Guided Selling   🐷 John Doe

Default ⓘ   Product Configuration Initializer ⓘ
☐

Auto Select Product? ⓘ   Product Search Executor ⓘ
☐

Guided Only ⓘ   Sort Order ⓘ
☐

Cancel   Save & New   Save

Figure 6.4 – The New Quote Process window

Let's learn about some important fields in the quote process:

- **Process Name**: Provide a meaningful quote process name. For this example, we have `Sample Guided Selling`.

- **Default**: Check this checkbox if you want this process to be the default for multiple quotes.

- **Auto Select Product**: If you select this, CPQ will automatically add the product to the quote when guided selling returns only one product.

- **Guided Only**: When this checkbox is selected, users can only search and add products using guided selling. When users access the product selection page for any quote containing this quote process, the filter panel button will be disabled.

Then, we need to create a new process input for all the process inputs we defined in *step 2*. Match the values of the input fields to the values of the product fields to ensure the sales rep returns the corresponding products. To do this, navigate to the quote process, which we created in *Figure 6.4*, **Quote Process → Related → Process inputs → New**. This will open the **New Process Input** screen.

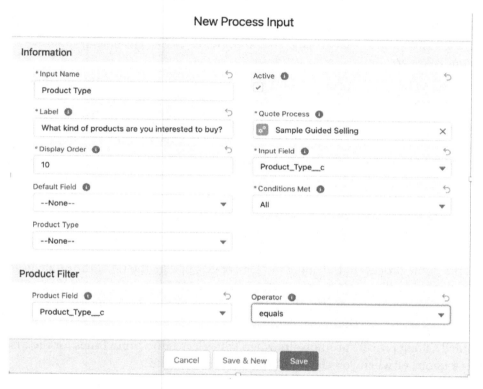

Figure 6.5 – Creating a process input field: Type – Product

Some important fields when creating a process input field include the following:

- **Input Name**: For each question we display in the QLE, there will be an associated input name, and this field is mainly for admins. In this example, we are naming this field `Product Type`.

- **Label**: This is the question displayed on the screen while using guided selling in the QLE.

- **Display Order**: The number entered here defines the order in which the process input is displayed. Provide some gaps while creating this order so that new requirements can be inserted. For this example, let's enter `10`.

- **Active**: This is used to activate the process input field.

- **Quote Process**: Provide the quote process name. In this scenario, choose the quote process name created in *Figure 6.4*.

- **Input Field**: This is the answer picklist that we created for the Process Input object. In this example, we choose **Product_Type__c**.

- **Conditions Met**: When there is more than one condition, we can choose between the picklist values – **All** or **Any**. The relevant prompt will be displayed if the conditions are met.

- **Product Field**: The answer picklist field is going to match the picklist field on the product object.

- **Operator**: This is used to compare the process input field to the product field. For this example, we want to match the field exactly, and therefore we choose **equals**. If this is a numeric field, we can choose greater than or less than as needed.

> **Important Note**
> At the time of this writing, Salesforce does not recommend creating more than five **Process Inputs** for a **Quote Process** when reps use **Lightning Experience**.

To link the quote process to the quote the rep creates, update the ID of the quote process that you created in *Figure 6.4* in the standard **Process ID** field on the quote. For this example, we are manually copying the ID and pasting it in the field. We can make this update using Salesforce automation rules.

The guided selling process prompts fire when you select **Edit Quote Lines** for the first time on a quote, or when you click **Add Products** in the QLE.

In the next section, let's learn how to create dynamic process input fields.

Creating dynamic process input

We can configure guided selling to dynamically display the questions based on the previous response. Admins can use the **Process Input conditions**-related list. Based on the conditions defined here, the search will dynamically display the products.

In the example shown in *Figure 6.1*, the second question is dependent on the first question's answer. If the answer to the first question is *Hardware*, then we want to display the questions related to *Hardware*. Similarly, if the answer is *Software*, the second question will ask what kind of *Software* product the user wants to buy.

To configure this dynamic input, admins need to create a new picklist field, **Hardware Type**, on the **Product** object (refer to *step 1* of the previous section for configuration details) and on the **Process Input** object (refer to *step 2* for configuration details) with the picklist values `Desktop`, `Printer`, `Smart Devices`, and `Laptops`. Next, they need to add the picklist field API names to **Input Field** and **Product Field** on the **Process Input** object.

The first question cannot be conditional as we don't have a dependency on the user input. The second question is dependent on the answer to the first one. When the rep chooses **Hardware**, we want to display the question: *What type of hardware product are you looking for?* This question needs to display conditionally only when the answer **Hardware** is selected. If the answer is **Software**, the corresponding question related to software needs to be displayed.

To configure dynamic process inputs, we will choose **Sample Guided Selling**, which we created in *Figure 6.4*, in the **Quote Process** box by navigating to **App Launcher** → **Quote Process** → **Sample Guided Selling** → **Related** → **Process Input** → **New**. Link `Hardware Type` on the process input and product objects in the quote process, as shown here:

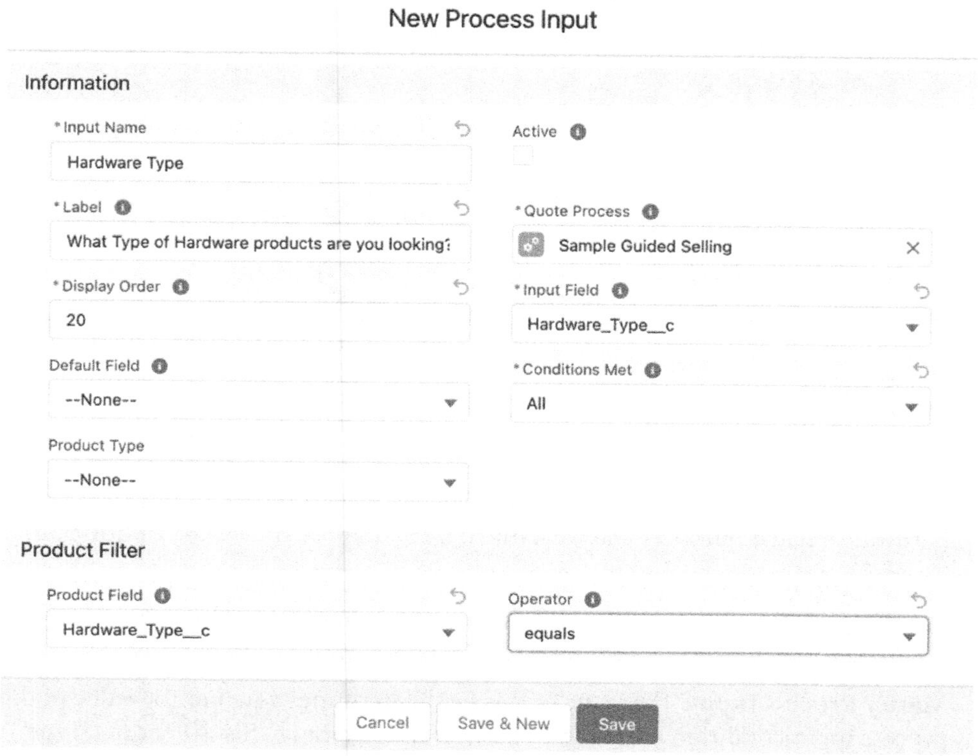

Figure 6.6 – Creating a process input field: Type – Product

Fill in the mandatory fields and save the record.

To create a **Process Input Condition**, navigate to **Quote Process → Related → Process Input**. Select **Hardware Type**. For this example, navigate to **Related → Process Input Conditions → New**, which will open the screen shown here:

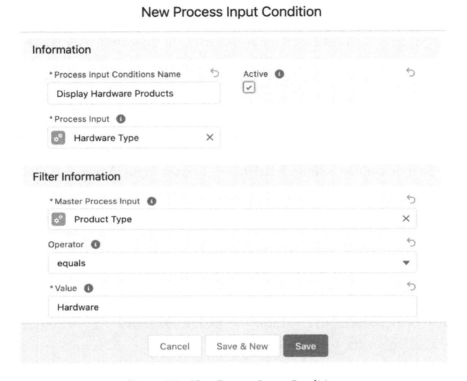

Figure 6.7 – New Process Input Condition

Fill in the following mandatory fields:

- **Process Input Conditions Name**: This field provides a meaningful name for the input condition. For this example, we are creating this condition to display hardware-related questions, so we name it `Display Hardware Products`.

- **Process Input**: This will default to the process input for which we are creating the condition. In this example, we want the hardware question (*What type of hardware product are you looking for?* from the example in *Figure 6.1*) to appear.

- **Master Process Input**: The value of this field determines whether the value of this process input condition evaluates to true. In this example, this is **Product Type**.

- **Operator**: This is a picklist value with different operators, such as **equals**, **not equal to**, **contains**, **greater than**, and **less than**. For example, in *Figure 6.7*, we are using the **equals** operator to check whether **Product Type** equals Hardware.

- **Value**: This is the answer value on which this question is dependent. In this example, we want this question to be displayed only when the previous answer is Hardware.

In the next section, let's see how guided selling can be tested in QLE.

Testing guided selling in QLE

In the previous section, we saw how guided selling can be configured. This can be applied to a specific quote or multiple quotes. Let's see how we can test this for a single quote. To apply the guided selling to a quote, input the ID of the **Sample Guided Selling Quote** process into the **Quote Process ID** field on the Quote object. If you have multiple guided selling quote processes, based on the business criteria, specific quotes can be updated with the corresponding quote process ID. Salesforce automations such as Flow or Apex can be used to automatically update the ID. In this example, let's update this manually. To do this, navigate to the quote process created in *Figure 6.4*, copy the Salesforce ID and update it in the quote process ID field.

To test the guided selling, navigate to **Quote** (for which we have updated the quote process ID) → **Edit Lines** → **Add Products**. This will display the **Guided Selling** screen, as shown in the following screenshot:

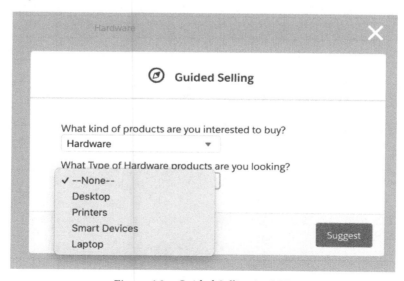

Figure 6.8 – Guided Selling in QLE

Based on the answer chosen, the next questions will follow. Clicking **Suggest** will display all the relevant products.

Summary

In this chapter, you have learned how to configure guided selling and seen why you should use it. We saw how guided selling can help businesses with complex product structures and help onboard new reps faster. Also, for scenarios where self-serving is needed without rep intervention, guided selling is very helpful to automate the sales process. Guided selling is like an experienced salesperson. It helps reps to ask questions about customers' needs and close deals faster. Guided selling also improves the customer experience by making their buying process much easier. The combination of search filters and guided selling makes for a well-rounded system. In the next chapter, you will learn about CPQ package configuration settings, which most configurations will be dependent on.

7
Creating Contracts, Amendments, and Renewals

So far, we have learned about configuring products, pricing, and quotes in CPQ. We have also detailed how a sales rep can create an opportunity and progress a deal. When the rep has an understanding of what the customer needs, a quote can be created.

Products are added to the quote and products and bundles are configured as needed. Based on the configuration, discounts, price rules, and product rules can be applied. Once the quote is approved, the quote document can be generated. If we have any external integration for e-signatures, the quote document is automatically sent to the customer for signatures.

Generally, once the document is signed by the customer, the deal will be closed by marking the opportunity as **Closed Won**. If orders are implemented, they are created now. For all the **subscription products** that we sold, we need a **contract** to keep track of which products need to be renewed later. The contract can then be used for future sales transactions. They are also used to facilitate amendments and renewals for the customer.

Contracts capture the subscription products and prices a customer has agreed to and are managed over time as a customer's install base changes.

In this chapter, you will learn about contracts, amendments, and renewals.

A contract will have subscription or asset records based on the type of products on the quote. These products on the quote will be translated to subscriptions if they are subscription products, or assets if they are standalone products. Amendments and renewals ensure continuity across assets and subscriptions tied to the account. All the products that a specific customer has bought can be tracked under the account object in Salesforce.

In this chapter, we will cover the following topics:

- Creating contracts
- Creating amendments
- Amending MDQ products
- Creating renewals
- Contracted pricing

Contracts overview

Contracts are used to manage subscription products that you have sold to your customers. In Salesforce CPQ, once a deal is completed and an opportunity is marked as **Closed Won**, a contract can be created.

In this section, we will learn how CPQ creates a contract. We can use the out-of-the-box **Contracted** checkbox field on opportunities or orders to initiate the contracting process, which will automatically create a contract record. Contracts can be created from either opportunities or orders. Generating contracts from orders is most common because then subscriptions and assets are related to order products and not just opportunity products. If Salesforce Billing is in play, orders must be created and all contracts must be generated from orders. This ensures amendments and renewals are billed correctly to the customer.

When **Allow Multiple Orders** is set to **True** in the CPQ package setting, CPQ can create multiple orders to a single quote. Orders can be split by the quote line field or quote line group field.

If orders are implemented, a contract needs to be generated from the order; otherwise, contracts can be generated from opportunities. The contract generated can be used for managing amendments and renewals. Salesforce CPQ can easily handle updates to the products included in the contract by creating amendments. Amending a contract will generate an amendment opportunity and an amendment quote. The process for amendments will follow the same flow as the original sales until the amendment opportunity is marked as **Closed Won** and it will be linked to the original contract.

Contracts can be renewed when they reach the contract end date. Tracking the contract end date for renewals is a tedious task and CPQ helps to automate this by creating **renewal opportunities** and **renewal quotes**. Renewals also help the sales team forecast accurately. When the same process is applied to renewals, a renewal opportunity and renewal quote can be created.

The **Renewal Model** setting in CPQ package configurations will determine how CPQ tracks the products on your quote. The renewal model can be either **Contract Based** or **Asset Based**. If your company sells both non-subscription and subscription products, you need to set this configuration to the **Contract Based** renewal model, which will help in creating a contract. If your company doesn't sell subscription products, you can set the renewal model to **Asset Based**. Renewal model setting should be done *before* creating subscriptions and assets with CPQ. Changing the renewal model after record creation is basically impossible.

Let's look at a simple example where Packt is selling a *Packt Pro 13" Laptop* (a sample product), which is a non-subscription product, and a *Loss and Damage Warranty*, which is a subscription product.

The following diagram shows the high-level contract creation process:

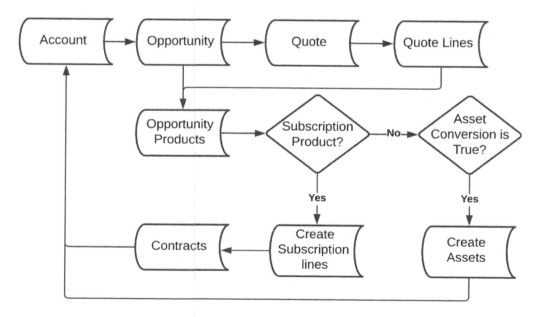

Figure 7.1 – Creating contracts

A rep has created an account for a customer who is interested in buying products and services from Packt. The sales process has progressed and an opportunity has been created. The customer looked at a few sample quotes and has finally accepted one quote, which is set as the primary, where all the products have been added. The rep has also added complimentary swag to this quote. Finally, the sale is completed and the opportunity status has been set to **Closed Won**. For the *Loss and Damage Warranty*, which is a service charged based on the number of years applicable, the quote lines will have a start date and an end date. This has been set up as a subscription product in Salesforce. We can now create a contract for this initial sale.

While creating a contract, the Salesforce CPQ engine looks at the opportunity products and determines whether a subscription or an asset needs to be created. We already learned how to create a subscription product in *Chapter 3, Configuring CPQ Products*. In this example, let's imagine we have three products on the primary quote that were synced to the opportunity:

- *Loss and Damage Warranty*, which is a subscription product
- *Packt Pro 13" Laptop*, which is a non-subscription product, with the **Asset Conversion** field set to **One Per Quote Line** or **One Per Unit**
- *Swag*, which is a non-subscription product, with the **Asset Conversion** field set to **None**

Based on this, the CPQ engine will create a subscription line for the *Loss and Damage Warranty* product, an asset for the *Packt Pro 13" Laptop*, and complimentary swag will be left, just as a one-time-sale product on the original quote. No record will be created for *Swag*.

The **Asset Conversion** field on a product determines whether a product needs to be converted into an asset or not. This field has three possible values:

- **One per unit**: If we are selling five laptops on a quote with this setting, CPQ will create five individual asset records. This will be useful for products where you want to track the serial number. If your business has bigger pieces of equipment, you might want to track each asset individually in the system.

- **One per quote line**: If we are selling five laptops on a quote, with this setting, CPQ will create one asset record with a quantity of five.

- **None**: With this setting, the product will not be converted into an asset. For the complimentary swag in our example, the **Asset Conversion** field is set to **None**.

> **Important Note**
> When you contract an opportunity containing a subscription quote line with a quantity of 0, Salesforce CPQ creates a zero-quantity subscription record on the contract.

Unlike asset products, where you can exclude certain products from asset creation, there is no configuration for subscription creation. These subscriptions get created automatically for all the relevant products. When you **contract an order** or opportunity under the contract-based renewal model, Salesforce CPQ creates a contract record. CPQ creates subscription records for all the subscription products on the quote and asset records for non-subscription products.

When you have percent of total products, subscribed assets are going to be created to link the **percent of total** subscriptions to the assets they cover. We learned about percent of total product and pricing configuration in *Chapter 4, Configuring CPQ Pricing*. For example, let's imagine you have a *Warranty Extension* product set up as a percent of total product based on the total hardware products on the quote. The hardware products will be set up as assets and subscribed assets will be created to link the *Warranty Extension* to the hardware. A subscribed asset is a related list on a subscription. It is a junction object between the subscription product and the asset.

Contracts contain lookups to subscription records for each subscription quote line. Each account in Salesforce serves as a source of truth for everything that a customer currently possesses and everything that was purchased in the past. A **Closed Won** opportunity and an associated primary quote contain the details of what was purchased for a specific deal. If you have implemented orders, they will manage post-sales activities, such as shipping, fulfillment, and activations. Orders are also suggested points of integration for external systems and are necessary for Salesforce Billing.

In the following subsections, let's learn how to create a contract from an opportunity and order.

Creating a contract from an opportunity

Salesforce CPQ provides out-of-the-box functionality to create contracts from an opportunity to manage subscription products. To configure contract creation from an opportunity, we have a few prerequisites, which are listed as follows:

- We must have an opportunity with at least one subscription product.
- There must be a primary quote associated with this opportunity that has at least one subscription product.

- The renewal method on the account related to this opportunity should be set to **Contract Based**.

- At least one quote line must have the **Subscription Pricing** field set to **Fixed Price** or **Percent Total**.

- Every quote line must have a start date, which is why it is recommended to include the start date on either the quote or quote line group. This will ensure that a start date is included in every subsequent quote line.

To demonstrate contract creation, we will manually select the **Contracted** checkbox and save the record. During actual implementation, this can be set automatically using either a Salesforce **flow** or **Apex** automation. For example, you can automatically update the **Contracted** checkbox to **True** whenever an opportunity is marked as **Closed Won**.

The conditions will depend on your business process and when you want a contract record to be created. For this example, a test account, *Packt Communications*, is used to create an opportunity named *Packt Laptop*. This opportunity has a primary quote with a few products. One of the sample products is a subscription product. The following screenshot shows an opportunity with products and an associated quote:

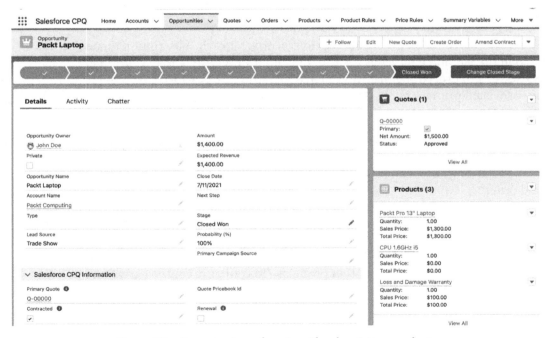

Figure 7.2 – Opportunity and quote with subscription products

As shown in the preceding screenshot, the **Contracted** checkbox on an opportunity has been selected and the opportunity's **Stage** property has been set to **Closed Won**. When this opportunity is saved, the CPQ engine automatically generates a contract with subscription lines and asset records using a **future Apex** method (`contractQuotesDeferred`).

As we have one subscription product for our example, *Loss and Damage Warranty*, the corresponding subscription line is created and attached to the contract. To view the contract, navigate to **App Launcher → Contract → Related**. This will display all the subscription lines associated with the contract, as shown in the following figure:

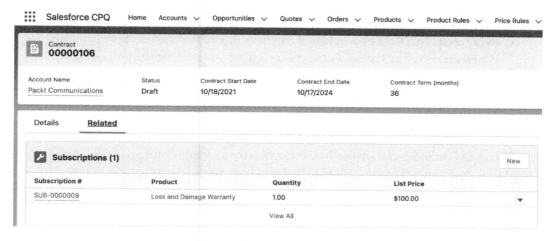

Figure 7.3 – Contract subscription lines

The subscription records contain pricing and date values for each of the subscription products on the quote. By default, the subscription product inherits its start and end dates from the quote line groups' start and end dates. If these are null, then the quote lines' start and end dates will be selected. Next, if the start and end dates are also null, then the quote lines' effective start date and effective end date values will be selected. The subscriptions inherit the values of all other matching quote line fields. This is a waterfall of **Quote Line → Quote Line Group → Quote**.

Salesforce CPQ sets a **Contract Start Date** and a **Contract End Date** and distributes subscription products based on the **Contracting Method** quote field. This has two possible values:

1. **By Subscription End Date**: This is the default value. CPQ groups subscription products by the end date into separate contracts. The contract start date for every contract is equal to the earliest start date among its subscription products.

2. **Single Contract**: CPQ creates one contract for all your opportunity's subscription products. This is not available for evergreen quote lines. Evergreen subscriptions go onto their own contract. **Evergreen** and **non-evergreen** subscriptions must be managed in different contracts:

   - **Evergreen**: This field on a contract can have one of two values: **True** or **False**. When this is set to **True**, CPQ users can create contracts with subscriptions that do not have an end date and these contracts do not need any renewals. They get auto-renewed until the customer cancels them.

Creating a contract from an order

Salesforce CPQ provides out-of-the-box functionality to create contracts from an order. It is used to manage subscription products that you have sold. To configure contract creation from an order, we have a few prerequisites:

- We must have an order with at least one subscription product.

- The renewal method on the account related to this order must be set to **Contract Based**.

- All the subscription order products you want to contract must be activated.

- We should have an uncontracted opportunity for the quote related to the order.

- Order products must be related to the quote line of the quote from which the order was generated.

To create a contract from the order, select the **Contracted** checkbox in the order and save the record. Salesforce CPQ will generate a contract with subscription lines and assets using a **queueable Apex**. In order-based contracting, CPQ distributes the subscription products based on the **Contracting Method** field on the order. This field inherits the **By Subscription End Date** and **Single Contract** values from the quote. Even if there are multiple orders, CPQ will attempt to create one contract based on this setting.

Contracting an opportunity or order locks the original quote lines and prevents them from being edited. To edit these quote lines, Salesforce CPQ provides two options:

- Amend the contract by creating an **amendment opportunity** and an amendment quote. The amendment quote lines can be edited and changes can be made as required.

- If the contract is ready for renewal, then a renewal opportunity and a renewal quote can be created. Renewal quote lines can be edited as required.

Service Cloud for Salesforce CPQ

So far, the contracting process that we have learned about is for Sales Cloud. Contracting for Service Cloud differs from Sales Cloud. Salesforce CPQ has an optional **connector package** that we can install for Service Cloud. This will help Service Cloud to be more CPQ focused.

For subscription products, this will generate **service contracts** instead of contracts and contract line items instead of subscriptions. For a percent of non-subscription products, CPQ will create assets, which is the same as for Sales Cloud. For percent of total products, CPQ will create entitlements in place of subscribed assets. Service contracts and service contract line items are the standard objects in Salesforce Service Cloud.

The following table shows the high-level differences in the contract process for Sales Cloud and Service Cloud:

Sales Cloud	Service Cloud
Subscription products on the quote will become subscription lines on a contract.	Subscription products on the quote will become contract line items.
Contracts will be created for **Closed Won** opportunities and all the subscription lines will be associated with the contract.	Service contracts will be created for **Closed Won** opportunities and all the contract line items will be associated under the service contract.
Subscribed assets will be created to link percent of total products to the assets they cover.	Entitlements will be created to link percent of total products to the assets they cover. Entitlements can also be created for fixed-price assets.
Amendment price books are supported out of the box.	Does not support an amendment price book ID field for service contracts.
Supports asset-based renewal.	Asset-based renewal is not available.

Table 7.1 – Contracts for Sales Cloud versus Service Cloud

Once the contract is created and activated, if the customer requests any changes to the existing contract, Sales Cloud CPQ amendments can be used. In the next section, let's learn how amendments can be created.

Creating amendments

As we all know, changes are inevitable in any business. After a contract gets created, your customers may request changes. Contract amendments are used to add or remove products. Price changes and subscription end date changes must be managed via a cancel and replace amendment.

For example, some requests may be to increase the quantities of existing products or services or buy additional products or services after the initial deal is closed. These changes can be handled in CPQ by creating **amendments**.

When the customer calls a sales rep, the rep needs to have access to information such as what the customer is currently subscribed to, when their current subscriptions end, whether or not the customer can upgrade to a different level of service, how much the upgrade costs, and where we can track changes to current subscriptions. This is a lot to handle for your sales team without automation. CPQ has built-in functionalities to track all this information on your subscriptions automatically. The account object provides a 360-degree view to the rep.

When do customers need amendments?

Amendments are created when a customer needs an upgrade or an add-on. A customer may need amendments typically when there is a need for the following:

- **A change of quantity**: When the customer wants to buy more products or services.

- **A different start date than the contract being amended**: An amendment opportunity or quote can have a different start date than the contract being amended. Changing the start date signifies when exactly the amendment is effective. For example, even though the contract may start from January, the amendment may be effective from March.

- **Adding or removing products**: The customer may have already bought a few products and be interested in buying different products. Instead of creating a new opportunity and quote, you can amend the existing contract.

- **Early contract termination**: You can create amendments with zero quantity from the end date of the contract. For example, say you have a contract from January 1 to December 31 for 20 products. You want to terminate the contract by October 31. You create an amendment from November 1 to December 31 and change the quantity to 0 for all the products.

When a customer calls to make changes to their existing contracts, CPQ knows what they have already purchased and uses that information to quickly create an amendment quote. The starting point for amendment creation is an existing contract. The following diagram describes the amendment creation process in CPQ:

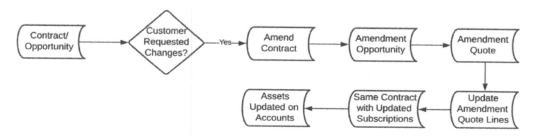

Figure 7.4 – Creating amendments

Let's learn about the standard CPQ amendment process, which can be customized for specific businesses as needed:

3. Initially, you have an opportunity that is marked as **Closed Won** and a contract created for all the subscription products and assets created for non-subscription products.

4. When you amend a contract, you are telling CPQ that you want to make changes to your existing subscriptions and assets.

5. Amending a contract will take you to the **Quote Line Editor** (**QLE**) where you see all the existing subscriptions with a zero **Net Total** price because the customer has already paid for these products and services.

6. You can add new products and make changes to the existing quantities. There are a few limitations when altering the existing quote lines in amendment quotes. You can change the quantity but it will not allow you to change the price or discounts on the original quote lines because these have already been negotiated with the customer and the sale is complete.

7. When you make changes to the quote lines and save, the CPQ engine will automatically create the amendment opportunity and associate an amendment quote. These are different from your original opportunity and quote where the customer has purchased the goods. CPQ provides a link to all these details under your contract.

8. The amendment opportunity and quote can be progressed and contracted similarly to how the initial deal was closed and contracted. If you are using orders, an order product is created for each new quote line or each quote line whose quantity was modified. Order products are *not* created for quote lines that were not modified in the QLE.

9. When you contract the amendment opportunity, CPQ recognizes that there is an existing contract associated with it and it updates the subscription lines on the original contract. CPQ will add subscription lines with positive/negative quantities unless you are terminating a quote line. Then, it will update the quote line.

10. It also updates the assets on the account for any non-subscription products.

11. In addition, it adds a co-terminated quote against the original contract. *Co-terminating a contract* means having the same contract end date. For example, if you have an original contract that has an end date of December 31, 2022, and in the process an amendment has been created, Salesforce CPQ matches the termination date of the amendments to the termination date of the original contract.

We now have an overview of standard CPQ out-of-the-box amendment functionality. Remember this process can be customized as per your business needs.

> **Important Note**
> To change the pricing and discount of existing quote lines, cancel the quote lines, which is similar to terminating the contracts by updating the quantity to 0, and re-add the same product, which allows you to change the pricing.

Cancel and replace

Salesforce Labs provides a free, open source **AppExchange** product for the cancel and replace functionality. This functionality will cancel the existing contract and create a new one. It will be useful for scenarios where multiple contracts need to be combined and will extend the contract beyond the original term. This is supported only in Salesforce Lightning. The cancel and replace functionality is not supported for **percent of total** and **MDQ** products.

The full code base is available in the public GitHub repo: `https://github.com/rjhalvorson/cancelAndReplace`.

Salesforce administrators can install the cancel and replace package by following these steps:

1. The cancel and replace managed package can be installed from AppExchange in your Salesforce instance. Navigate to **Account → Setup → Edit Page** and add the custom **ActiveContracts** Lightning component to the screen.

2. Navigate to **Setup → Users** and add the **Salesforce CPQ Cancel and Replace** permission set for the users who need this functionality.

The cancel and replace functionality is ready to use. To use it, do the following:

1. Navigate to any account in your Salesforce instance where you have more than one contract.

2. On the **Account** page, find the Lightning component that was added during installation.

3. Select the contracts that you would like to cancel and replace. Click the **Cancel and Replace** button and fill in all the required data on the Salesforce screen that opens:

   - **When do you want to start**: This is the start date for the new quote as well as cancellation quotes.

   - **Term**: This is the length of the replacement quote (new contract).

   - **Opportunity**: This is the name of the opportunity that will be created.

   - **Stage**: This is populated from the opportunity stage in your Salesforce org. You can set it to any stage where you require a new opportunity to be generated.

Once you have filled in the details, click **Continue**. Salesforce creates queueable jobs that will perform the necessary steps:

1. Amend all the selected contracts using the API and create the amendment opportunity and amendment quotes. These quotes will be canceled to generate negative orders.

2. The quantity of all the line items in the cancellation quote will be set to 0.

3. After all the contracts are amended, a new replacement quote will be created.

4. The system will loop through all the cancellation quotes, aggregate the line items and quantities, and add them to the new quote.

Amendment fields on a contract

Let's look at the fields that influence the creation of amendments and renewals in a contract. Navigate to **App Launcher → Contract → Salesforce CPQ Amendment Information**, as shown in the following figure:

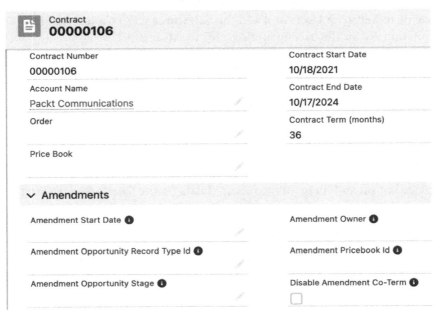

Figure 7.5 – Amendment fields on a contract

In the preceding figure, you can see the following fields that can be configured:

- **Amendment Start Date**: By default, the start date is set to the current date and we can override this value if needed.

- **Amendment Pricebook Id**: If you have a different price book for the amendments that you want to use, you can update the Salesforce ID for that price book in this field.

- **Amendment Opportunity Stage**: An amendment opportunity does not have to go through all the same stages as an initial opportunity. We can set the stage at which we want the amendment opportunity to be created by setting a stage value in this field.

- **Amendment Opportunity Record Type Id**: If we have a separate sales process for amendments, we can link it to the specified record type so that the amendments are created with that record type.

- **Amendment Owner**: You can set a default owner for amendment opportunities using this field. The default owner is the admin user who authorized the API.

- **Disable Amendment Co-Term**: This determines whether you are co-terming the amendments or not. The best practice is to co-term but you can override that if you want to by selecting this checkbox. When you select this checkbox, the end date is not populated for amendment quotes.

Let's take an example where Packt is selling a 12-month subscription to their customers. Packt always want to capture a full year of pricing when they are selling the license. Packt initially sold 10 licenses with a 12-month term starting on January 1, 2021. In March, the customer requested an additional five licenses.

The subscriptions on the amendment will inherit the contract end date December 31, 2021. But because we need 12 months for these additional licenses, these amendments need to have an end date of February 28, 2022. To change the end date before creating the amendment, set **Disable Amendment Co-Term** to **True**. When the amendments are created with this setting, the amendment quote will be created with a start date of March 1, 2021, and an end date of February 28, 2022. This ensures Packt sold the licenses for a 12-month term. When the original contract comes for renewal on December 31, 2021, CPQ renews all 15 subscriptions in the same renewal quote.

Creating a sample amendment

Let's revisit the previous example where the customer bought a *Packt Pro 13" Laptop* and the related *Loss and Damage Warranty*. The customer returns after a few months and wants to buy two additional products that Packt is selling, one a *Home Security Console*, which is a non-subscription product, and the other *Home Security Monitoring*, which is a subscription product.

The original contract has amendment lines and assets related to the account. As stated, an amendment can be created from either the contract or an opportunity. Many opportunities can relate to one contract. In this example, we are creating an amendment from the contract. To do this, follow these steps:

1. Navigate to **App Launcher → Contract → Amend**. The following figure shows an existing contract where we have the **Amend** button:

Figure 7.6 – Creating amendments from a contract

Clicking the **Amend** button will open a screen displaying all the existing subscriptions related to the contract, as shown here:

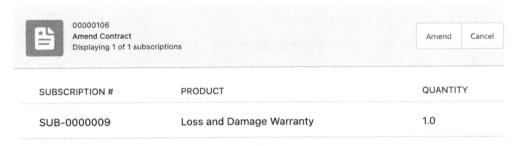

SUBSCRIPTION #	PRODUCT	QUANTITY
SUB-0000009	Loss and Damage Warranty	1.0

Figure 7.7 – Creating amendments from a contract

2. Again, click on the **Amend** button. This will take you to the QLE, where you can make changes and save.

    The net total in our example is 0 as we have already charged the customer in the initial quote. The end date is always co-terminated with the contract. It is advised not to change the end date as we want all the lines to be co-terminated at the same time.

    We can change the start date and the CPQ prorate functionality will calculate the prices accordingly. CPQ supports a native prorate functionality for amendments. Refer to the prorate multiplier setting configurations in *Chapter 8, Configuring CPQ Package Settings*, for details on how to set up proration. The following figure shows the QLE with existing subscriptions:

Quote Information

| Start Date | 11/29/2021 | | | End Date | 10/17/2024 | | Subscription Term | |

Additional Disc. (%)

. #	PRODUCT CODE	PRODUCT NA...	QUA...	UNIT C...	MAR...	LIST UNIT PRICE	ADDITIONAL DISC.	NET UNIT PRICE	NET TOTAL		
1	LDWARRANTY	Loss and Damage Warranty	2.00			$100.00		$97.22	$97.22		>
2	HOMESECURITYCONSOLE	Home Security Console	1.00	$100.00		$300.00		$300.00	$300.00		>
3	HOMESECURITYMONITORING	Home Security Monitoring	1.00	$30.00		$200.00		$583.33	$583.33		>

SUBTOTAL: $980.55

QUOTE TOTAL: $980.55

Figure 7.8 – Amendments QLE

3. The QLE can be edited to make changes. In this example, we have increased the quantity of **Loss and Damage Warranty** to **2.00** (initially the quantity was set to **1.00**).

The net total is calculated, but only for the additional quantity, as the original unit has already been paid for. You are also seeing that even though the list price is **$100.00**, the net total is calculated using CPQ proration and instead of **$100.00**, the total is **$97.22**. Also, this is only calculated for the updated quantity, and in this example, it's a quantity of 1.

4. We have also added two new products: **Home Security Console** and **Home Security Monitoring**. For these additional products, we can also apply discounts as required.

5. Save the record and this will take you to the **Amendment Quote** screen. The CPQ engine will create the quote and the opportunity in the background. The amendment opportunity will have only the changed products and new products.

6. If needed, we can also remove a product by updating the quantity to 0.

7. Now set **Opportunity Stage** to **Closed Won** and select the **Contracted** checkbox on this opportunity to create a contract.

Navigate to the account and view the asset and contract details. You will notice that the asset records have been created for all the non-subscription products, in this example, for *Home Security Console*. We see in the following figure that we still have only one contract and CPQ has updated the existing contract with the new subscription lines:

Figure 7.9 – Contract lines post amendment

As shown in the preceding figure, **SUB-0000009** is the original subscription line. **SUB-0000010** is the amendment subscription for the additional quantity. **SUB-0000011** is the amendment subscription line for the new subscription product that we have added as part of amendment creation. In the next section, we will discuss amending MDQ products; MDQ quote lines require different treatment than a standard quote line.

Amending MDQ products

In *Chapter 4, Configuring CPQ Pricing*, we learned how to create an **MDQ** quote. We also saw that CPQ creates a separate quote line for each segment. When you add an MDQ product and standard product to the same quote, they are separated in the QLE. CPQ allows a rep to make changes to the segmented product using the **quote lines drawer**. Products can be segmented either monthly, quarterly, or yearly or by a custom term. For products with custom segments, a rep can create the segment start date and end dates in the QLE.

A few considerations about MDQ quoting, contracts, and amendments are as follows:

- The quote start date is mandatory to calculate the MDQ quote line prices.

- MDQ products support daily, monthly, yearly, and quarterly based subscription term units.

- MDQ products cannot be parent bundles and you cannot have product options associated with them.

- The standard bundle parent can contain MDQ child options. When you add this bundle to a quote, a bundle parent will appear as a standard product table, and the MDQ product will be separated in a segmented table.

- MDQ products cannot be configured and cannot have configuration attributes.

- The user experience for MDQ quotes for a large number of segments is limited. If you have price dimensions set to a monthly basis, there could be instances where you will end up with a large number of segments, which may not display well in the QLE.

- Contracting works differently for MDQ products. Let's take an example of Packt subscription MDQ products segmented yearly, as shown in *Figure 7.10*:

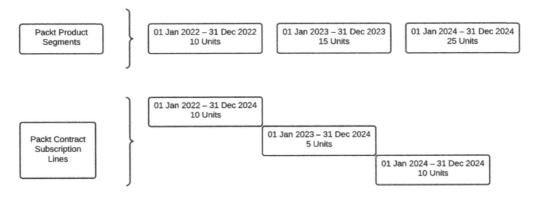

Figure 7.10 – MDQ subscription lines

- When MDQ is contracted, the subscriptions will be different from the standard CPQ contract. The first subscription will be created with a start date of the first segment, which is January 1, 2022, and the end date of the last segment, which is December 31, 2024. This subscription will have the number of units of the first segment. The next subscription starts from the second segment start date, which is January 1, 2023, until the end of the last segment, which is December 31, 2024. In the first subscription, we have added 10 units and CPQ maps the remaining units for the second subscription; in this example, it's 15 – 10, which is 5 units. The third subscription considers the last segment and the remaining units: 25 – 15, which is 10 units.

- You can only amend the current and future segments of an MDQ subscription. Past segments will not be available.

- CPQ doesn't support amending multiple MDQ subscriptions that have different start dates.

- The product record for an amended MDQ subscription contains a lookup to the subscription record from which it was amended.

From the previous discussion, you will realize that amendments and subscriptions become a little complex for MDQ products.

Now that we have learned how to configure and create amendments, we will see how to create renewals in the next section.

Creating renewals

As the contract progresses closer to the end date, you may need to renew it. We can extend subscriptions or make changes for up-selling or down-selling. The rep needs to talk to the customer and make sure that the renewals are successful and whether the customer is interested in up-selling the deal. This is again similar to negotiations that take place in the initial sales process, offering discounts for renewals, and up-selling is also common for a few businesses.

Contract-based renewal process

Let's learn how Salesforce CPQ creates renewals using the contract-based renewal model. We have a contracted opportunity and the contract has subscription lines with start dates and end dates. Renewals will be created for subscription products and percent of total products.

> **Important Note**
> If **Preserve Bundle Structure** is on, then CPQ will try to recreate the assets, which is a hassle.

The following are the steps to create a renewal:

1. First, there is an out-of-the-box **Renewal Forecasting** checkbox on contracts that need to be selected for creating renewals.

    By selecting this checkbox, you are telling the CPQ engine that there is a renewal that needs to be created. This checkbox can be selected as soon as the initial contract is created so that the forecasting can be accurate. Subscription products are added as **renewal opportunity** products with the existing pricing information from the **original opportunity**.

    To create these opportunity products, Salesforce CPQ creates a quote in the backend, which is primarily used to sync all the products from a quote to the opportunity and deletes this quote. This is also referred to as the **ghost** quote, as it is just used to sync the renewal products.

    The following figure shows the CPQ out-of-the-box renewal opportunity process:

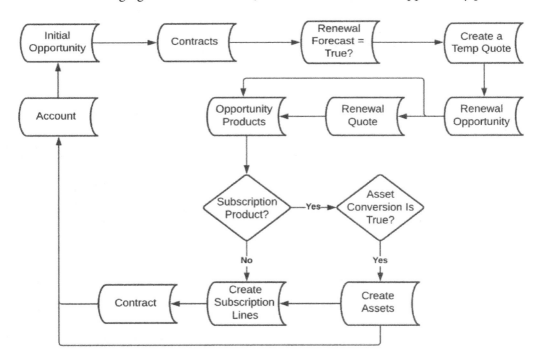

Figure 7.11 – Renewal opportunity process

2. Next, you want to create a renewal quote for which the **Renewal Quote** checkbox on the contract needs to be selected.

The reason why these two (a temporary quote to sync the products and the actual renewal quote) are kept separate is to make sure that the renewal quote has all the subscription products in the sales process when the deal gets closer to the renewal date. For example, if the original contract was created for 3 years, there might have been a few new subscription products in these 3 years. If we created the renewal quote as soon as the initial sale was closed, then it will only have the initial sale subscription products.

Also, there might have been amendments that were created on this contract after the end of the original sale, when the deal was closer to renewal. This may happen even though the renewal opportunity has been created with the original subscription products. The renewal quote generated now will have all the contract subscription line items. Technically, the renewal quote should be created when the rep is ready to negotiate with the customer. Then, it follows the same sales process.

> **Important Note**
>
> If your sales rep creates any amendments after the renewal quote creation, then the CPQ out-of-the-box functionality will not sync these new amendment products to the renewal quote. The rep needs to manually sync these amendment products to include them on the renewal quote.

The difference between a renewal quote and an amendment quote is that the renewal quote is exactly the same as a new quote. You can change prices, add discounts, and perform all the actions that can be performed on a new quote and create a new contract.

Asset-based renewal process

When you have an **asset-based** renewal model, you can renew your assets from the account for percent of total products and at least one covered asset. Creating asset-based renewals is much simpler compared to contract-based renewals. The following figure shows the asset-based renewal process:

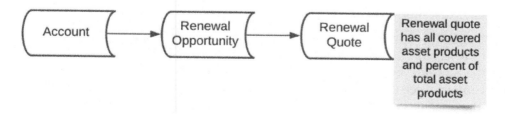

Figure 7.12 – Asset-based renewal process

Let's see the important steps in creating renewals for an asset-based renewal model:

1. To renew an asset, navigate to the account and click the **Renew Asset** button. This will display the **Asset Selection** page containing all the assets on this account that are covered by a percent of total product.

2. Select the assets that you need to renew and click **Renew**. Salesforce CPQ creates a renewal quote, associates it with a renewal opportunity, and opens the QLE.

3. Edit the quantities of the assets from your original quote if required. You can also add new products as needed and save the record. Salesforce CPQ updates your renewal opportunity to reflect the assets you added or removed on your renewal quote.

4. For asset-based renewals, Salesforce CPQ always uses the standard price book to price the renewed quote lines, unlike contract-based renewals where you have an option to select a different price book. **Large Scale Amendment** and **Renewal Service** do not support asset-based renewals, so the number of quote lines supported by CPQ is lower.

Before creating a sample renewal opportunity using the contract-based renewal model, let's look at the renewal pricing and renewal-related fields on a contract that controls the renewal process.

Renewal pricing

There is a field called **Renewal Pricing Method** on the account object that drives the pricing behavior for products on renewals. It can have three values:

- **Same**: This is the default option. This value will take the same price, including discounts from the original opportunity, and apply that to the renewal opportunity and quote at the time of renewal creation. For example, if you had a list price of $100 and a discount of 10%, then the initial discounted sale was at $90. The renewal will have the same prices applied.

- **List**: This value will take the list price of the product based on the price book used in the original opportunity. If we have an updated renewal price book ID on the contract, then renewals will take the list price from this price book. The original sale's discounts will not be applied in this case.

- **Uplift**: This option will be used when you want to have the renewal price increased by a percentage each time the renewal is created. In addition to marking the field on the account, you will need to set **Renewal Uplift Rate** at either the subscription or contract level. If both are set, the subscription takes precedence over the contract. The discounts will flow from the original opportunity and then **Uplift** will be applied on top of that. The additional discount field will not be null when this is used and may result in negative values in the discount field on account of the uplift.

> **Important Note**
>
> If contracted prices exist for the defined pricing method, they will be overridden by injecting **Special Price** with a **special price type**. CPQ will calculate the additional discount as the discrepancy between regular and customer prices.

Renewal fields on a contract

A contract has several fields related to renewals that can be used to customize the renewal process. Navigate to **App Launcher** → **Contract** → **Salesforce CPQ Information**, which will open the screen shown here:

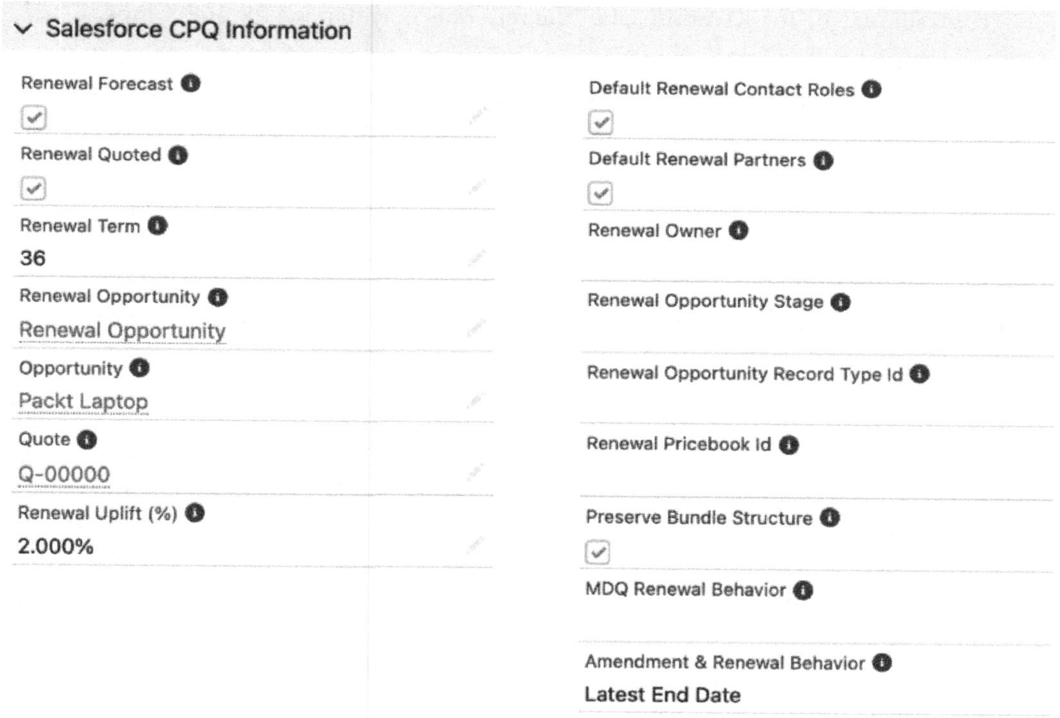

∨ Salesforce CPQ Information

Renewal Forecast ⓘ
☑

Renewal Quoted ⓘ
☑

Renewal Term ⓘ
36

Renewal Opportunity ⓘ
Renewal Opportunity

Opportunity ⓘ
Packt Laptop

Quote ⓘ
Q-00000

Renewal Uplift (%) ⓘ
2.000%

Default Renewal Contact Roles ⓘ
☑

Default Renewal Partners ⓘ
☑

Renewal Owner ⓘ

Renewal Opportunity Stage ⓘ

Renewal Opportunity Record Type Id ⓘ

Renewal Pricebook Id ⓘ

Preserve Bundle Structure ⓘ
☑

MDQ Renewal Behavior ⓘ

Amendment & Renewal Behavior ⓘ
Latest End Date

Figure 7.13 – Renewal fields on a contract

Let's learn about some of the important renewal fields shown in the preceding figure:

- **Renewal Forecast**: When this checkbox is selected, CPQ will automatically create the renewal opportunity and sync all the existing subscription product lines to the renewal opportunity. The ghost quote will be created in the backend and deleted.

- **Renewal Pricebook Id**: If you want to use a different price book for renewals, you can set that price book ID here. We can create renewal opportunities in a different record type. This may not go through all the same steps as the initial opportunity.

- **Renewal Opportunity Stage**: This field represents the stage at which you want the renewal opportunity to be created. You can directly assign a stage from your sales process and skip the other stages prior to the selected one. Sometimes the initial contract may be for 12 months, but the renewals may happen for 36 months.

- **Renewal Opportunity**: This field is the lookup for the renewal opportunity that gets created. This will be automatically updated based on the period you select for the renewal forecast. Salesforce CPQ by default names this **Renewal Opportunity**. You can customize this to have a different name as needed.

- **Renewal Term**: This value is the term of the renewal and will be used for the new contract creation. This will default to the term we have in the original contract. You can override this value if needed.

- **Renewal Owner**: This is the opportunity owner; you can preset this to the required owner from the Salesforce user object as needed. The default owner is the user who authorized the API.

- **Renewal Uplift**: This field can be used to apply an uplift to the original opportunity products. If you want to increase the price of the products by a certain percentage every time a deal is due for renewal, then the percentage increase can be specified here.

- **MDQ Renewal behavior**: This field is used for multidimensional quoting and can have two picklist values. By default, this is set to **None**. If you have an MDQ product in your original contract, the same MDQ product will be added to the renewal opportunity. You can opt out of the MDQ process by setting this picklist value to **De-segmented**.

- **Renewal Quoted**: When you are ready to work on the renewal opportunities and negotiate with customers, this checkbox can be selected. Selecting this checkbox and saving the contract record will automatically create a renewal quote. In typical business scenarios, the **Renewal Forecast** checkbox can be automatically selected using flows or Apex based on business needs or as soon as the deal is closed. A sales rep can also select this manually to generate the renewal opportunity.

- **Amendment and Renewal behavior**: You can set the renewal start date and amendment end date. When you have multiple subscriptions that have different end dates on a quote, you can choose which end date you want to use for the renewal start date. You can then pick either the latest one or the earliest one.

There is one more important feature for renewals, which is the ability to swap products while creating renewals. This field is on the product record. Navigate to the **Product →
Renewal Product** field. This field is a **lookup** field to the product. When you set this field, this new product will be considered at the time of renewal, replacing the original product. If this product is part of a bundle, then the renewal product needs to be specified at both the product level and the product option record level.

All of these fields can be set manually but you can automatically update them as needed using a flow or Apex logic. For example, contract activation can automatically set the **Renewal Forecasting** checkbox to **True**. These are some of the controls that can be customized as per the business needs.

Creating a sample renewal

In this section, we will see how to create a sample renewal opportunity and complete the renewal process using the contract-based renewal model.

Let's revisit the previous example where we created a contract from the initial sale and have an associated amendment. We have one subscription from the initial sale and another from the amendment.

For this example, we will manually select the **Renewal Forecast** checkbox and save the contract. The CPQ engine will create a renewal opportunity in the backend and the renewal opportunity field on the contract is populated.

The following figure shows the renewal opportunity. It has all the products from the initial contract, including amendments, and is available for all forecasting and pipeline reporting in Salesforce:

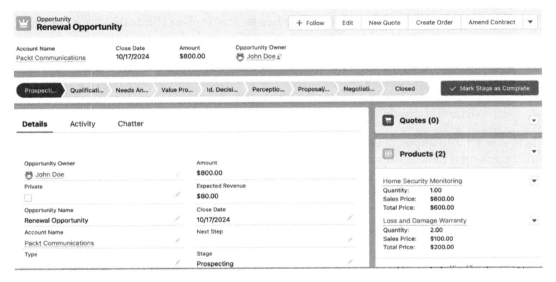

Figure 7.14 – Renewal opportunity

Let's imagine that you are nearing the initial contract end date and your rep needs to create a renewal quote. We can create the renewal quote by checking the **Renewal Quoted** checkbox on the contract manually. We can also have this selected automatically based on the business process. Once the contract is saved with this checkbox selected, a renewal quote is created automatically and set as the primary. Navigate to **Quote → Edit Lines**, which will open the QLE, as shown here:

. #	PRODUCT CODE	PRODUCT NA...	QUA...	UNIT C...	MAR...	LIST UNIT PRICE	ADDITIONAL DISC.	NET UNIT PRICE	NET TOTAL		>
1	HOMESECURITYM ONITORING	Home Security Monitoring	1.00	$30.00		$200.00		$600.00	$600.00	☆ 🗐 🗑 ↗	>
2	LDWARRANTY	Loss and Damage Warranty	2.00			$100.00		$100.00	$200.00	☆ 🗐 🗑 ↗	>

Q-00057 Edit Quote

Service Products | Add Products | Add Group | Delete Lines | Quick Save | Calculate | Cancel | Save

Quote Information

Start Date 10/18/2024   End Date 10/17/2027   Subscription Term

Additional Disc. (%)

SUBTOTAL: $800.00

QUOTE TOTAL: $800.00

Figure 7.15 – QLE renewal quote

The renewal quote has all the initial subscription lines and pricing from the original subscriptions. The rep can also update discounts and make changes to this quote like any other new quote.

As the sales process progresses, the renewal opportunity **status** can be set to **Closed Won**. Once the deal is closed, the **Contracted** checkbox can be selected on the opportunity, which will generate a new contract, as shown here:

		Contract Number ↑		Contract Start Date		Contract End Date		Status		
1		00000106		10/18/2021		10/17/2024		Draft		▼
2		00000107		10/18/2024		10/17/2027		Draft		▼

Figure 7.16 – Account with related contracts

The new contract starts from the next day after the previous one ends based on the term and the contract end date. If we have added non-subscription products to the renewal quote, the corresponding assets related to the account can be created. New subscriptions are created, with new start and end dates.

So far, you have learned how a typical renewal process works. In the actual implementation, we will often have situations where we need to migrate contracts from a legacy system.

Having multiple contracts is a common scenario in CPQ implementation. One of the use cases is legacy data migration. If businesses have implemented CPQ from the beginning, then all the contracts would have been generated in CPQ. But often we need to migrate data from a third-party system to CPQ and these contracts might have been created differently and may not align with CPQ.

The end dates for each of these contracts might be different. Salesforce CPQ provides a feature to merge all the contracts into one master contract. Refer to *Figure 7.16*, which has a **Renew Contracts** button. This button allows you to select all the contracts that need to be merged and decide which one is the master. When you select a particular contract as a master, the end date of that contract is inherited by all the quote lines.

Let's look at one advanced feature available in creating renewals, which is early renewal.

Early renewals

Early renewal is the process of renewing your contract before the end date. Let's see why we might need to perform an early renewal.

Imagine we have already created the renewal quote and the customer has decided to make some changes to the contract and they do not want to wait until the renewal start date to make these changes. They want to make the changes to the contract now and sign for the upcoming renewal. This needs an early renewal. Setting an early renewal is a two-step process:

1. Extend the start date of the renewal opportunity. First, we need to adjust the renewal quote to make the changes required by the customer. In this scenario, let's imagine the customer needs additional licenses. Navigate to **Renewal Quote →** **Edit Quote Line**. Reconfigure the QLE and add additional products as needed. For example, we have two *Loss and Damage Warranty* licenses, as shown in *Figure 7.14*, and we need to increase the number of licenses to five.

    Also, the customer needs these five licenses on August 17, and they don't want to wait until the renewal date, which is October 17. So, we need to adjust the start date of the renewal quote to the date the customer needs these changes. When we adjust the renewal quote start date, we are double-charging the customer because the customer has already paid for the two licenses as part of the initial renewal and when we backdate the renewal quote to August 17 (2 months earlier), we are charging for all five licenses.

2. To avoid double-charging, we need to credit the additional period, in this example, 2 months for quantity 2, for which we have already charged the customer, for the same products under the initial contract. To make this adjustment, we need to create an amendment. To do this, navigate to **Contract → Amend → Amend**. Set the start date to the date when the early renewal starts, which in this scenario is August 17. Make sure you select only the products for which you are creating the early renewal and set the quantity to 0. This will create a negative line for which credit can be created.

In the next section, let's learn about contracted pricing.

Contracted pricing

Imagine you have sold a particular product to a customer for $100 and you want to keep that price on hold every time the customer renews the contract irrespective of any price updates in the price book. For this, Salesforce CPQ offers a feature called **contracted pricing**, which is set at the account level. Contracted pricing will help you to honor the initial deal price. To configure contracted pricing, navigate to **App Launcher → Account → Related → Contracted Prices → New**, which will open the screen shown here:

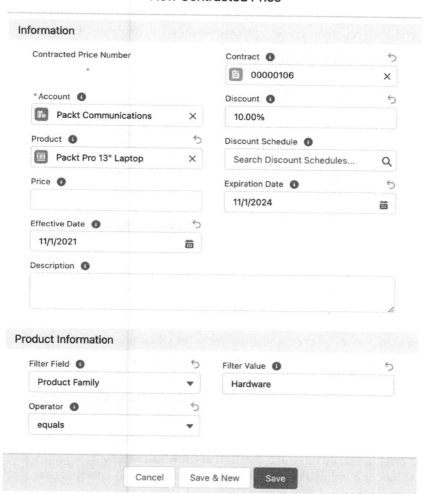

Figure 7.17 – Contracted pricing

Let's learn about a few important fields in contracted pricing creation:

- **Product**: Select the product for which this special pricing needs to be applied.

- **Price**: Add the specific price that needs to be applied to this product. If you remember the CPQ price waterfall diagram (*Figure 4.13* in *Chapter 4, Configuring CPQ Pricing*), the contracted price comes in the special price field. When we are setting this price, remember that this is the price for the subscription term of the product. For example, if the term is 12 months, then this price will apply to the entire term.

- **Discount**: The percentage of discount to be applied.

- **Discount Schedule**: This discount schedule will override the discount schedule at the product level. This is specific to the account or customer that you are selling to.

- **Effective Date** and **Expiration Date**: These define the start date and end date when the contract pricing is applicable.

- **Product Information**: This section contains the information related to product filters. Instead of setting this at the product level, you can apply filters so that contracted pricing is applicable at the product family level. For example, you want to discount all the `Hardware` products to 10% and when the customer is renewing the contract, this filter can be used.

  When you are setting this up, do not use the **Price** field as you have different products with different prices and you cannot apply the same price to all the products. It's always advisable to use the **Discount** field for setting up contracted pricing for a range of products.

  While calculating the quote line price, Salesforce CPQ verifies whether your quote line has a contracted price. If it does, then Salesforce CPQ passes that price to your quote line's special price. It then updates the quote line's **Special Price Type** field to **Contracted Price**. As a best practice, set only one contracted price per product. If you create more than one, it shows an error when you create a quote. Also, it is preferred to generate a contracted price on a quote rather than the product.

If **Generate Contacted Price** on a quote is set to **True**, when you add a product to the quote, the price of the product is added as the contracted price to that customer only. When you set it at the product level, it gets applied to all the quotes, which may throw an error.

Contracted pricing can be inherited through **account hierarchy** by cascading down the hierarchy. When in conflict, the one set at the lowest level will take precedence. We can set **Ignore Parent Contracted Prices** at the account level if needed.

You can retrieve the contracted price from an alternate account by creating a `ContractedAccountid__c` CPQ special field on a quote set as an account lookup or formula so that it stores the ID of the alternate account.

Summary

In this chapter, you learned when and how to create contracts, amendments, and renewals. Several use cases can be configured using these out-of-the-box features.

This is a complex functionality in CPQ that will help you configure products for any specific business. Renewals are as important as your initial deals. Creating and negotiating renewals promptly will help generate a lot of revenue by up-selling. You have also learned how the contract-based renewal model helps in managing the recurring relationship with customers after the initial sale. You have also understood how to customize renewals and amendment processes. You have seen how accounts can be a single source of truth for contracts, amendments, and renewals. While CPQ manages all the record-keeping for amendments and renewals, reps can focus on closing more deals.

In the next chapter, you will learn about the CPQ data model and the object relationships for some of the major CPQ objects.

8
Configuring CPQ Package Settings

In the previous chapters, we learned about different CPQ configurations and how the CPQ package can be customized as per specific business needs. CPQ's out-of-the-box functionality is dependent on the package settings that provide global control across the CPQ platform. With these settings, we can enable or disable certain CPQ features, configure aspects of a specific feature, and control the overall package behavior.

When implementing CPQ, we need to make sure we capture the high-level requirements that will help in selecting the right configurations, as making these changes later becomes difficult and very involved. In this chapter, we will discuss different package settings and how these settings will affect automation.

We will be covering the following topics:

- Configuring the CPQ package
- The **Documents** tab
- The **Groups** tab
- The **Line Editor** tab
- The **Plugins** tab
- The **Pricing and Calculation** tab

- The **Subscriptions and Renewals** tab
- The **Quote** tab
- The **Order** tab
- Additional settings

Configuring the CPQ package

CPQ package settings can be configured to control the Salesforce CPQ functionality. These settings can be enabled or disabled as per the business needs and govern how the CPQ **installed package** functionality is available. These settings are at the organization level and apply to the entire package. When implementing CPQ for any business, we need to understand the business process and the high-level requirements. This will help administrators configure the package settings correctly so that CPQ's out-of-the-box functionality can be used with minimum customizations. For example, an electric panel for a home would control the power for the whole home. This is similar to the org-level configuration. When power to a specific room needs to be controlled, then a specific switch panel can be operated.

Let's learn about these configurations and how they can be customized in a Salesforce CPQ test instance. These settings can also be configured and tested in a sandbox instance before configuring them in a production instance.

To create or modify package settings, navigate to your Salesforce instance where you want to configure the settings: **Salesforce → CPQ setup → Quick find → Installed packages**. In the list of installed packages, search for `Salesforce CPQ` and then click **Configure**. This will open the package configuration screen, as shown here:

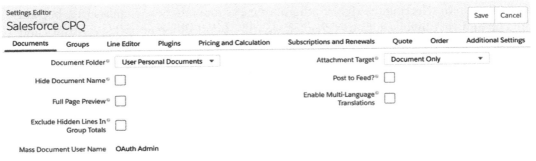

Figure 8.1 – CPQ package settings

As shown in the preceding screenshot, the package settings are grouped into different tabs. Each of these settings controls different functionalities of CPQ. Most of these settings have Salesforce help: when you hover over the question mark symbol next to the label, you can see what that setting refers to. In the following sections, we will learn about some of the important settings. Not all these configurations are required for implementation; only a few of these may be applicable as per your business process. Let's begin by looking at the **Documents** tab.

The Documents tab

This tab includes settings that will help you customize the creation, distribution, and storage of your quote documents. Let's learn about a few important configurations in the **Documents** tab. This is not an exhaustive list, and we can refer to Salesforce Help for additional details:

- **Attachment Target**: This field determines where to store the generated quote documents, based on the target object chosen. We can select the following values:

  - **Document Only**: Choosing this value means that the quote documents will be available in the chosen Salesforce document folder only. Users even without a Salesforce CPQ license can access the quote documents when this picklist is selected.

  - **Quote**: If you choose this value, the quote document will be available in the notes and attachment section of the quote. This setting allows those with access to the record to have access to the document.

  - **Opportunity**: When this option is selected, the quote documents will be available in the notes and attachment section of opportunities. This will grant any user with permissions to the opportunity object the ability to view the quote document without a CPQ license.

- **Enable Multi-Language Translations**: This setting allows your reps to generate CPQ quotes in one of the languages supported by your org. Enabling this setting will add a local **Document Language** picklist to the **Generate Document** page. Before getting the translated content, you must have the translated values stored for the intended language.

- **Hide Document Name**: This setting allows you to hide the filename when generating the document. This setting prevents reps from changing the default filename that is specific to your organization.

> **Important Note**
> The aforementioned list is not exhaustive and we can refer to the Salesforce
> Help for additional details: `https://help.salesforce.com/s/`
> `articleView?id=sf.cpq_package_settings.htm&type=5`.

Next, we'll look at the **Groups** tab.

The Groups tab

Settings in this tab will determine the **quote line group** and **solution group** management and their functionalities. This tab has the following settings:

- **Solution Groups Enabled**: This setting is helpful when your business has a standard set of predefined products in a quote line group. For example, you may want to group hardware and software items separately in your quotes. Solution groups allow you to group and create subtotals that are independent of other quote lines and quote line groups.

- **Require Group Name**: Selecting this checkbox will make the group name mandatory in the QLE.

Now that we have learned about the settings on the **Groups** tab, let's learn about the **Line Editor** tab.

The Line Editor tab

This tab contains all the configurations related to the line editor. We have already seen some of these settings during the QLE configuration in *Chapter 2, Configuring Opportunities and Quotes*. A few important settings are as follows:

- **Visualize product hierarchy checkbox**: This setting will help indent the components of bundle products, including nested bundles. By selecting this checkbox, you will see the breakdown of products and their components in the **Quote Line Editor** (**QLE**). When you add a product bundle in the QLE, the indentation will help reps see the parent bundle and all the components associated with it.

- **Keep Bundle Together**: When this setting is enabled, the bundle's components will always be displayed along with the bundle. When the bundle is dragged and dropped to a new location in the QLE, all the corresponding components will also move automatically.

- **Preserve Bundle Structure**: Selecting this setting will display the product options in the same order as they exist in the **renewal quotes**. This setting can also be enabled at the contract level if your business only needs this functionality for renewals under a specific contract. Enabling this setting at the package level means it will be applicable globally.

- **Quote Batch Size**: CPQ loads and saves quotes in the QLE in batches of the quote line. This setting controls the number of lines in a batch. When this field is blank, CPQ engines use a default value of 150. This value can be edited as per business requirements. A smaller batch size is optimal and less likely to hit a **governor limit**. It's recommended not to have a bigger value to avoid performance issues. Post-implementation, once the number of quote lines is known for most scenarios, this field can be set to increase performance.

- **Large Quote Threshold**: This is a user-defined number. For **user interface** (UI) calls, CPQ will send all quote lines to be evaluated until it hits this threshold. If the number of quote lines meets/exceeds the threshold, then the quote line batch size setting is utilized to parse the QLE calculation. Once the threshold is reached, CPQ will also ignore the quote scoped **product rules** for that quote. If we need to include these validation rules, and then we need to enable another package configuration: **Enable Large Quote Threshold Validations**. This field has a null value by default. This setting needs to be enabled only if your business uses large quotes with several lines. This value can be adjusted when you start hitting the governor limit.

- **Enable Large Quote Experience**: Enabling this setting will enhance the user experience for quotes containing large quote lines.

- **Enable Expand/Collapse Bundles**: Admins can choose this setting if product bundles in the QLE can be expanded or collapsed. This feature will be useful for bundles with several products enhancing the rep experience. To make use of this functionality, make sure the following CPQ settings are also enabled:

  - **Enable Large Quote Experience**

  - **Visualize Bundle Hierarchy**

  - **Keep Bundles Together**

- **Enable Multi Line Delete**: When this setting is enabled, reps can select multiple quote lines and delete them.

Next, we will learn about the **Plugins** tab.

The Plugins tab

Using this tab, we can link optional third-party plugins. These plugins help extend the CPQ features and integrate the package with third-party tools.

> **Important Note**
> Plugins require either APEX or JavaScript skills.

Let's learn about a few important configurations in the **Plugins** tab:

- **Electronic Signature Plug-in**: This will integrate Salesforce with electronic signature plugins, which can be used to e-sign a quote document automatically. The e-signature tool will have instructions for how to fill in this detail.

- **Quote Calculator Plug-in (QCP)**: This feature extends the Salesforce CPQ quote calculator by adding a JavaScript quote calculator plugin. Never use the legacy calculator as it is no longer supported by Salesforce.

- Additional functionalities can be added to the QLE with custom JavaScript code. Certain third-party **AppExchange** applications such as Vertex will provide the QCP to integrate with CPQ. You can refer to the Salesforce developer guide documentation for further information on how to use the QCP at `https://developer.salesforce.com/docs/atlas.en-us.cpq_dev_api.meta/cpq_dev_api/cpq_dev_jsqcp_guidelines.htm`.

The next tab we will learn about is the **Pricing and Calculation** tab.

The Pricing and Calculation tab

These settings manage the price calculations on CPQ quotes:

- **Unit price scale**: By default, this is set to 2. Unit prices are rounded to two decimal places.

- **Calculate Immediately**: By enabling this field, you can enable real-time calculations. In previous chapters, we saw that reps can click the **Calculate** button in the QLE to see the calculated values. With this setting, the calculations are performed automatically. This has a huge impact on QLE performance. Do not enable this setting unless this is absolutely necessary and the impact is validated. Reps can click the **Calculate** button to see the changes, but they still need to click **Quick Save** and **Save** to update the changes.

- **Enable Quick Calculate**: This improves the quote calculation time by disabling price rules and quote line formula fields that depend on parent relationships, and displaying roll-up summary fields in the QLE. This setting needs to be enabled only if you are not using the affected features, such as price rules, quote line formulas, or displaying roll-up summary fields.

- **Use legacy calculator**: By default, this configuration will be enabled in the org when you install CPQ. Admins need to disable this setting as it is no longer supported by Salesforce. When you disable this, you need to authorize the new calculation service. This will appear only once and disappear after you authorize the new calculation service. This enables the CPQ Advanced Quote Calculator.

Next, let's learn about the **Subscriptions and Renewals** tab.

The Subscriptions and Renewals tab

These settings are related to **contract subscriptions** and **renewals**. Let's learn about a few important settings in this tab (this list is not exhaustive – please refer to the Salesforce Help documentation (`https://help.salesforce.com/s/`) for the complete list):

- **Renewal Model**: This field can have two values:

  - **Contract Based**: For contract-based renewals, the admin configures the order or opportunity with at least one subscription product. A contract-based renewal model creates subscription records for subscription products and asset records for non-subscription products with asset conversion. The contract-based model is useful for businesses that sell a lot of subscription products and want to keep track of contract details such as the subscription start date and end date.

  - **Asset Based**: In the asset based renewal model, only an asset record is created for non-subscription products when an order or an opportunity is contracted. The asset-based method is mostly used for non-subscription products.

The renewal model that you set at the package level will be applied to all accounts by default. Alternatively, the renewal model can be changed at the account level to a different value, and this overrides the renewal model that was set at the package level. Changing the renewal model after records are created is nearly impossible, it is advised to make the appropriate selection at the beginning of the implementation.

- **Contract in Foreground**: Enabling this setting can help perform immediate user actions right after the contract is created, but it increases the risk of CPU timeout. By disabling this setting, CPQ runs the contract process in the background. Users can continue working on the Salesforce contract amendment process in progress.

- **Enable Evergreen subscriptions**: When this setting is enabled, CPQ creates contract subscriptions that do not have an end date. Customers can cancel or terminate the contracts at any point. The product's **Subscription Type** can be **Evergreen** or **Renewable/Evergreen** when this setting is enabled. Admins cannot disable this setting once enabled. To prevent users from creating evergreen subscriptions, admins need to remove the picklist values from the product subscription type field. CPQ will create evergreen subscriptions on a different contract than renewable subscriptions.

- **Re-evaluate Bundle Logic on Renewals**: Selecting this package setting will automatically reconfigure a bundle on renewal. Renewing a bundle with this setting enabled executes all configuration rules and automatically adds the required products. This setting provides the same functionality as a user manually finding the renewal quote, reconfiguring the bundle, and then saving it. This setting will prevent users from manually re-configuring bundles.

- **Bypass Preserve Bundle Structure**: This setting removes the requirement to keep the original bundle structure on amendments. Enabling the **Preserve Bundle Structure** setting on contracts is not required when this setting is selected on the package setting, but it is advised not to use this setting and continue to use **Preserve Bundle Structure** on contracts to avoid unexpected price changes and unforeseen product and price rule changes.

- **Subscription term unit**: This field can have two values, **Month** and **Day**. This setting defines how your company is selling its subscriptions. When your company is selling services such as Amazon Prime and video streaming, it makes sense to set this value to a month, whereas if you are renting an industrial product, this can be set to days. Even though this value is set to a month or day, the unit of time for adding these subscription products to a quote can be customized.

  CPQ determines the subscription length by evaluating this package-level subscription unit with the quote's subscription term. For example, you can set a yearly subscription by setting the subscription term unit to **Month** and your quote subscription term to 12. For this same example, when the yearly subscription term is set to **Day**, then your quote subscription term needs to be set to 365.

- **Subscription Prorate precision**: This field is applicable when you have a start date and an end date for your subscription that includes partial months. For example, when you have the subscription term unit as **Month**, but the time duration between the start date and end date is greater than a month, this picklist tells CPQ how to calculate the **prorate multiplier**. When the subscription term is a month, the subscription prorate has values: **Day**, **Calendar monthly + Daily**, **Day With Calendar Month Weighted**, **Month**, and **Monthly + Daily**. When the subscription term unit is **Day**, the subscription prorate has only one value, **Day**.

Let's look at the prorate multiplier in more detail in the following subsection.

Prorate multiplier

When a rep adds subscription products to a quote, the pricing is calculated by the CPQ engine in the backend using the prorate multiplier. It is important to understand how integrated systems handle part-period proration. An admin should understand what systems may be consuming CPQ data, commonly, revenue recognition engines and billing engines. The CPQ proration calculations should be evaluated against proration logic in these engines to ensure that bookings and billings match.

Let's learn how the CPQ prorate calculation works. It's important to choose which subscription term best suits your business when implementing CPQ and it is advisable not to change this setting as old quotes are not retroactively changed. Also, this affects how renewals and active quotes are calculated. Changing this could have a substantial impact on forecasting. The subscription term unit that is configured in package settings applies to all the subscription products. A quote's prorate multiplier is calculated based on the default subscription term and the length of the subscription. For example, let's imagine *Packt Subscription* is a subscription product in a Salesforce instance with a unit price of $30. We have a quote with a 24-month term in this subscription product and the **Default Subscription Term (DST)** for this quote is 12.

The prorate multiplier is calculated by dividing the subscription term (24) by the default subscription term (12), which is 2. So, the price of this product on the quote will show as 2*30, which is $60.

The prorate multiplier is easy to calculate when subscription terms are used for subscription lengths. This gets complex when we have start dates and end dates to calculate the term, as these calculations need to consider the number of days in a month, partial months, leap years, and so on. To handle various business needs, CPQ provides five different methods of prorate calculations. Each of these calculations is applicable by setting the **Subscription Prorate precision** field accordingly. Let's consider the same example of the *Packt Subscription* product with a 12-month DST. But now, instead of a 24-month term, we have the quote start date as Jan 5, 2020, and the end date as May 10, 2021. Let's see how the prorate precision is calculated for this use case:

- When **Subscription Prorate precision** is set to **Day** in the CPQ package settings, the prorate multiplier is calculated as days divided by the number of days necessary to complete the DST from the start date. In this example, it will be 492 / 366 = 1.3442. The price of the product in the QLE will be 1.3442 * 30 = 40.326.

- When **Subscription Prorate precision** is set to **Calendar monthly + Daily** in the CPQ package settings, the prorate multiplier is calculated as *([Partial days in start month / days in start month] + Whole months + [Partial days in end month / days in end month]) / DST*. In this example, it is ([27/31]+16+[21/31]) /12 = 1.4623. The price of the product in the QLE will be 1.4623 * 30 = 43.869.

- When **Subscription Prorate precision** is set to **Day With Calendar Month Weighted** in the CPQ package settings, the prorate multiplier is calculated as *Years + (Remaining days / X)*, where $X = 366$ if the remaining days include February 29, otherwise $X = 365$. In this example, it is 1+(121/365) = 1.3315. The price of the product in the QLE will be 1.3315 * 30 = 39.945.

- When **Subscription Prorate precision** is set to **Month** in the CPQ package settings, the prorate multiplier is calculated as *Months (rounded up) / DST*. In this example, it will be, 17/12 =1.4166. The price of the product in the QLE will be 1.4166 * 30 = 42.498.

- When **Subscription Prorate precision** is set to *Monthly + Daily* in the CPQ package settings. The prorate multiplier is calculated as *(Months + [Remaining days / {365/12}]) / DST*. In this example, it will be (16 + {6/{365/12}])/12 = 1.3497. The price of the product in the QLE will be 1.3497 * 30 = 40.491.

Now that we have learned about the prorate multiplier, let's look at the **Quote** tab settings.

The Quote tab

These settings manage quote creation and maintenance for CPQ quotes:

- **Disable Initial Quote Sync**: When a rep creates the first quote from an opportunity, by default, Salesforce CPQ creates quote lines for each of the opportunity products. When this setting is active, CPQ will not create these quote lines.

- **Primary Quote Keeps Opportunity Products**: In the previous chapters, we have seen that when a quote is marked as primary, the quote products are synched from quote to opportunity. When the primary quote is moved from quote A to quote B, the related products are pushed to the opportunity.

  For example, let's think that quote A has two products, product A and product B, and quote B has two other products, product C and product D. When quote A is set as primary, product A and product B will be synched to the opportunity. When the primary quote is moved from quote A to quote B, the opportunity products will be automatically changed to product C and product D. With this setting, if there is no primary quote associated with an opportunity, the previously synched products will not be deleted from this opportunity.

- **Default Quote Validity (Days)**: This field describes the time duration for which a rep is allowed to edit a quote. This depends on your company's business process and how you would want your reps to edit quotes. By default, this is set to 30 days. Using customization, admins can enforce security to lock the quote so that reps cannot edit the quotes past this limit.

Next, let's learn about the **Order** settings.

The Order tab

The following are the settings related to orders:

- **Allow Multiple Orders**: This will allow reps to split a quote into multiple orders. If your business requires this functionality, then using this configuration, the quote can be split into orders, as per the inventory available, or as per the location, and much more. This setting is available only in **CPQ +**.

- **Create Orders Without Opportunities**: This setting allows you to create an order from the quote without an opportunity. This is useful for organizations with high volumes of orders.

- **Default Order Start Date**: This will allow the order to default with the quote start date or the current date.

- **Require Approved Quote**: If this setting is enabled, sales reps cannot create an order until the quote's **Status** field is set to **Approved**.

After learning about the various settings, let's now look at some of the additional settings that CPQ offers.

Additional settings

The following are the additional settings available in the CPQ package settings:

- **Triggers Disabled**: This setting disables CPQ triggers temporarily. This is useful when you are performing data migration or when you are debugging or testing in CPQ. This needs to be enabled once the activity is completed.

- **Multiple Bundle Views**: This configurator has two values, **Wizard** and **Classic**, for quotes with multiple bundles. The wizard option displays each bundle separately. With the classic option, all the bundles are displayed together on one page, separated by the section layout.

- **Enable Large Configurations**: This setting allows users to include more than 400 products in product bundles. This setting has a performance impact as it slows down processing for all bundles.

- **Execute Scripts**: This setting needs to be enabled during the installation or upgrade. Post CPQ implementation, executing scripts is very helpful.

> **Important Note**
>
> Whenever there are configuration changes made and CPQ functionality doesn't work, it is advisable to execute scripts. This is very helpful for troubleshooting, when CPQ throws an error related to "Field Metadata," or when a price rule or any configuration stops working. Also, when you add a new field summary variable or picklist values, executing scripts will resolve the issue.

Summary

In this chapter, you have learned how to configure the CPQ package settings. You have also learned how the package settings can control the other configurations in CPQ. You saw that these settings apply across the entire package. It is very important to thoroughly understand these settings for successful CPQ implementation. With these master configurations, you should be able to minimize the customizations and leverage the out-of-the-box functionality.

In the next chapter, we will learn about CPQ data model and Migration concepts.

Section 3: Advancing with Salesforce CPQ

This section describes the CPQ data model and some of the major objects that are related to each other. We will then learn how CPQ changes can be migrated from one Salesforce instance to another. You will explore how legacy data can be migrated to Salesforce CPQ.

You will be provided with a high-level overview of Industries CPQ and how it is different from the standard Salesforce CPQ. Finally, you will learn some of the implementation best practices that impact the performance of your CPQ implementation and things that you need to watch out for.

This section comprises the following chapters:

9
The CPQ Data Model and Migration Concepts

In the previous chapters, we learned about Salesforce's **Configure, Price, Quote (CPQ)** out-of-the-box configurations and used them to optimize the quote-to-cash process. Typically, many businesses won't have an existing CPQ implementation.

Often, a business uses spreadsheets, ad hoc software, in-house tools, or Salesforce standard objects to store data. When you decide to migrate such businesses to CPQ, you need to have a strategy for migrating data from those legacy sources into Salesforce, as well as being ready to anticipate a business process transformation. In this chapter, we will learn about successfully implementing CPQ and data migration.

Implementing CPQ is like building a home. You first need to lay the foundation for it. Understanding the data model is like building this foundation. Then, you can build relationships using CPQ with the products, bundles, options, features, price rules, product rules, approvals, quote templates, and so on that we have learned about so far in the previous chapters. For your convenience, you can configure some of the aforementioned stages in parallel too, but you need to be aware of the interdependencies in the implementation. In this chapter, you will learn about the CPQ data model and the interdependencies.

Finally, we will understand how the deployment of CPQ changes, from Sandbox to Production, play a crucial role in the implementation. All the changes need to be developed in a sandbox, following a project methodology that works for your company before migrating them to production.

Specifically, we will be covering the following topics:

- Understanding the CPQ implementation strategy
- Deploying CPQ changes
- Understanding the CPQ data model
- Legacy data migration
- CPQ localizations

Understanding the CPQ implementation strategy

In the previous chapters, we saw that Salesforce CPQ can dramatically improve the quote-to-cash process. Proper implementation is the key to success. Unlike Sales Cloud or Service Cloud, CPQ, across the platform, impacts several business stakeholders. As CPQ involves changing product configurations, pricing, contracting, order management, and much more, it involves different groups from your organization, such as product engineering, finance, sales, sales operations, and legal. Communication is important for a successful project implementation. In addition, not engaging the right people in a project is one of the biggest failures. Identifying key internal resources and building an implementation team consisting of management, business **Subject Matter Experts (SMEs)**, and technical SMEs becomes crucial for successful implementations.

CPQ is a managed package; once installed, it's going to be embedded into the standard Salesforce package. You can use a standard data model, such as accounts, opportunities, products, and price books. You can use the standard Salesforce data from these objects to configure products, pricing, and other automation. You need to evaluate the state of this data to see whether the current data can be effectively used.

CPQ implementation is a major change in the way reps sell products and deliver quotes to customers. It is more than a system deployment; it's an organizational change. The following are some of the key points to be considered during CPQ implementation:

- **Project phasing**: Every project has it; we don't recommend all business units in all regions go live at the same time with completed data migration. Rather, we usually phase by geography, customer segment, or product line.

- **Integrations/dependent systems**: Only focusing on CPQ and the requirements driven by rep behavior can cause certain integrations to be overlooked. It is equally important to consider the existing integrations as part of the CPQ implementation and migration project.

- **Design for the rule, not the exceptions**: Do not try to automate the edge cases in a business process. Leave them as manual processes. For example, if the automation only impacts a small percentage of use cases or corner-case scenarios, then it doesn't make sense to work on that and over-engineer things for automation. These one-off scenarios can be handled manually.

- **Low-hanging fruits**: Focus on the use case that provides the most value and keep it simple.

- **Maximize CPQ configurations**: CPQ comes with its own set of tools – line summary variables, price rules, product rules, and much more. As a best practice, it is important to note that a CPQ implementation should rely on CPQ tools and not Salesforce tools. For example, to calculate a price, use a price rule and not a workflow rule. To summarize a variable, use a summary variable and not a roll-up summary field. It can be hard to predict how standard Salesforce configurations operate with the CPQ module.

- **Engage users early and often**: Adoption is the key. Implementing CPQ is not rolling out a fancy tool; it is a business transformation.

- **Requirements**: Identify key pain points in the current system and see how CPQ can help with minimum or no customization. Simplify and standardize the current business processes. This will be a drastic change in the way the quote-to-cash process was used before. With automation, businesses may lose flexibility.

- **What type of transactions are to be supported when going live?**: Is it just net-new (no data migration) or is it a migration/conversion of existing customer and contract data that is required to support day-one amendment transactions?

- **Iterative design**: Incorporate feedback and refine CPQ configurations.

- **Deployment**: Make sure you maintain a deployment sheet from the beginning of a project. This ensures that you don't miss any components during the project deployment. There are three primary types of CPQ configuration to be mindful of when deploying:

  - Metadata

  - Record data

  - Package settings

- **Post-development**: Use key SMEs to help with training and enablement.

Deploying CPQ changes

In any implementation, development can happen in multiple sandboxes. These can be either **dev** or **dev pro** environments. All the changes from a development environment need to be migrated to an integrated **QA** environment. Once the changes are tested, these changes need to be deployed into a **full sandbox** so that **User Acceptance Testing (UAT)** can be performed in this instance.

A UAT instance can be thoroughly tested end to end to complete testing of new and regression cases. CPQ testing and UAT should be conducted in a fully integrated environment. Once a business sign-off is complete, the changes can be deployed to a pre-production or staging environment. Then, finally, the changes can be deployed to the production environment. The following figure shows a standard linear development strategy:

Figure 9.1 – The development strategy

It is always strongly advised to perform **smoke testing** following a CPQ deployment to production. Smoke testing should include two things:

- Testing of the new features
- A light regression test across major use cases

> **Important Note**
>
> It is always recommended to have a rollback strategy so that if things go wrong in production, changes can be rolled back and business can continue.

Metadata changes, such as objects, fields, and workflows, can be easily migrated from one Salesforce instance to another using tools such as changesets for easy environments and DevOps and release management for complex environments. Record data containing relationships is not easy to deploy between different instances of Salesforce. We know that Salesforce allocates a unique 15- or 18-digit ID to each record we create.

We cannot maintain relationships between records when deploying changes through multiple development environments and then, finally, to the production environment. It's important to note that all CPQ configurations, such as product rules and price rules, are data records and not metadata, which makes CPQ deployment difficult. The metadata changes need to be deployed before the data changes. For example, consider deploying a price rule and associated metadata (for example, a new field). The new field needs to be deployed before deploying the price rule. For the price rule, you will have multiple records in multiple objects. You will have a price rule record, a price action record, and a price condition record, all of which need to be deployed.

Your organization should have several standard test scenarios that are used to test-exercise a system for errors and compatibility. These scenarios need to be executed before deploying the changes to production. This is included as part of the internal release schedule.

Let's look at a few guidelines for deploying CPQ changes from one instance to another:

- Consider an external deployment tool, such as **Prodly** or **Copado**. This is one of the best options for deploying CPQ data from one environment to another. Using these deployment tools will help to automatically deploy all the dependencies. In the price rule example, by choosing to deploy a price rule, the deployment tool will automatically deploy all its price actions, price conditions, and much more.

- Manually creating the changes in each environment is not advisable, as it is error-prone and doesn't keep the environments in sync.

- Evaluate the existing DevOps process and include the CPQ metadata migration.

- Using external IDs connected to the records will help the deployment, as these values will never change. Admins need to create an ID field to stamp the record ID from the development environment. Then, as a record is promoted through higher environments, it has a consistent ID and makes deployment validation/reconciliation easier.

- The internal release schedule will help streamline the deployment process and choose the best time for deployment. It is considered a best practice to avoid major deployments during the quarter-end and year-end periods.

- There is no right or wrong tool for deployment. Choose the tool that fits your organization's existing deployment process.

In the next section, let's learn about another important concept, which is the CPQ data model.

Understanding the CPQ data model

CPQ uses standard Salesforce objects and CPQ objects. All the CPQ object API names start with SBQQ__, which identifies a specific object that is linked to Salesforce CPQ. All the CPQ field names that come out of the box are also prefixed with SBQQ.

In *Chapter 1, Getting Started with Salesforce CPQ Implementation*, we learned about the high-level CPQ object model. But that model was basic and didn't provide extensive information about all the objects and fields. CPQ is an enterprise-level application with more than 80 objects, 1,000 fields, 28 fieldsets, and 500 classes; the scale of the product is huge.

The most important and major Salesforce objects are **products** and **opportunities**. Most organizations, before implementing CPQ, might have customized these two objects heavily. As businesses grow further, they implement CPQ; so, we may need to decouple the existing customization in these objects and move the functionality to CPQ objects.

The following figure shows the object model for major objects:

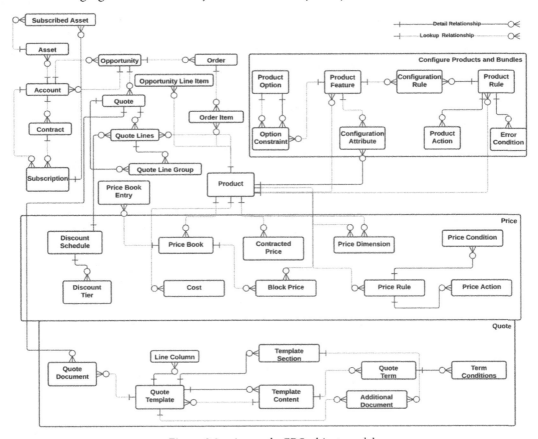

Figure 9.2 – A sample CPQ object model

Refer to the Salesforce help documentation for an exhaustive list of the lookup and master-detail relationships: `https://help.salesforce.com/s/articleView?id=sf.cpq_object_relationships.htm&type=5`.

For your specific implementation, you will be building a data model that will include major objects and their relationships. This is not a one-time activity; as part of your implementation progress, you can revisit these objects and/or their relationships as needed.

The **Salesforce Schema Builder** can be used for extracting a data model. You don't need the 500+ objects from the CPQ package and the thousands of fields to build the object model. But even for the objects that are needed for your implementation, this is a cumbersome task. However, this object model will be very useful, and you'll have an overview of the data structures. You can view the relationships between the major CPQ objects listed as follows using Schema Builder:

- Opportunity
- Opportunity product
- Quote
- Quote line
- Order
- Order product
- Contract
- Subscription

The detailed relationships between objects can be reviewed in many ways. Schema Builder is an out-of-the-box Salesforce tool that helps to visualize the object model. In the next section, let's learn about Schema Builder.

Exporting a Salesforce object model

The Schema Builder is an easy and out-of-the-box Salesforce tool that helps you visualize an object model and its relationships. Navigate to **Setup** → **Quick Find** → **Schema Builder**. On the left-hand side of the panel, you can select objects and clear objects. You can also select specific objects whose relationships you want to display. Select **View Options** to display the field only with **relationship**; that way, you can get a simpler object view. Click on **Auto-Layout** to view all the selected options in the display.

The following figure shows a **Schema Builder** example with a few sample objects - opportunity, quote, quote lines, and products:

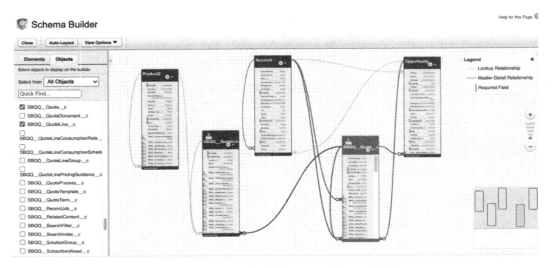

Figure 9.3 – A sample of objects in Schema Builder

As you can see, Schema Builder displays the lookup and master-detail relationship between objects. You can choose standard and CPQ objects as needed. In this example, we are showing the relationship between **Account**, **Opportunity**, **SBQQ_Quote__C**, **SBQQ__QuoteLines__C**, and **Product2** objects. This is a user-friendly and intuitive tool that can be used to understand the Salesforce object model very well.

Exporting Salesforce objects to Lucidchart

Another method of creating a data model outside Salesforce is using **Lucidchart**. This provides an out-of-the-box integration to export Salesforce objects.

To do this, navigate to **Lucidchart → File → Import Data → Entity Relationship (ERD) Import your Data → Import from Salesforce**. Lucidchart will prompt you to connect to either a sandbox or a production instance. Provide the Salesforce credentials. Choose the objects that you want to import from the search window, as shown here:

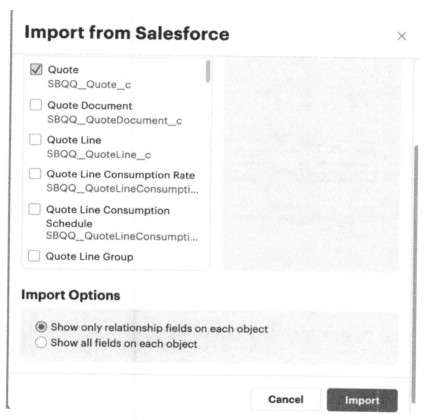

Figure 9.4 – Importing Salesforce objects

Select the **Show only relationship fields on each object** option to display only the required fields. The objects will be added to the left-hand panel of the Lucidchart window under the **Entity Relationship Diagram (ERD)**. These objects can be dragged and dropped to the chart. The following figure shows sample objects in a chart:

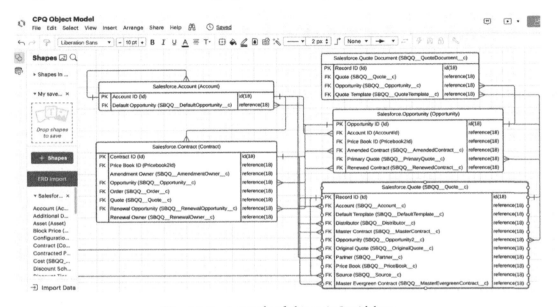

Figure 9.5 – A sample of objects in Lucidchart

Once you import the objects, you can see a list of the objects on the left-hand side, and you can add objects as needed. The fields on these objects can be deleted to simplify the ERD view. Deleting fields from Schema Builder will delete them from the database.

In the next section, let's learn about data migration from legacy systems to Salesforce.

Legacy data migration

Data migration is the process of moving data from one system to another. Migrating legacy data to Salesforce CPQ has a few prerequisites to ensure that all dependencies are migrated accordingly. For example, if you are migrating a contract, the dependencies to the account and the initial opportunity need to be migrated before migrating contract data. If the account already exists in your Salesforce instance, then you will need to map the relevant properties to the Salesforce objects to auto-populate the account fields when you migrate the contract. While migrating, make sure that the field API values are not changed.

Data migrations need to be performed in a full sandbox for business validation and regression testing. Make sure that the test scenarios include historical data, new data, and in-progress (in-flight) data. Once the business validates and provides a sign-off, the same migration can be performed in production. When you have large historical data volumes, check with business stakeholders whether they need all the data to be migrated. Note that for businesses, the current fiscal year/quarter data is much more important than historical data.

Make sure that you check the amount of time taken to load the data to a full sandbox to estimate the production data load times. Communicate to business stakeholders in advance the implementation dates and possible downtimes (if applicable).

When importing data to Salesforce objects, we can use the external ID to prevent duplicate record creation. These are unique IDs for each record in your organization. External IDs can also help with moving data from one organization to another. The external ID keeps the original record ID in a field so that when we have records related to it, we can easily find them. But the drawback of using the external ID is that cloning will fail, as these are unique.

There are several steps that CPQ admins need to perform to maintain data integrity and manage these dependencies. Admins need to make sure that in the data migration, they are migrating the prerequisites for historical data and new data as well.

Data migration tools

As the Salesforce platform is very flexible for exchanging data between internal or external systems, we have several tools for migrating legacy data. There is no right or wrong tool to choose for migration, and you need to choose the tool that best suits your migration needs. Some tools include the following:

- **Salesforce tools**: Data from Salesforce can be easily exported to Excel or into .csv files using Salesforce reports. Data can be imported using the data loader application without writing any code but only in .csv format. If you have used Salesforce, your admins will be familiar with reports and the data loader. The only limitation to be aware of is that this activity is manual. Data from other systems needs to be cleaned and formatted before loading it into Salesforce.

- **Application Programming Interface (API) integration**: Salesforce developers can use an API to upload and download data. Developers can write code to insert, update, or delete data from either a standard object or a custom object. The main drawback of this approach is the need to program for data migration.

- **Third-party tools**: These tools are in between the manual migration process and using code. Most of these tools have drag-and-drop interfaces that make them easy to use. These third-party tools promise faster implementation and in-built data validations. The drawbacks of this approach include high costs, vendor management, and no single tool being the best fit.

Now that we know how to choose the best method of migration to import and export data, let's learn some of the important considerations for organizing and migrating data.

Data migration best practices

Data migration is always a complex process in CPQ implementation. Data quality plays a crucial role in a successful migration. Make sure data is validated in the test system thoroughly before migrating to the production system. A few important considerations in CPQ legacy data migration include the following:

- If data migration is owned by a certain migration team, this team must be engaged throughout the entire project.

- Data migrations are a very large effort. Expect data migration to be one of many, if not the largest, efforts in a CPQ rollout.

- Plan many mock migrations. We always push for a minimum of three test loads (which includes a full simulation of data migration), which is rarely enough.

- If possible, avoid using CPQ to calculate pricing on the quotes being migrated. If you are creating quotes/quote lines because you are recording an already completed sale, stamp the final price to the quote line as opposed to having CPQ calculate this price. For example, you may need to create quotes as a means for arriving at a migrated contract.

- Identify the data you need to migrate. Choose which objects need to be migrated and the relationships. Consider the order of operations for these objects for data loading.

- Always back up your data before performing a data loader operation.

- Create templates for data – for each object, create an Excel template and validate the data before loading.

- Start off small – load a small subset of data. Validate and test before performing the complete load.

- Prepare the destination organization and make sure all the metadata and prerequisites are available.

- Package setting plays an important role in data migration. Disable triggers, as this is critical for migration. Make sure triggers are enabled again after the migration.

- Make sure the production version of the CPQ package is the same as the sandbox.

- Testing – thorough testing is the key. Once the data is migrated, perform regression testing with that data. The data will drive functionality in CPQ.

    One of the key concerns while migrating your data to Salesforce CPQ is to ensure its integrity and accuracy. Ignoring the quality of the data migrated will end up affecting all your business processes carried out using the concerned records.

- Run reports for validation. For example, a pipeline report before and after migration needs to be the same. Check the invoicing and billing details of existing and new systems to make sure there is no revenue impact.

- While migrating, make sure the field API values are not changed.

- CPQ configuration is data-driven. Missing data in CPQ is missing functionality. Run your test scripts while moving data from one organization to another. Picklist values cannot be added using a data loader; this must be done manually. Picklist values migrated in a changeset must be activated in the new organization.

The data migration sequence

Irrespective of the tool chosen, the migration process is implemented in sequence so that the prerequisites are migrated as required. For example, you cannot migrate opportunities without migrating accounts because you need the parent records to migrate any child records.

Each stage must be executed and completed before executing the next stage. Some stages are executed by an external **Extract, Transform, Load (ETL)** tool, and other stages can be executed directly in Salesforce using **batch Apex** or **queueable Apex**. Migration initially needs to be performed in a full sandbox environment where regression testing needs to be completed. Once the business validates and provides a sign-off, the same migration process needs to be executed in the production organization.

For example, if you have used a data loader to migrate the data in the sandbox, the same .csv file and data loader mappings need to be used for production migration. Additional records can be added to the .csv file based on the business. You may have loaded the contracts into the sandbox using a .csv file on January 1, 2021. The actual go-live date may be on January 15 after the UAT. Additional contracts that were generated in these 15 days need to be appended to the .csv file.

Alternatively, if you have used migration scripts, the same migration script needs to be executed in the production organization. Email deliverability needs to be turned off while migrating the data to production to avoid sending emails to users associated with the records. While using the data loader, verify the time zone of the target organization and make sure the data loader has been correctly configured.

Make sure the order of migration is determined correctly. You can decide your organization's object dependencies using Schema Builder. The following are the major stages in CPQ data migration:

- **Account stage**: In this stage, the existing accounts can be modified to support account-dependent migration. For example, you may have to migrate or create the corresponding account when you have a dependent opportunity or a contract from the legacy system.

- **Contact stage**: Billing contacts are required for invoicing. Parent accounts related to the new contacts should have already been migrated.

- **Price books**: At this stage, we can create a legacy price book that can be used specifically for migration.

- **Product2**: At this stage, products from third-party or **Enterprise Resource Planning (ERP)** systems can be migrated to the Salesforce `Product2` object.

  Products and related records drive most of the CPQ functionality. Missing product data can break the functionality. The product metadata schema needs to be migrated completely. For example, when you are migrating a bundle, you need to make sure all the dependencies are migrated.

- **Pricebook entry stage**: Legacy products that were migrated will be associated with legacy and standard price books. For multi-currency, a price book entry is created for each currency.

- **Opportunity stage**: Active subscriptions and orders from the legacy system can be created as closed-won opportunities. In progress, opportunities can be migrated by mapping the opportunity stage.

- **Migrating opportunities to quotes**: With CPQ, the entire sales process is changing, and data needs to change along with it. Opportunity/quote lines need to be migrated to CPQ quote lines in this stage. For active contracts, a historical quote is no longer necessary to process an amendment or renewal. Quotes need to be created only for in-flight opportunities.

  Field-level data, configurations, automation, and so on need to be taken care of. Do you need all the versions of the legacy quotes to be migrated? Think about an archival plan for old data.

CPQ migrations can take days or weeks. Involve sales teams/stakeholders. Close as many deals as possible for the CPQ implementation so that you will have a minimum number of open deals to migrate.

Identify Salesforce reports and a list view that might break and needs rework.

The timing makes a lot of difference. Avoid migration during the quarter end or the year end, where reps need to meet targets and close deals. For example, closed-won opportunities can be migrated automatically. After year end or by quarter end, we may have minimum in-progress opportunities, and these can be created manually to avoid errors.

- **Quote stage**: In-flight quotes can be extracted and transformed to map CPQ quotes before migration.

- **Quote line item stage**: Products on quote lines need to be remapped to the Salesforce products object. Once quotes and quote lines are loaded, we enter into the stage(s) of the migration where we can generate subsequent records using the standard package triggers (namely, orders, order products, contracts, and subscriptions). We don't necessarily need to load orders and contracts. We can have the package create these records if it is possible without performance concerns.

- **CPQ pricing engine stage**: The CPQ engine summarizes all the line items to calculate the total amount on the quote. Migration provides the quantity, list price, term, and discount values. For deals being migrated that are already closed-won, avoid running the calculation sequence on migrated quotes. There are performance guardrails around the CPQ pricing sequence that seriously hamper the number of records that can be migrated.

- **Contract migration stage**: Standard contracts are migrated with related subscription and asset records. Another option is to mass-create the contract by setting the opportunity stage to closed-won. The contract start date, renewal date, and total amount need to be validated thoroughly. Use migrated opportunities to bulk-create contracts by updating the opportunity stage to closed-won. A contract is not useful without subscription records.

When we don't have subscriptions in a legacy system, we need to gather the subscription data from external information and assets and create contracts in Salesforce. Test the **renewal opportunity** generation with a manual contract and product data.

When you have Salesforce contracts, archive contracts that you don't need.

Make sure that CPQ contract fields are added to existing contracts and create subscription lines.

- **Renewal opportunity stage**: Renewal opportunities can optionally be provided at this stage.

- **Order migration stage**: Standard orders and line items are generated from CPQ quotes at this stage. Orders represent the next steps following an opportunity being closed-won. As a best practice, never use opportunities for order data; leverage the order object for updating order-related data. Orders are also the point for integrations. Fulfillments and delivery processes can be best used with orders.

- **Billing migration stage**: For active subscriptions, make sure only unbilled charges are invoiced to the customer. For example, while you are migrating customers, you may have a 3-year subscription with yearly billing. A legacy system may have already billed for 1 year; the remaining 2 years need to be billed in Salesforce. Invoice schedules can be created at this stage. A payment gateway and configuration need to be set up.

These are some of the common stages. They can be modified, and other custom object migrations need to be included as needed.

In the next section, let's learn how CPQ can be used for multi-language requirements.

CPQ localizations

When selling your products in different countries, you might need to display the product information in a country-specific language. You may also need translations when you are selling in a country supporting multiple languages. Salesforce CPQ provides a localization functionality, extending the standard Salesforce metadata translations. CPQ also supports all the languages supported by native Salesforce. The Salesforce CPQ localization object provides translations for text, text area, long text area, and rich text area fields on the following objects:

- Product
- Product feature
- Product option
- Price dimension
- Quote template
- Line column
- Template content
- Quote term

Salesforce CPQ stores the translated values in a localization record. On the page layout of the record that needs to be translated, add the **Translate** button. For example, let's create translations for a product. Navigate to a sample product record in your Salesforce instance and click **Translate**. This will open the page shown in the following figure:

| Loss and Damage Warranty | | | | | |
| Translations | | | Save | Quick Save | Cancel |

Language

Select translation output language	French	

FIELD NAME	FIELD VALUE	TRANSLATED VALUE
Product Name	Loss and Damage Warranty	nom du produit
Product Code	LDWARRANTY	
Product Description		
External ID		

Figure 9.6 – Creating product translations

In this example, we navigated to the **Loss and Damage Warranty** product. Select the language to be translated; in this example, we selected **French**. For all the fields to be translated, provide the translated values, and save the record. In the previous figure, the **Product Name** field has been translated.

Summary

In this chapter, you learned how to extract and work with the Salesforce object model, which helped you understand object dependencies and relationships. We also saw the important role legacy data migration plays in the successful implementation of the CPQ project.

Migration may sound as simple as migrating data from point A to point B, but in this chapter, we realized that there are a lot of complexities involved in this process, and it is very challenging. We also realized that the data in each legacy system is different, and thus it is very important to understand the legacy data mapping to Salesforce CPQ objects. We learned how CPQ changes can be migrated from one Salesforce instance to another. There is no right tool that fits all migration needs. Based on the business process and the functionality, the solution needs to be analyzed and implemented.

In the next chapter, we will learn about Salesforce Billing.

10
Salesforce Billing

In the quote to cash process that you have learned about so far, you have seen how the sales process progresses by creating opportunities and configuring products, prices, and quotes. Your business generates contracts, orders, amendments, and renewals as needed. Finally, an invoice needs to be sent to the customer for processing payments and recognizing revenue.

Traditional business models store invoicing, payment, and financial functionalities in a third-party system in **Enterprise Resource Planning (ERP)** systems. Extending these models for subscription and usage products requires a lot of customization and has its own challenges. When sales and finance are disconnected, invoices are often sent with errors. There will be a lot of manual complexities to integrate sales and finance and support new business models. Transforming the business process to subscription- and usage-based products therefore calls for a new revenue model.

Salesforce Billing is a part of **Revenue Cloud**, which is designed for recurring customer relationships. It helps with automating invoice creation and payment processing. Billing is just not a finance function; it is a customer touchpoint and impacts sales in a subscription model, unlike traditional one-time sales. Having Billing on the same platform where we maintain the rest of the customer relationship has many advantages. Sales reps can collect billing-related data early in the sales process and Billing can use this data seamlessly.

Salesforce Billing connects sales and finance in one unified system. Billing enhances CPQ capabilities with invoice generation, payment, and revenue recognition functionalities. Implementing Billing provides the ability to create quotes, orders, and invoices all in a single system without integration with an off-platform billing application.

In this chapter, we will be covering the following topics:

- Salesforce Billing overview
- Installing Salesforce Billing
- Creating invoices
- Creating payments
- Understanding the revenue recognition process

Salesforce Billing overview

Salesforce Billing is an add-on package for CPQ. The **order** object acts as a bridge between Salesforce CPQ and Billing. Billing uses the order object to create **invoices**, **payments**, and **revenue recognition**.

Billing can help automate the invoicing process. Debit and credit memos can be generated for any change required to the invoices. The invoice contains all the products and services for which the customer has been billed. In the previous chapters, we saw that after a primary quote with the required products has been created and the opportunity is set to **Closed Won**, an order and a contract will be created.

Contracts serve as a source of truth for future customer transactions including amendments and renewals for subscription products. The order serves as the source of truth for all the billing transactions. It is recommended to create an order from the quote, and then create a contract from the activated order. In *Chapter 7, Creating Contracts, Amendments, and Renewals*, we learned how to create a contract from an order object.

Salesforce Billing assesses several fields and settings to determine when an order product is ready for invoicing. Invoices can be created for the different types of products that we learned about in *Chapter 3, Configuring CPQ Products*. These invoices include the following:

- **One-time products**: This charge is invoiced once for the total order quantity and price.
- **Subscription products**: Salesforce Billing creates recurring invoices for subscription products. Order Products' date fields and billing fields determine how frequently a recurring invoice will be created.
- **Evergreen subscriptions**: For order products of the **evergreen** subscription type, Salesforce Billing creates invoices for each billing period indefinitely. Customers will be charged for subscription products until they cancel the subscriptions.

- **Products with billing schedules**: Salesforce Billing invoices an order product based on the billing schedule with pre-determined dates. For example, you can create a billing schedule to invoice 20% upon order activation and the remaining 80% after 3 months.

- **Usage summaries**: A usage summary is used to invoice usage independently from its parent product. The customer pays a given amount based on their usage. An order may have multiple consumption schedules. Salesforce Billing can create usage summaries for each of the consumption schedules and store them in the usage summary object. Each **usage summary** represents the period where the usage is captured and billed.

Salesforce Billing can also prevent an order product from being billed by setting the order product's **Hold Billing** field to **Yes**. Billing creates invoices for different groups of order products by matching their billing account fields. If the billing account has order products with different payment terms, then it groups order products by matching the payment terms. Admins can define more levels of groupings using the order product's **Invoice Group** field.

Configuring products for Salesforce Billing

The standard product object that you have configured for Salesforce CPQ can be configured for Billing by updating several Billing-related fields. Let's navigate to a sample product, the **Packt Pro 13" Laptop**, in your Salesforce organization and view the billing data, as shown in the following screenshot:

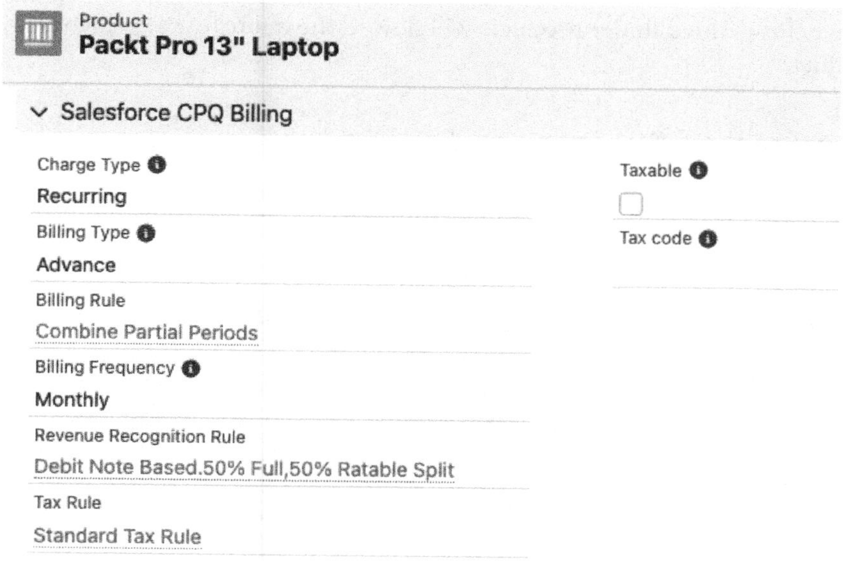

Figure 10.1 – Product billing data

Some of the important Billing fields on the product object include the following:

- **Charge Type**: This field defines whether the product is billed one time, as a recurring subscription, or based on usage.

- **Billing Type**: This field can have one of these two values: **Advance** or **Arrears**. Advance billing bills a product or service before you provide it. Arrears billing charges a product or service after you provide it. Salesforce Billing evaluates the billing type while calculating the product's next billing date.

- **Billing Rule**: Billing rules influence invoice creation. Pricing and date values on invoice lines will influence the billing period's dates and the billing cycles. In this example, we are using a sample billing rule, **Combine Partial Periods**.

- **Billing Frequency**: This determines how often an order product will be invoiced. For this example, we selected **Monthly**. You can override this on the **Quote Line** and **Order Product** so you do not have to create a new product record for the same product to support different billing frequencies.

- **Revenue Recognition Rule**: This determines whether Salesforce Billing creates a revenue schedule for an order product. This also contains the revenue treatments and provides revenue recognition reporting through a revenue schedule.

- **Tax Rule**: This field defines tax calculations and also determines whether to calculate tax or not for a specific product. Tax rules determine how to calculate tax based on tax integrations. In this example, we are using **Standard Tax Rule**.

The billing fields defined under products will flow to the quote line and eventually, to the order product.

Advantages of Salesforce Billing

Using Salesforce Billing, you can create and automate invoices, payments, and revenue recognition. Sales reps can create accurate quotes with any revenue model. Here are some of the advantages of implementing Billing:

- Salesforce Billing helps to streamline the quote to cash process. It also helps the ongoing customer relationship. Salesforce Billing is a unified transactional billing engine that helps with recurring time-bound customer events. Using Salesforce Billing, we can handle the change orders, co-terminated add-ons, prorated pricing, and so on.

- It can be used to generate error-free billing for subscription and usage-based products and allows billing data to flow seamlessly and accurately from order to invoice.

- It helps to configure complex billing and tax rules.

- It accelerates the payment collection process and improves cash flow. Billing can also create powerful revenue recognition systems.

- Salesforce Billing helps with data and reporting to understand profitability across systems.

- It improves sales performance by automating billing data transfer from CPQ to billing objects.

- It eliminates the need to integrate with a third-party system for invoices and payments and improves customer satisfaction.

- Salesforce Billing can integrate with payment gateways that process credit card and ACH transactions.

- The native quoting and pricing schemas are supported by the billing package. If you can quote it, you can bill it.

- It provides a 360-degree customer view to the rep and eliminates the need to log into multiple systems for financial details.

In the next section, let's learn how to install Salesforce Billing.

Installing Salesforce Billing

We need to install Salesforce CPQ before installing Salesforce Billing. It is recommended to install the same version of Billing as CPQ.

The following CPQ package settings need to be configured before installing Billing:

- In the **Subscriptions and Renewals** settings, if your organization uses **Percent of Total (PoT)** products that cover assets, the **PoT Renewals (Contracting from Orders)** setting must be unselected.

- Within the **Subscriptions and Renewals** settings, the **Subscription Term Unit** field must have a value of **Months**.

To install Salesforce Billing, navigate to `https://install.steelbrick.com/`, search for `Salesforce Billing`, and click on the **Production** or **Sandbox** instance based on where the package needs to be installed. Follow the similar installation steps you saw in *Chapter 1, Getting Started with Salesforce CPQ Implementation*, for installing Salesforce CPQ.

Once the installation is complete, the package can be configured by navigating to **Setup** → **Quick Find** → **Installed Packages** → **Salesforce Billing** → **Configure**.

For testing billing functionality in a test environment or creating a **Proof of Concept (PoC)** for business users, the admin can insert sample data that can be added by navigating to **Setup** → **Quick Find** → **Installed Packages** → **Salesforce Billing** → **Configure** → **Additional settings** → **Insert Sampledata** → **Save**.

> **Important Note**
> Salesforce CPQ and Billing have separate proration settings in package configurations. Make sure that the proration settings in both packages are aligned to ensure accurate order product and invoice line totals.

Salesforce Billing also provides separate page layouts for **account**, **order**, **order products**, **product**, **consumption schedule**, and **order product consumption schedule** objects. These page layouts can be assigned to the required Salesforce profiles. The standard Billing page layouts can be cloned or customized as needed.

Salesforce Billing consists of a permission set that grants permissions for the package custom objects. Admins can customize permissions for standard objects as needed. Orders and order products are standard objects that contain standard fields, CPQ fields, and Billing fields. In the next section, let's learn how an invoice can be created in Billing.

Creating invoices

An **invoice** is a legal document that denotes the customer's agreement to pay you for services. Invoices display the products or services sold, and the amount that the customer needs to pay. The invoice record contains important information such as the balance, due date, and payment status.

Salesforce CPQ Billing invoices support multiple revenue types, such as one-time, recurring, or usage-based models. Multiple invoices for multiple orders can be consolidated using billing configurations. To make sure customers are billed efficiently, invoices for a single order can be split as required.

Invoices can be created in two ways:

- Salesforce Billing allows you to create an invoice manually from a single order when you select the **Bill Now** checkbox on an order and save the record. This is recommended only for testing. For the actual implementation, it is advisable to automate invoice creation based on business rules. The reason it is advised only for testing is Salesforce Billing can bill multiple orders together based on configuration, but the **Bill Now** checkbox only looks at that order, so you risk having multiple orders (that bill together) getting out of sync.

- Invoice creation can also be automated using an **Invoice Scheduler**. Based on the user-defined rules in Billing, the Invoice Scheduler creates invoices for unbilled order products.

Creating a sample invoice

Let's see how we can create an invoice manually using the **Bill Now** checkbox on an order. We learned about creating orders from opportunities in the previous chapters. Let's take an example where we have a sample opportunity.

Imagine the sales process has progressed. We have a primary quote created for this opportunity and have added a sample product, **Loss and Damage Warranty**. This is a subscription product with recurring billing. Selecting the **Ordered** checkbox on the opportunity and saving the record will create an order. All the quote lines will be translated to order products. The order needs to be activated to generate an invoice.

Each order product will be converted to an invoice line. The invoice inherits the **Service Start Date, Service End Date, Subscription Term, Payment Terms**, and **Order Products** from its parent order. A few prerequisites to create an invoice include the following:

- The Order Product must be activated.
- The following Order Product fields should be populated:

  - **Charge Type**.
  - **Billing Rule**.
  - **Tax Rule**.
  - **Revenue Recognition Rule**.
  - **Next billing** date.
  - **Billable unit** price.
  - The **Hold billing** field must be set to **No**.
  - The **Invoice run processing** status should be **Pending Billing**.

Selecting the **Bill Now** checkbox on an order and saving the record will create an invoice as shown in the following screenshot:

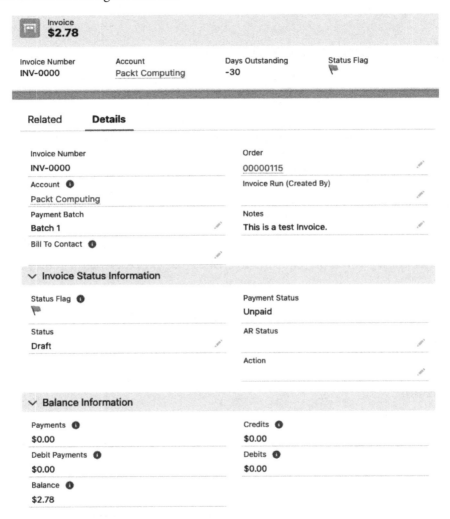

Figure 10.2 – Invoice created from an order

Let's look at a few of the important fields on an invoice:

- The **Related** tab contains all the invoice lines related to this invoice.

- **Invoice Number** contains a unique number generated by Salesforce Billing.

- **Account** and **Order** are related to this invoice.

- **Notes** can be used to hold information related to the invoice.

An invoice can have the following **Status** values:

- **Draft**: By default, invoices are generated with a **Draft** status. This will allow admins to review and correct any errors before sending them to customers.

- **Error**: During the calculation, if there are any errors, the invoice status will be set to **Error**. The errors can be reviewed in the invoices' error log-Related List.

- **Initiated**: The status of the invoice will be set to **Initiated** when Salesforce Billing is calculating the field values for invoice lines and invoices.

- **Posted**: Salesforce Billing has finished posting and the invoice is ready to be sent to a customer. Once the invoice is posted, you cannot make any changes to the invoice or invoice lines. Changes to the invoices will be handled by creating credit or debit notes. This will ensure that the organization will have a record of all the legal requirements.

- **Canceled**: When a user process has canceled an invoice, the status is set to **Canceled** and a credit note will be created for the remaining balance.

- **Rebilled**: When an invoice is canceled, it can be rebilled using the **Cancel and Rebill** button.

- **Post In Progress**: This is the status while the posting is in progress. When the posting is successful, the invoice status is set to **Posted**. If there is any error, it will be set to that **Error**.

Invoices contain the tax information that Salesforce Billing provides, an internal tax engine, and an ability to integrate with external tax engines. Invoices also contain the payments and the balance information. Posting an invoice will lock it, preventing any changes from being made to it. A posted invoice is ready for payment and revenue recognition. Posting an invoice will initiate the following actions:

- **Payments**: Allocate payments to the invoices and invoice lines. Customers can select the payments in the **Payment Center** and complete the invoice payments. Customer payments can be handled manually or processed via a third-party payment system. The payment terms defined in the quote will flow to the order.

- **Revenue Recognition**: Creates a **revenue schedule** for invoice lines covered by a **revenue schedule creation action set**. Salesforce Billing allows the revenue schedules to be managed through specific rules associated with each product.

Once the invoice is posted, it cannot be changed as the transaction will be recorded in financial books. Changes to the posted invoice can be made by using **credit notes** and **debit notes**. This will be useful when we have errors in paid or partially paid invoices. Both the credit note and debit note objects have a lookup relationship to the account object.

Credit note lines and debit note lines track the actual amount to be allocated to one or more invoice lines. A credit note will decrease the invoice line balance and a debit note line will increase the invoice balance. A credit note can be created by clicking the **Cancel and Rebill**, **Credit**, or **Convert Negative Lines** buttons on the invoice. A credit note can be created with tax or without tax as needed. Credit notes and credit note lines can also be created manually.

Debit notes can be created from the **Debit Note** tab by clicking on the **New Debit Note** button or can be created from **Related List** on the account.

In the next section, let's learn how to automate invoice creation.

Configuring an Invoice Scheduler

Using an **Invoice Scheduler,** Billing can automatically create invoices. An Invoice Scheduler uses an invoice run to evaluate when to invoice an order product. It considers all the unbilled order products and evaluates the user-determined criteria to generate invoices and invoice lines. Order products will be mapped to invoice lines. To create an Invoice Scheduler, navigate to **Setup** → **Quick Search** → **Invoice Scheduler** → **New**. You'll see the following:

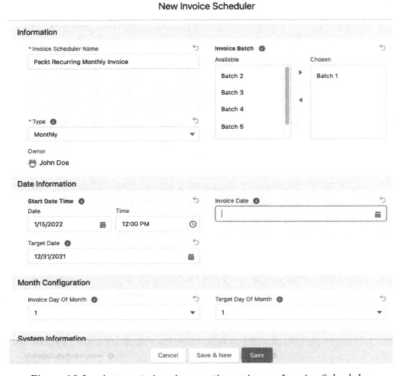

Figure 10.3 – Automate invoice creation using an Invoice Scheduler

Let's look at some of the important fields in creating an Invoice Scheduler:

- **Invoice Scheduler Name**: The name of the invoice scheduler.

- **Type**: This defines the time frame for the invoice run. This can be set to **Daily**, **Weekly**, **Monthly**, or **Once**. In this example, we are creating a monthly invoice scheduler.

- **Batch**: This is a **multi-select** picklist on **Invoice Scheduler** and **Order** objects. This is mainly used to distribute the load of invoice generation and reduce time-out errors. This batch value is compared against the **Invoice Batch** value on the order record. Only orders with matching invoice batch values will be picked up for the **invoice run**. The batch value selects the orders to be considered for invoicing. If required, additional values can be added to the invoice **Batch** fields. Make sure these values are added to both **Invoice Scheduler** and **Order** objects. When you use invoice batches, they need to be defined on every order for the batch to be selected for invoice generation.

> **Important Note**
> Using invoice batches will result in separate invoices being generated for the same account if the orders have different batches, so you need to make sure the batches won't result in invoice splits. If needed, use Salesforce automation to set batch values to their defaults.

- **Start Date Time**: The **Invoice Scheduler** process begins at this date and time.

- **Invoice Date**: This field is for one-time invoice creation. An invoice will be created on this date.

- **Target Date**: All eligible active order products before or equal to the target date will be invoiced.

- **Invoice Day Of Month**: This is used for monthly invoices to specify the day of the month that will be invoiced.

- **Automatically Post Invoices**: By default, all invoices are generated in draft mode. If there are any corrections, draft invoices can be edited and corrected. No changes will be allowed once an invoice is posted. At the beginning of the Billing implementation, it is advisable to create all the invoices in **Draft** status, and once the system stabilizes after going live, this can be changed as needed.

The invoice run object stores all the information related to invoice execution. This is a Related List on the Invoice Scheduler.

An invoice run is created when the Invoice Scheduler hits the target date. All the unbilled order products meeting the invoice run criteria will be selected for invoice generation. Salesforce Billing keeps invoice run criteria as a record in the Invoice Scheduler's invoice-run-Related List. Invoice runs are subject to Salesforce governor limits. If the invoice runs and processes many order products, you may encounter Apex errors.

Make sure the invoice runs are tested in a sandbox environment for scalability. Invoice Scheduler target dates can be used to generate invoices ahead of the actual invoice date. The invoice run's **Clean Up Invoices** button cancels any invoices that have a status of **Error**, **Initiated**, or **Draft**, and rolls back the order product status to **Pending Billing**. This will be useful for resetting when there are a lot of incorrect invoices.

Salesforce does not publish benchmarks for Invoice Scheduler performance because the overall performance is dependent on the specific implementation. Invoice creation can trigger the creation of records related to revenue recognition and payments.

Salesforce Billing provides several options to create invoice documents. If you have any third-party tools such as **Conga** or **DocuSign** for quote document generation, it is advisable to use the same application for invoice document generation as well. Salesforce Billing out of the box does not create and send invoice documents. Now that you have learned creating invoices in Billing, next let's learn how to create payments.

Creating payments

Salesforce Billing can be used to manually collect and allocate payments, or alternatively to automate the payment process. Payments can then be posted to keep the books up to date. Salesforce Billing allows multiple ways to create payments:

- Payments can be manually created by accounts receivable users.

- Admins can create a payment run that evaluates the posted invoices at scheduled intervals. Payments will be processed based on the given account's payment methods.

- Customers can directly pay invoices using their own payment methods in the Salesforce Billing Payment Center.

- Using external payment gateways – payment gateway records in Salesforce contain information for establishing the connection between Salesforce Billing and an external gateway.

- Salesforce Billing also supports self-service payment options using the Salesforce Billing API or Salesforce Communities.

Once the payment is completed, Salesforce Billing creates a payment record in the payment object. Once Billing verifies the funds, the **Payment Status** field will be updated to **Completed**. Admins can also import payments using the **data loader** or by updating payments manually.

The following diagram shows a high-level billing data model:

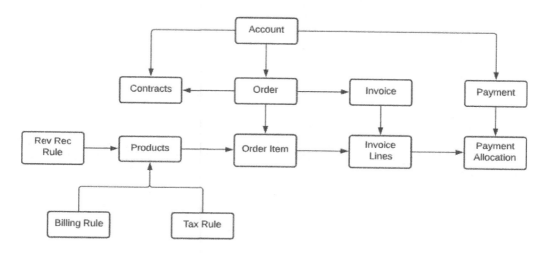

Figure 10.4 – Billing data model

Salesforce Billing tracks payments using several objects. Each product has an associated **Billing Rule**, **Tax Rule**, and **Revenue Recognition Rule** that defines how these transactions are scheduled for the product. Payments have an optional lookup relationship to the invoice record.

A **payment object** represents a payment event such as receiving a check or a credit card payment. A **payment record** stores information about the payment amount and payment-related details. Payments can be applied to any posted invoice with a balance. A payment has a master-detail relationship to an account. Payment allocation represents the payment amount applied to an invoice line's balance. When a payment is created for an invoice, it automatically creates allocations against the full balance of each invoice line. Let's learn about the revenue recognition process in Billing.

Understanding the revenue recognition process

Billing offers support for ERP systems by converting the Salesforce CPQ quote to cash data into transactional data. This conversion helps ERP systems to inherit matching data that can be used for accounting functions for general ledger and financial reporting. Salesforce Billing uses several objects to manage the revenue recognition system. Revenue recognition is controlled by accounting standards and can be complex.

For example, revenue for a warranty subscription product of 120 dollars for a period of 12 months can be recognized as 10 dollars a month. Revenue can also be partially recognized. For example, 50% of the revenue can be recognized in full and the remaining 50% is based on the product subscription start date and end date. The revenue recognition process in billing can be automated by configuring the following:

- **Revenue distribution method**: This defines how billing spreads revenue over a time period.

  Let's create a sample revenue distribution in Salesforce Billing by navigating to **Setup → Quick Find → Revenue Distribution Methods → New**. This will open the screen shown in the following screenshot:

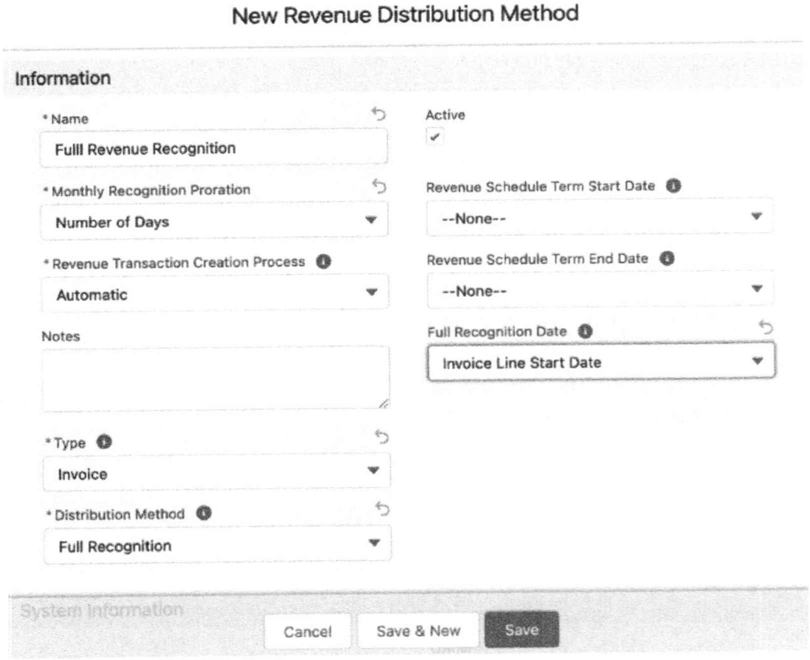

Figure 10.5 – Creating a revenue distribution method

Let's look at a few important fields in the revenue distribution method creation process:

- **Name**: Provide a meaningful name for the revenue distribution method.

- **Revenue Transaction Creation Process**: This can have two values: **Automatic** and **Manual**. Select **Automatic** to automatically create the revenue recognition.

- **Type**: This determines the record based on which revenue can be distributed. In this example, we are choosing **Invoice**.

- **Distribution Method**: This determines how the revenue can be recognized. This can have three values: **Daily**, **Monthly**, and **Full Recognition**. For this example, we are selecting **Full Recognition**.

- **Full Recognition Date**: This is required if the **Distribution Method** is **Full Recognition**. This is the date on which the revenue will be recognized. When the **Distribution Method** is set to **Daily** or **Monthly**, then the **Revenue Schedule Term Start Date** and **Revenue Schedule Term End Date** fields are mandatory.

Additional revenue distribution methods can be defined as required for your company's financial requirements.

- **Revenue Recognition Rule**: These rules specify whether Billing creates a revenue schedule for an invoice order or invoice line. Using Revenue Recognition Rules, Billing creates revenue transactions for a specific time. Products for which we need to recognize revenue require a **lookup** to a Revenue Recognition Rule.

To create a Revenue Recognition Rule, navigate to **Setup → Quick Find → Revenue Recognition Rules → New**. This opens the following window:

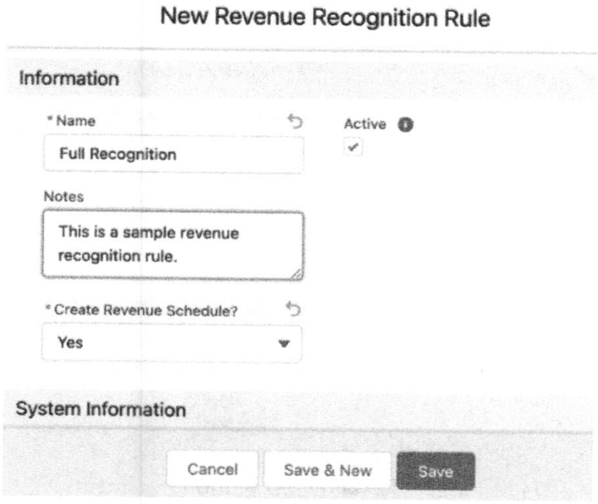

Figure 10.6 – Creating a Revenue Recognition Rule

Provide a meaningful name and set **Create Revenue Schedule?** to **Yes**.

Admins can create additional Revenue Recognitions Rules as required by your company's finance team.

- **Revenue treatment**: This controls how and where Salesforce Billing identifies a product's revenue. Revenue recognition treatments specify how Salesforce makes revenue schedules. They also describe how Salesforce Billing records revenue transaction data in finance books and general ledgers.

A Revenue Recognition Rule can have numerous treatments. To create a sample treatment, navigate to **Setup → Quick Find → Revenue Recognition Treatments → New**. This will open the following window:

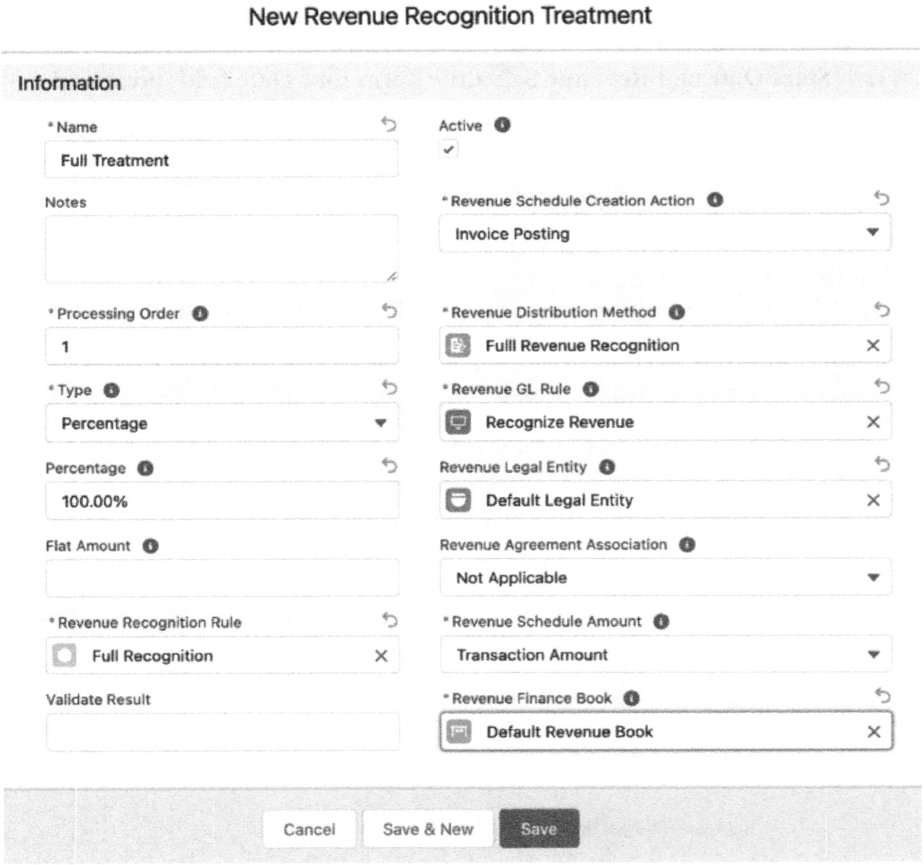

New Revenue Recognition Treatment

Information

* Name	Active
Full Treatment	✓
Notes	* Revenue Schedule Creation Action
	Invoice Posting
* Processing Order	* Revenue Distribution Method
1	Full Revenue Recognition
* Type	* Revenue GL Rule
Percentage	Recognize Revenue
Percentage	Revenue Legal Entity
100.00%	Default Legal Entity
Flat Amount	Revenue Agreement Association
	Not Applicable
* Revenue Recognition Rule	* Revenue Schedule Amount
Full Recognition	Transaction Amount
Validate Result	* Revenue Finance Book
	Default Revenue Book

Cancel   Save & New   Save

Figure 10.7 – Revenue recognition treatments

Let's look at a few important fields when creating a revenue treatment:

- **Name**: Provide a meaningful name.

- **Processing Order**: When we have multiple revenue recognition treatments, you can provide a processing order. This is the sequence in which revenue treatments will be processed. A **Processing Order** value of 1 will be executed before 2.

- **Type**: This can have three values: **Percentage**, **Flat Amount**, and **Remainder**. This is how the amount will be calculated.

- **Revenue Recognition Rule**: We are using the revenue rule that we created in *Figure 10.6*.

- **Revenue Distribution Method**: This sets the revenue distribution method used for assigning revenue. In this example, we are using the revenue distribution method created in *Figure 10.7*.

- **Revenue GL Rule**: All transactions administered through this treatment record journal entries founded on this GL rule.

- **Revenue Legal Entity**: Legal entities can be created in Salesforce Billing. All the treatments applied to order products under the parent Revenue Recognition Rule will have a matching legal entity.

- **Revenue Finance Book**: Finance books are helpful for organizing your transaction records into several groups for reporting and recordkeeping purposes. Finance books can also be created in Salesforce Billing.

This will create a full revenue recognition transaction based on the invoice start date. We have seen how revenue recognition can be automated in Salesforce Billing. Next, let's learn how **General Ledger** (**GL**) accounts can be created.

Creating GL accounts

Salesforce Billing can also be used to configure general ledger accounts for financial transactions. To summarize the financial transactions for invoices, tax, and revenue, we need an **Account Receivable** (**AR**) account, a revenue account, and a tax payable account. These are generic accounts chosen to demonstrate the account creation in Salesforce Billing. In a real-world implementation, the accounts required by your organization's finance department need to be created and configured as required.

GL accounts can be created by navigating to **Setup** → **Quick Find** → **GL Accounts** → **New**. This will open the following window:

Figure 10.8 – New GL Account

Let's learn about some of the important fields in GL account creation:

- **GL Account Name**: This is the name of the GL account we are creating. In this case, we are creating a Revenue Account.

- **GL Account Number**: This is a unique number for each business. A company's **Financial Management System** (**FMS**) will provide this unique number. This value will be mapped to the FMS.

- **GL Account Description**: Add an appropriate description to provide users with more information as to what this account is for.

- **Active**: Click the checkbox next to this option to activate the account for use in Salesforce Billing transactions.

Saving this will create a GL account. Repeat the same process for different GL accounts that you need to create as per your organization's FMS requirements. After creating the GL accounts, let's learn how to create GL rules and GL treatments. GL rules define how Salesforce Billing records transactional data in your finance books. You can create a GL rule by navigating to **Setup → Quick Find → GL Rule → New**. Next, you can create the GL treatment by navigating to **Setup → Quick Find → GL Treatment → New**. This will open the following screen:

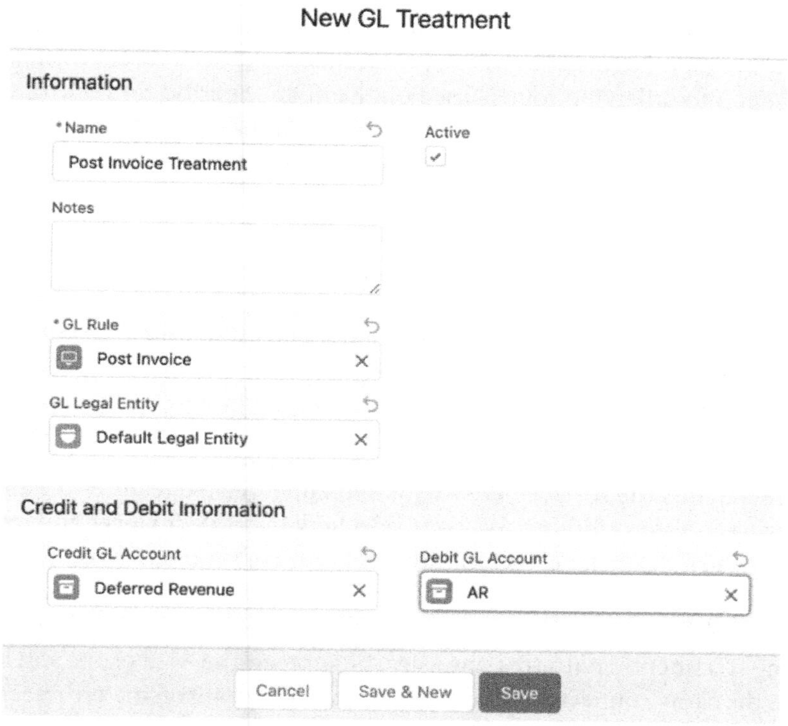

Figure 10.9 – New GL Treatment

A few important fields in the GL treatment creation process include the following:

- **Name**: Provide a meaningful name for the GL treatment.

- **GL Rule**: This is the GL rule to which we want to apply this treatment.

- **GL Legal Entity**: When a GL rule evaluates an order product, Salesforce Billing applies one of the rule's treatments if the order product and GL treatment are part of the same legal entity.

- **Credit and Debit Information**: GL treatments contain lookups to a credit GL account and a debit GL account.

GL rules can be organized by GL treatment. Similarly, we can also create tax rules and tax treatments in Salesforce Billing to define how Billing processes taxes for the transactions.

Invoice lines contain lookups to revenue recognition rules, GL rules, and tax rules. These lookups help to establish the relationship between a transactional object and a GL account every time a transaction is performed. These relationships can be used for finance bookkeeping in external GL systems.

Salesforce Billing provides **finance books**, which are an out-of-the-box Billing object to store transactional data such as invoice lines, payment allocations, credit note lines, and revenue schedules. Finance books can be used to track this transactional data by organizing them into different groups based on the finance period for reporting and recordkeeping. Billing can help group a finance book's transaction records by date and legal entity into finance periods. Finance books can be used to ensure a seamless handoff to an ERP or accounting system.

Summary

In this chapter, we have learned how Salesforce Billing helps to unify the sales and finance teams in any business and helps to improve the customer experience. We also gained an understanding of the advantages that Salesforce Billing provides in the quote to cash process.

We have just scratched the surface here – a lot of finance-related features can be configured using Salesforce Billing. We have seen how to create invoices and invoice lines in Billing using the CPQ order object for different types of products. We have realized that Billing offers a lot of out-of-the-box configurations for setting up GL accounts. We have learned about revenue recognition rules, GL rules, tax rules, and the corresponding treatments. With this, the sales, finance, and service teams will be able to work from the same connected system. This helps reduce invoicing errors, creates an empowering customer experience, and allows us to close the books faster.

In the next chapter, we will learn about Salesforce Industries CPQ.

11
Understanding Industries CPQ

Salesforce has two CPQ solutions – **Salesforce Configure, Price, Quote (CPQ)** and **Industries CPQ**. Salesforce CPQ is a general CPQ application that can fit any business, given the right configurations and customizations. We will refer to Salesforce CPQ as standard CPQ and compare it with Industries CPQ in this chapter.

Salesforce acquired Vlocity in February 2020 and renamed it **Salesforce Industries**. Salesforce Industries covers 12 **industry clouds**: six of these are from the Vlocity acquisition and the remaining ones are from Salesforce. Salesforce Industries drives digital transformation by providing businesses with industry-specific solutions to meet their unique needs.

Industries CPQ, formerly known as Vlocity CPQ, is one of the many modules within a specific industry cloud. It is a cloud-based quote- and order-capturing system built on the standard Salesforce platform and extends the native Salesforce capability to the industry-specific Quote-To-Cash (Q2C) process.

Industries CPQ also provides tools for **customer life cycle management, quoting, order capture, billing,** and **service inquiry** resolutions across channels and devices. For these complex ordering systems, Industries CPQ provides a digital customer experience that offers the ability to configure the right products for customers. Sales agents can use the conversational omnichannel **User Interface (UI)** and guided selling capabilities. A shared catalog and industry-specific communication data model supports all industry applications with catalog-driven order capture and fulfillment, using Industries CPQ order management. This allows businesses to quickly design and launch new products and promotions.

Industries CPQ uses **asset-based** ordering to define prices, configure products, and enable shopping cart interactions. It is built using standard Salesforce **objects** and extends features to **discounts, bundle pricing, cancelation fees,** and **customer preferences**.

Industries CPQ improves usability with a consistent UI and coherent functioning across marketing, sales, and services. This is very adaptable for high-volume and complex CPQ processes.

In this chapter, we will learn about the following:

- Industries CPQ overview
- Comparison of Salesforce CPQ and Industries CPQ
- Enterprise Product Catalog (EPC)
- Industries CPQ's UI

By the end of this chapter, you will understand Industries CPQ and some of its features at a high level. This is *not* meant to be an in-depth overview of Industries CPQ.

Industries CPQ overview

Before we learn about Industries CPQ, it is important to understand what Salesforce Industry Cloud is. Industry Cloud is a combination of CPQ and digital commerce. Industry Cloud helps customers increase sales and digital adoption, and it enhances services, marketing, and operational efficiency. Salesforce Industry Cloud includes 12 clouds, 6 of which used to belong to Vlocity, as shown in the following figure:

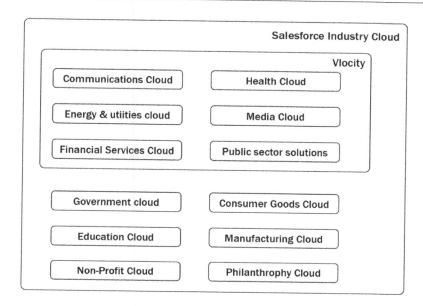

Figure 11.1 – Salesforce Industry Cloud overview

Industries CPQ can be used to configure products using the **Enterprise Pricing Catalog**. Admins can build reusable pricing components to support complex pricing strategies, create discounts and promotions, and override product offers for a limited amount of time. In addition, Industries CPQ helps generate accurate quotes, orders, and quote documents for B2B and B2C businesses. It also provides guided selling for Salesforce users and customers in Community Cloud and Commerce Cloud.

Industry Cloud has built-in integration with the sales and service clouds. We have seen that Salesforce CPQ uses a custom quote object, whereas Industries CPQ uses out-of-the-box objects. Opportunities, quotes, and orders are all standard Salesforce objects that make integration seamless. Industries CPQ extends the CPQ functionality with additional fields and object relationships.

Industry Order Management (OM) is another module that is specific to an industry. **OM** helps with the decomposition and fulfillment of orders. Order line items get converted to assets. We can perform **Move, Add, Change, Delete (MACD)** orders on these assets.

For example, imagine Packt is a cell phone service company. If a Packt customer has a medium plan and they want to add additional roaming, we can perform a MACD order to add roaming and modify the existing asset without service interruption.

Comparing Salesforce CPQ and Industries CPQ

Salesforce CPQ is a general CPQ and billing application (billing needs to be purchased separately) that can be used for any industry with some customizations. Industries CPQ is a module in Salesforce Industry Cloud and is specific to an industry. The standard sales process and B2B or B2C customer journey are the same as what we saw in the previous chapters. Industries CPQ leverages most of the standard Salesforce objects, such as accounts and opportunities.

We have seen that Salesforce CPQ fields are in the format `SBQQ__fieldname__c`. If we used Industries CPQ for Communications Cloud, a custom field would be `vlocity_cmt__fieldname_c`, and if we used it for Insurance Cloud, it would be `vlocity_inc__fieldname__c`.

Industries CPQ follows a similar order of operations to the standard sales process we learned about in *Chapter 1, Getting Started with Salesforce CPQ Implementation*. When a customer is interested in our products, a lead will be converted into an account and an opportunity will be created. Then, for the configured price and quote functionalities, we use Industries CPQ.

From the opportunity or quote, we can use the CPQ configurator to configure, price, and quote. From the quote and the order, we can have the contract and contract life cycle management module within Industry Cloud. We can use the B2C Commerce cloud connector between Industries CPQ and the B2C Commerce cloud. The Industries CPQ sales process is similar to the standard sales process, replacing the configure, price, and quote sections with Industries CPQ. The following diagram shows an industry-specific sales process with some of the prerequisite configuration modules, such as **Catalog Management**:

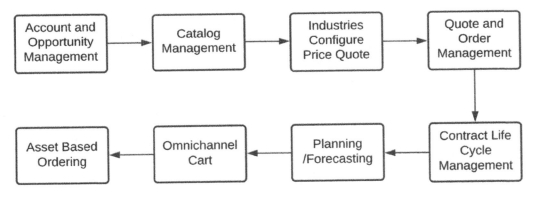

Figure 11.2 – Industries CPQ sales process

At a high level, Salesforce CPQ and Industries CPQ support similar functionalities, even though they have different UIs:

- We can create a quote or order, configure products, and add products.

- We can configure complex pricing arrangements, including contracted, slab, and range-based pricing.

- Quote approval is supported.

- We can generate quote documents.

- Contract life cycle management is supported.

- OM is supported. Salesforce OM is horizontal across all industries and Industries OM is specific to a vertical.

- There is support for amendments and renewals.

We cannot compare the pricing of these two as Salesforce CPQ is a separate application and Industries CPQ is a module in Industry Cloud.

Key features of Industries CPQ

Industries CPQ has several key features out of the box, making it the perfect tool to implement for a specific industry. Industries CPQ supports high-volume transactions using efficient APIs.

Some of these features are listed here:

- We can build B2B and B2C applications using a third-party web or mobile app. Using APIs, CPQ can handle the rules and pricing.

  Customers may have their own websites and they can implement CPQ in the backend. This results in a great customer experience as they will be using the website that best suits their business and the UI they like the most. CPQ operates in the backend for configuring and pricing.

- Industries CPQ provides seamless integration with OM.

  OM is another module in Industry Cloud. Industry OM can help hide the complex product configuration in the backend and display a simple product to the customer on the UI.

- Industry Cloud can modify assets and in-flight orders.

  After an order has been placed, customers can make modifications. For example, you might order a cell phone and select a mobile plan for it. But before the order ships, you want to make changes to the plan and update the limited calling plan to unlimited calling and international texting. In some situations, the shipment might reach the customer, which would mean making changes to an existing service. With Industry Cloud, you can modify a shipped order without any service interruption.

- Industries CPQ supports multi-site quoting and ordering at the same time; we can manage quotes and orders for multiple locations without needing to shuffle through multiple screens.

  For example, say Packt is providing internet services to corporate offices in multiple locations and each site has a different configuration. This can be managed in a single quote without needing to generate multiple separate quotes for each location.

To decide which CPQ best suits a customer implementation, we can do the following:

- We can simply check whether the customer has a communication, media, or energy business. If so, it's better to consider Industries CPQ.

- Work with the company's business users to make sure their main use cases are documented and perform a **Proof of Concept** (**POC**) in a test environment.

- Customers may also have a high number of orders, too many for Salesforce CPQ to support. Industries CPQ has a programmatic interface that allows for a highly customized quoting UI that does not come out of the box with Salesforce CPQ.

- Alternatively, the Salesforce account team can also help with proposing the right product for any business.

Industries CPQ test environment

To create a test environment for configuring sample use cases and examples using Industries CPQ, refer to the Industry Cloud documentation on Vlocity University: `https://help.salesforce.com/s/articleView?id=000357469&type=1`. We can request a training environment by filling in the form at `https://vlocitytrial-prod.herokuapp.com/?templateid=SFI_IPQ`. This is a free instance that is available for a limited amount of time. A new instance can be created if required. The training instance comes with pre-loaded data that can be used as is or modified for performing testing, or creating a POC for your implementation.

Once you decide to move forward with an Industries CPQ implementation for your business, the corresponding Industry Cloud licenses can be bought from Salesforce. A Salesforce account manager can provide you with the actual costs of the Industry Cloud licenses.

For the implementation, you will follow the standard path for the environment strategy from **Developer Instance → Full Sandbox → Production**. Based on the industry, the corresponding Industry Cloud package can be installed from AppExchange.

For example, for a communication-based cloud, you can install the corresponding Industries CPQ package: `https://appexchange.salesforce.com/appxListingDetail?listingId=a0N3000000B5hsoEAB`.

Enterprise Product Catalog

Enterprise Product Catalog (EPC) is an input for CPQ, digital commerce, and OM. This is where you perform product design, pricing, product life cycle management, product versioning, and product publishing. Vlocity EPC helps you to effectively manage a portfolio of products that are relevant to industry customers.

EPC provides a unified UI with common tools that enable your teams to collaborate and create, manage, and deliver product offers, eliminating data silos. Vlocity DataPacks can be used to move products from the development environment to the production environment. Vlocity EPC provides an industry-leading catalog-driven platform using a **metadata** approach. It provides the core components required to centralize, configure, integrate, and maintain product and service portfolios across the enterprise. Vlocity EPC provides commercial and technical elements needed to define reusable products and services. EPC provides a lot of business benefits. Some of the important benefits include:

- Decreased time to market for new products and offers
- Improved responsiveness to changing market conditions
- Easy catalog maintenance with industry-specific standards
- Improved product life cycle management
- A cohesive and consistent catalog view across CPQ, OM, and customer life cycle management
- Support for multiple languages

EPC's out-of-the-box functionalities can also be configured. Businesses can build their own Lightning web components to customize EPC. The EPC UI includes the following:

- **EPC**: This is an Industry Cloud module used to manage end-to-end processes and product data related to product life cycle management.

- **Product Designer and Pricing Designer**: These are Salesforce Lightning pages and Industry Cloud Lightning web components for configuring and maintaining EPC.

- **Product Console**: The original UI for EPC built on AngularJS.

In the following sections, we'll learn how to create products in Industries CPQ.

Creating products

Commercial products are products that the customers can see, while technical products communicate with backend systems for fulfillment. For example, broadband internet is a commercial product that can be decomposed into two technical products, a port and an authentication. Products added to the cart are the commercial products sold to the customer, while technical products are used for OM fulfillment. All the products inherit attributes from object types and assign additional products unique to the products. Products can be standalone products or bundles containing other products.

For example, a cell phone and a mobile data plan are sold together as a bundle. We can also define cardinality for products, and the min, max, and default quantities. We should define a price to use for a product in CPQ. Products can be created using product objects or **Vlocity Product Console**. Let's create a sample product by navigating to **Setup** → **App Launcher** → **Vlocity Product Console** → **Product**. Then, click on the + icon next to the product, and you will see the following:

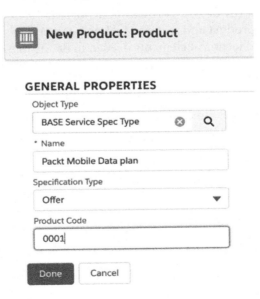

Figure 11.3 – Creating a new product

Let's learn about some of the fields here:

- **Object Type**: These are templates to create products. Using **Object Type**, we can define the product hierarchy. For this product, I am using an existing template from the test org. These templates can be created based on the business and the products that your company will be selling.

- **Name**: This field specifies the name of the product; in this example, we are creating a `Packt Mobile Data plan` offer.

- **Specification Type**: This is a picklist field with the values **Resource**, **Service**, **Product**, and **Offer**. In this example, we are creating an **Offer** product.

- **Product Code**: Provide the product code for the product that you are creating.

Click **Done** and the product will be created. Now open the product in the product console. Navigate to **App Launcher → Vlocity Product Console → Product**. Click the search icon and search for the product you created in *Figure 11.3*. This will open the following screen:

Figure 11.4 – Vlocity Product Console

The options on the left-hand side are called **facets**:

- **General Properties**: The product needs to be set as **Active** and **Orderable** for it to be visible in the cart. Other attributes can be filled in as per the product you are creating. In this example, as we are creating `Packt Mobile Phone`, we have set **Product Family** to **Mobile**. The product's effective start date and end date can be set.

- **Pricing**: We need to set the price for this product. The price can be set to zero, but it can never be null. The product price is defined in the price list. Each price list must be associated with a price book. More than one base price can be associated with a product by creating price list entries stored in different price lists. When a product has more than one base price list entry in a price list, you can use a **context rule** to determine which price to apply to the product. Clicking on the Pricing facet will open the following screen:

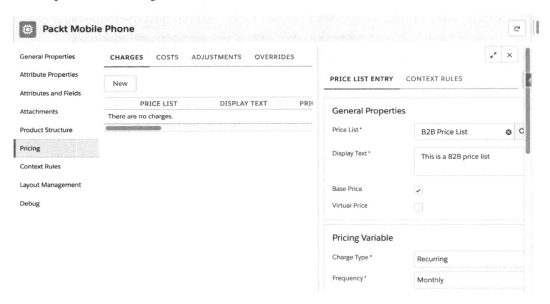

Figure 11.5 – Pricing facets

When you are creating a bundle, you can set the price to Virtual, meaning the bundle itself will not carry any price and the price of the bundle is the sum of all the products within the bundle. In this example, this is set to the base price. We want the price to be associated with this product. You can set all other pricing attributes, such as the charge type, deciding whether this is a one-time or recurring charge. **Frequency** can be set to Weekly, Monthly, or Yearly. Pick the start date. We can also create promotions that apply only to a specific period, and a promotion can end automatically.

In Industries CPQ, we have two types of rules. These rules will control product visibility and product functionality in the cart. These are similar to standard CPQ product rules or price rules:

- **Context rules**: These determine what products, promotions, and pricing appear in the cart. A context rule will contain a rule and one or more conditions associated with the rule.

- **Advanced rules**: These allow you to determine the compatibility, pricing, availability, and eligibility of products. For example, you can create a **product relationship** between a phone and its compatible charger. Creating an advanced rule using this product relation will add the compatible products automatically when the product or bundle is added to the cart.

The combination of products, price lists, context rules, and advanced rules determines product visibility in the cart. When the configurable rules don't meet the implementation needs, Industries CPQ can also be customized by custom Apex interface implementation.

In the next section, we'll learn about the UI of Industries CPQ.

Industries CPQ's UI

In Salesforce CPQ, we saw that the **Quote Line Editor** (**QLE**) is the UI that reps use. In Industries CPQ, we have a few UIs that enhance customer experience and also aid in self-service that can be leveraged based on the kind of business and the sales process.

We have a few UI options for Industries CPQ:

- **CPQ cart**: An out-of-the-box shopping cart UI where agents can add, configure, and remove products. The cart can be configured as per the specific business needs. Currently, this is **Angular**-based on **Vlocity Cards**, which may be converted to **Lightning Web Components** (**LWCs**). Vlocity Cards provide **configurable cards**, **layouts**, and **templates**, which can be customized as required.

- **Omni scripts for guided selling**: Build your own guided flow using **OmniScripts**. Using APIs, you can build additional functionality.

- **Digital commerce LWCs**: Prebuilt out-of-the-box LWCs are available that provide additional functionality on top of the UI, which can help agents select the right products.

Industries CPQ's cart

The cart is a responsive digital experience UI provided by Industries CPQ. It has the following features:

- It was developed using Vlocity Cards.

- The cart optimizes the shopping experience and helps in accurate order creation based on the rules defined in Industries CPQ.

- The cart helps dynamically configure products and simplifies selling, pricing, and order capture, allowing users to search product catalogs and create orders.

- The cart is an out-of-the-box Industry CPQ solution used to reduce the cost of building an order capture from scratch.

For example, let's imagine Packt is selling cell phones and the agent is ready to create and configure an order. First, let's create an order. To do this, navigate to **App Launcher** → **Account** → **Related** → **Orders** → **New**. This will open the following screen:

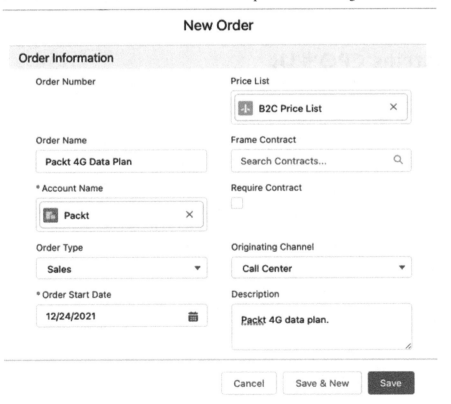

Figure 11.6 – New Order

Let's look at some of the important fields for creating an Industries CPQ order:

- **Order Name**: Provide a descriptive order name.

- **Account Name**: Choose the customer account for which this order needs to be created. This is a **lookup** for the account object.

- **Price List**: This is like the standard Salesforce CPQ price book. For this example, we have selected a B2C price list.

Fill out the rest of the information as needed and save the record. This will create an order.

Now let's configure products and add them to this order. To do that, navigate to **Order →** **Configure**. This will open the cart, as shown in the following screenshot:

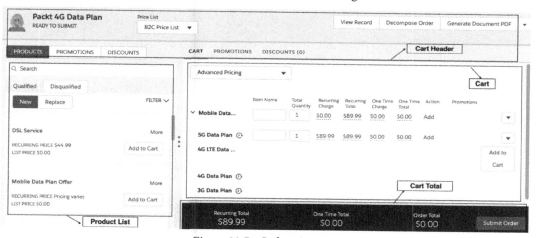

Figure 11.7 – Industries cart

Let's look at the cart UI:

- **CART** has a **PRODUCTS** tab on the left-hand side where you have the product list. In the product selector, you can also search the products and click **Add to Cart**. This will add product lines to the cart on the right-hand side. In the backend, they get stored in standard Salesforce objects: order and order line items. In this example, we have added the **Mobile Data Plan** bundle. This has added all the child items under the bundles to the cart.

- You can add the bundles or products from the product list to the cart section and, here, you can view the order line items. The concept of bundles in Industries CPQ is the same as in standard CPQ, which we learned about in *Chapter 3, Configuring CPQ Products*. In the cart section on the right-hand side, we can see the quantities and the pricing details. Not all the pricing details are required to be applied to a product. Based on the type of product the rep is selling, the corresponding pricing can be configured by the admin in the backend.

- We have different pricing options available in Industries CPQ. More than one price can be applied to a product:

  - **Usage Price**: The price for using a product. For example, if you are buying a roaming plan, you can choose pay-as-you-go, rather than paying upfront.

  - **Usage Margin/Recurring Margin/One Time Margin**: They apply to B2B. We can show the sales rep the cost versus the price.

  - **Recurring Charge**: Recurring charges for a specific service. For example, they apply to monthly product line internet services, phone subscriptions, and so on.

  - **Recurring Total**: This is the total of all the products in a bundle. This total is the same as the bundle price we learned about in *Chapter 3, Configuring CPQ Products*.

  - **One Time Charge**: These are one-time charges, such as installation charges or activation charges.

- To configure products, Industries CPQ provides a feature called **product attributes**. Product attributes are stored in JSON and not in custom or standard fields. These are used for order capture and fulfillment.

  These attributes are additional information about products. Reps can click the down arrow next to the **One Time Margin** field and click **Configure** – this opens the product attribute screen.

  Product attributes are dictated by rules, and they will determine the pricing. They are stored in JSON.

  For example, for the Packt mobile data plan, admins can define a product attribute that can influence the pricing. The initial 1,000 messages can be free, and any additional messages can be charged. Reps can override the attribute pricing and provide an additional discount.

- The cart header section categorizes products, promotions, discounts, and price list options. A cart header also has some Vlocity actions, for example, **Generate Document PDF**, which will create a quote document.

- In the cart total section, you can view all the related totals for the line items that have been added so far, and the order can be submitted to fulfillment using the **Submit Order** button.

When the products are added to the cart, the total may be outside of the customer budget. In this example, in *Figure 11.8*, reps can click the **Recurring Charge** label, which displays a pencil icon, as shown here:

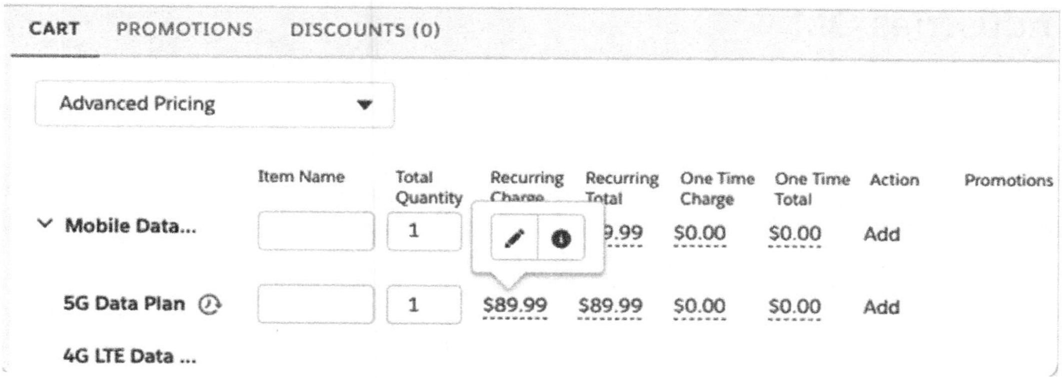

Figure 11.8 – Editing cart prices

Clicking the pencil icon will open the Adjustment screen. Reps can then make price adjustments as needed. For example, in this scenario, the rep has given a $5 discount. This reduces the recurring charge to $84.99:

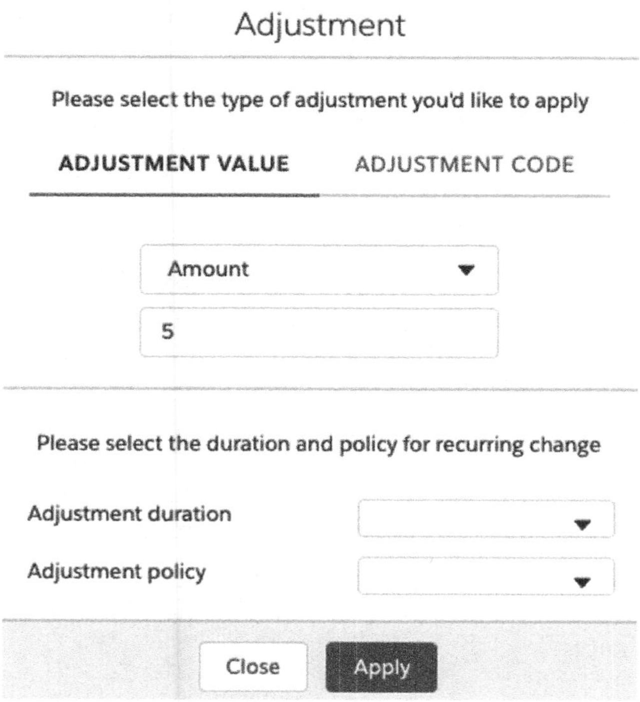

Figure 11.9 – Price adjustments

Reps use **Adjustment** to modify the price based on the product price amount or percentage.

Industries OM

Once the customer is ready, the sales rep can submit an order to the cart, which will kick off the OM flow. In the backend, the order is decomposed between commercial products and technical products.

To view the decomposition details, navigate to **Accounts → Orders → View Order → Decomposition**. This displays the mapping between the commercial products that have been decomposed to the technical products.

In the backend, Industries CPQ has mapped commercial products to technical products so that fulfillment can happen correctly. The following actions take place:

- OM picks up the details and completes the processing and fulfillment of order lines.
- OM orchestration will decompose the commercial plan and fulfillment is completed considering all the technical order dependencies.
- An asset will be created related to the order, and it provides additional functionality to disconnect or modify the asset. This uses the standard asset object in Salesforce.

Industries OM is a separate module and has a lot of industry-specific features.

In CPQ, we can perform order capture using the configurator or API. Multi-site quoting functionality comes out of the box. We can also perform MACD orders.

Industries CPQ OmniScripts

In *Chapter 6, Configuring Guided Selling*, we saw that Salesforce CPQ has a guided selling feature. Similarly, we can build guided flow in Industries CPQ using OmniScripts. This provides the customer with a guided path for completing a business process and creates a seamless customer experience:

- OmniScripts use *drag and drop* to configure complex logic in the backend and interactive dynamic forms in the UI.
- OmniScripts can be Lightning-enabled and can be reused as required.
- They also help to configure interactive and easy-to-use business processes with branching. This will help to provide only the required processes based on the customers' choices.

For example, if a customer wants to choose a mobile plan, an OmniScript can be configured with the required logic.

To create an OmniScript, navigate to a Vlocity Salesforce instance and go to **App Launcher → OmniScripts → New**.

In OmniScripts, different elements can help you to configure the guided flow, such as the following:

- **Actions**: These are used to perform various actions, such as fetching data, saving data, and calculating pricing and discounts. We can also call Apex using actions.

- **Display**: This can be used to enhance the UI for displaying any text or images on the screen.

- **Functions**: These are used to perform calculations within the OmniScript for displaying conditional messages and providing geo-locations.

- **Group**: This is used to group elements together.

- **Inputs**: This is used for system or user input.

- **OmniScripts**: These are nested Omniscripts that are also reusable.

Vlocity CPQ provides another feature, DataRaptors, that can be used in OmniScripts. DataRaptors allow you to read and write data to and from your Salesforce org. This is the extract, transform, and load functionality application in CPQ.

Digital commerce

There is a cloud-based solution in Salesforce Industry Cloud that enables high-volume browsing and product configuration using a self-service UI. The open architecture of the Industries CPQ platform allows us to use CPQ components, services, and UIs as individual components and to integrate process flows with external systems, all using a unified UI. There are high-volume APIs that are built on a caching layer (to accommodate high-volume API call activity). Digital commerce APIs work for guest and authenticated users, unlike CPQ APIs, which work only for authenticated users. Salesforce also provides a B2C Commerce cloud connector as part of Salesforce Industry Cloud to use digital commerce.

Digital commerce APIs extend catalog-driven product selection and configuration. They are built for additional scalability and performance when it comes to high volumes. API caching allows businesses to offload static calls from constrained services and accelerate website performance during peak events. Using digital commerce APIs, you can retrieve a list of products, promotions, and configurations without needing a Salesforce opportunity, quote, or order record.

Summary

In this chapter, you learned about Industries CPQ and how it is different from standard Salesforce CPQ. Industries CPQ is a whole different implementation, and in this chapter, we have just scratched the surface. The basic knowledge from this chapter will help you gain an overview of what Industry Cloud is and where CPQ falls within Industry Cloud.

As a consultant and business partner, you will be able to decide how to choose the right CPQ for your business. Having the right CPQ also helps in making the sales process simple and easy to use with minimum customizations. This helps to increase revenue and grow your business.

In the next chapter, we will learn about some CPQ implementation best practices.

12
CPQ Implementation Best Practices

So far, you have seen how Salesforce CPQ helps businesses close complex deals with speed and accuracy while improving customer satisfaction. It also helps you automate the sales process and avoid manual steps that may be error-prone. We have learned that CPQ helps in configuring customer-specific products, pricing them correctly, and selling the right products to the right customers. We have also discussed how using **Salesforce Billing** adds additional advantages by providing out-of-the-box billing for subscription, usage-based, and non-subscription products. This also helps create and automate invoices in one platform, avoiding additional integration costs.

The CPQ package provides you with all the customizations and controls that you need to automate your business processes. CPQ and its related customizations can be built on top of the Salesforce platform, and this gives you all the Salesforce automation, including standard configurations, code, and other capabilities, with integrations and third-party applications.

The way CPQ is implemented impacts the performance and scalability of a system when end users start using it. During implementation, it is critical that your company takes care of system optimizations and tunes automation accordingly.

In this chapter, we will learn some of the best practices related to CPQ:

- The best practices for improving CPQ performance
- The best practices for CPQ implementation

The best practices for improving CPQ performance

The term *performance* refers to the ability to process an action faster. For example, you want data to **load**, **add**, **quick-save**, and **save** records, complete calculations in the **Quote Line Editor** (**QLE**), and generate quote documents faster. When considering scale, we are discussing the increase in processing capacities. For example, you want to process as many records as possible. In addition, you want to load and save more quote lines, select more products, and calculate more rules.

CPQ performance and optimization depend on the Salesforce platform's and Sales Cloud's performance, as CPQ is built on top of them.

Make sure that your Salesforce environment is ready for a CPQ implementation and that you're not just adding the managed package to an already overburdened environment. For example, if the existing release management process continuously fails due to performance issues, then you should attack that problem first before trying to implement CPQ.

Within CPQ, you have several customizations that might have been configured as per the specific implementations for your business needs, as shown in the following figure:

Figure 12.1 – CPQ customizations on top of the Salesforce platform

CPQ is a **managed package** and all the **Salesforce platform governor limits,** such as **Apex CPU time, Apex heap, SOQL queries,** and **DML** statements, apply to it. For more details on Salesforce governor limits, refer to the Salesforce governor limit documentation here: https://developer.salesforce.com/docs/atlas.en-us.apexcode. meta/apexcode/apex_gov_limits.htm.

If a managed package developed by a Salesforce **Independent Software Vendor (ISV)** has passed a security review, then such a package is generally provided with a higher per-transaction limit. Also, CPQ is a qualified ISV-certified managed package. Salesforce CPQ has its own licensing and namespace, which is a unique identifier in the Sales Cloud. There's no limit on the number of certified namespaces that can be invoked in a single transaction. However, the number of operations that can be performed in each namespace must not exceed the per-transaction limits.

Configuration and customization complexity play a major role in CPQ performance. For implementation, we need to take into consideration both the CPQ system and Salesforce platform automation and customizations. In the CPQ QLE, the higher the configuration complexity, the higher the response time. Product selection plays a major role in the scalability of CPQ. More elaborate product selection criteria can only scale fewer number of quote lines. Any business will want to avoid these issues and complete the maximum number of quotes in the shortest time possible.

It is important to know which performance issues are annoyances versus which performance issues prevent deals from moving forward. For example, if my load time is latent because of the number of product rules being fired, that is frustrating. If my quotes fail to calculate because I have too many quote lines, that is a critical issue with the implementation.

Apex CPU Time Limit Exceeded is a very common error that users will encounter that prevents them from moving forward. For example, this error can occur while using an out-of-the-box contract or order generation method. It can also happen while saving and calculating a quote. This error can appear due to the following:

- The record that is being created, edited, or renewed is too large.

- The native Salesforce automation is being executed in parallel with CPQ package automation.

Salesforce package settings for large quotes can be used to resolve the error. The quote batch size will break down quotes into smaller chunks to send back and forth to **Heroku**.

Any transaction that fails with an Apex governor limit error message that points to the SBQQ namespace may not always be associated with the CPQ package. The underlying Salesforce platform and Sales Cloud customizations that interact with CPQ should be structured as shown in *Figure 12.1*.

The processes in the Salesforce CPQ namespace are not all designed to run multiple times in a single transaction. Custom code, flows, and process builders are some of the items that may cause managed package triggers to run multiple times, which can result in governor limit errors.

> **Important Note**
>
> Native Salesforce automation will add significant overload to a system while saving a quote. The general best practice in Salesforce CPQ is to avoid writing a **trigger**, workflow rule, flow, or process builder on a **quote**, **quote line**, or **quote line group** object. Updating fields on these objects using Salesforce CPQ configurations such as product rules, price rules, and the **Quote Calculator Plugin (QCP)** will optimize the performance.

There are three major functions performed on the **Add Products** page and the QLE that impact performance:

- Load
- Calculate
- Save

Loading includes the static resources, the editor (which includes all the quote lines, bundles, and so on), the rules, and all the calculation details that happen in the background. Calculations can happen at the server level or locally, while local calculations are more efficient. Some of the calculations are at both the local and server level, and they will have a larger performance impact.

Let's learn about the key contributors in performance and scale while configuring the QLE and selecting products on the **Add Products** page:

- The main performance and scalability impacts include Salesforce customizations and CPQ configurations and customizations. As per specific implementations, we have CPQ configurations such as the following:

  - **Price rules**, which perform automatic calculations and update the QLE fields. **Lookup queries**, which are used for fetching additional information that is not available on the quote, as well as **reference fields**, which are fields on the user interface and calculations.

- **Product rules** are used to perform actions on a product, based on the conditions and queries. We have product bundles containing options, features, and constraints. Then, we have reference fields, which are fields on the user interface, product entity, and product option entity.

- Standard Salesforce customizations, such as **Apex triggers**, and configurations such as **process builders**, **workflow rules**, and **flows** impact CPQ performance.

Any organization needs to balance these customizations as per their requirements and choose the right automation. We should minimize the number of automations for each object and only try to automate the most common uses cases. In this section, we will look at some CPQ configurations for achieving performance and scalability:

- For implementations where we have the scenario of large quote lines, the CPQ **Package Settings** can be used. In the line editor settings for a large quote, **Large Quote Threshold** is disabled by default. When we have issues saving large quotes, this setting can be enabled. The threshold can be adjusted to improve the performance when the system throws governor limit errors. It's recommended that this value be set slightly lower than the number of lines on the quote.

- Similarly, for loading large quotes, we can use the **Quote Batch Size** setting, which is set to 150 by default and can be changed as per a customer's needs. Quote load and save actions process the specified batch size. Smaller batches are less likely to hit governor limits. Larger batches cause better quote line performance because the editor makes fewer round trips to the server.

- Enable the **Improve Browser Performance** checkbox in the CPQ **Package Settings** under the **Additional Setting** tab to take advantage of technology advancements in web browsers.

- In *Chapter 3, Configuring CPQ Products*, we learned about **nested bundles**. But these have huge performance implications, and it is advised to avoid them as much as possible. Instead, we can use product features as an alternative. Nested bundles are more difficult to work within an integration layer as well, specifically creating quote lines via the CPQ API.

- The configuration action on the **Add Products** page has **load**, **edit**, and **save** options. For better performance in the configuration phase, we need to use the load and save options.

- There are a number of configurations that can be used in different ways. Using the right tools and automation can help improve performance. For example, formula fields with references are not good for performance, as they not only calculate the formula but also reference additional **sObjects**. Loading these formula fields to the QLE adds a significant load to a system, which is why we should minimize the usage of referenced formula fields. In this scenario, a price rule can be used because it is pre-cacheable and reduces the performance impact during loading.

- Reuse referenced fields across different price rules.

- Remove any unused fields from the QLE and referenced field sets.

- While calculating the quote, we saw that we can have local calculation and server calculation. Most standard price rules are cached in the background, minimizing the performance impact. Some price rules may have to go back to the server to calculate the rule lookup queries, require local information, and gather additional data from the server to complete the calculations. This will add a round-trip, impacting performance. Adding lookup queries will increase the performance load. We can use summary variables as an alternative and use rollup summary fields for reference in a price rule. This can help pre-cache the price rule and avoid server calculation.

> **Important Note**
> Avoid unnecessary lookup queries for calculations and use platform optimizations.

- For better performance, combine product rules/price rules with similar actions and conditions.

- An **evaluation event edit** is inefficient, as it needs a server request. Instead, use load and save, which are more efficient. While configuring the **evaluation scope**, the **quote-scoped** product rule increases the performance impact, as it evaluates all the data under the quote, whereas product-scoped rules are only going to be evaluated based on the current data and bundle that you are configuring.

- A combination of **option constraints** and **dynamic features** can be used as an alternative to price rules. These often perform similar types of actions and can be configured on products and bundles, rather than a product rule.

- Prefer feature and option constraints in simple cases, where product rules are not required.

- Avoid loading product images during configuration.

- We have two ways of implementing the QCP – with the **Apex legacy QCP** or the **JavaScript advanced QCP**. The Apex QCP runs the calculations on the server side, impacting performance. It is preferred to use the JavaScript QCP, as the scripts run locally in a user's browser.

- Automations built against **opportunity** and **opportunity product** will also have an effect, as users try to save a primary quote.

There are many things that can slow down CPQ performance. We can also measure some of the limitations on runtime, CPU utilization time, and other governor limits in test instances using **Salesforce Event Monitoring**, debug options, or third-party **AppExchange** tools. We are just scratching the surface here; there are lots of factors that can impact system performance.

In the next section, we will look into some of the implementation best practices.

The best practices for CPQ implementation

CPQ implementation is no different from any standard Salesforce implementation, and we need to follow the standard best practices. CPQ implementation is also a transformation product, and we need to think about additional best practices. Let's learn some of them:

- Thoroughly understand your company's sales process and analyze whether there is a need for CPQ. Are the sales reps struggling to close deals? Do you have disconnected systems? Generically, there needs to be a very strong business case for bringing CPQ into a Salesforce environment, but what that business case is can vary widely from client to client.

- Clearly define the implementation objectives and identify the right time to implement CPQ.

- Analyze whether you need Industries CPQ with Industry Cloud or the standard Salesforce CPQ.

- Understand how the existing processes and integrated systems will be affected by CPQ implementation and make sure that the user adoption is taken care of right from inception.

- Provide necessary training to the technical team and business stakeholders.

- It is equally important to understand your back office and finance processes along with the sales process.

- Make sure you have seamless integrations with all the dependent systems.

- Return on investment with CPQ implementation is significant. CPQ implementation will impact multiple stakeholders, such as legal, finance, sales, pre-sales, product management, product pricing, and downstream ordering systems. Make sure all these stakeholders are involved from the beginning by clearly defining the business process.

- It's always better to go with a **Minimum Viable Product** (**MVP**) solution in the first phase, and once the business process stabilizes, introduce automation to expedite deal velocity.

- Make sure you plan for phased deployment for a specific segment of the business or a specific region before expanding it to other regions.

- Product catalogs need to be cleaned up and maintained to remain up to date.

Again, there is no right or wrong way to perform a specific implementation. It totally depends on the budget, tools, and resources that are available to you and your business.

Summary

Salesforce CPQ provides your company with the tools you need to take control of the **Quote-to-Cash** (**Q2C**) process. Using CPQ, you can easily configure unique solutions for your customers. CPQ provides controls to your sales manager and sales operation team, which include controls over discounts, approvals, and processes.

CPQ helps generate proposals and contracts in minutes, whether it is a new sale, an amendment, or a renewal. You can track all the deal data in one system, as everything is built on top of the Salesforce platform. Closing the deal and using automatic order and invoice generation integrates billing into the same platform, unifying the sales and finance teams into one system.

Integrated payment options make collections fast and easy. Scheduled reports and dashboard alerts can help the sales and finance teams monitor any potential issues. You can also generate revenue recognition schedules for orders with multiple products and different subscriptions. Managers and executives will have complete visibility of the related data from forecasted opportunities to recognized revenue for all deals, including new sales and renewals. You can connect with your customer in a new and different way and produce accurate quotes using CPQ!

Further reading

CPQ implementation is complex, and it is recommended to involve an implementation partner. For additional help and CPQ knowledge, do the following:

- Use a Salesforce test organization to learn, practice, and test the implementation examples provided in this book.

- Refer to Salesforce Help for additional information.

- For each Salesforce release, refer to the CPQ enhancements and performance improvements: `https://help.salesforce.com/s/articleView?id=release-notes.rn_revenue_cpq_parent.htm&type=5&release=236`.

- Join Trailhead community groups (based on your location, you can also search for local meetups).

Index

Packt.com

Subscribe to our online digital library for full access to over 7,000 books and videos, as well as industry leading tools to help you plan your personal development and advance your career. For more information, please visit our website.

Why subscribe?

- Spend less time learning and more time coding with practical eBooks and Videos from over 4,000 industry professionals

- Improve your learning with Skill Plans built especially for you

- Get a free eBook or video every month

- Fully searchable for easy access to vital information

- Copy and paste, print, and bookmark content

Did you know that Packt offers eBook versions of every book published, with PDF and ePub files available? You can upgrade to the eBook version at packt.com and as a print book customer, you are entitled to a discount on the eBook copy. Get in touch with us at customercare@packtpub.com for more details.

At www.packt.com, you can also read a collection of free technical articles, sign up for a range of free newsletters, and receive exclusive discounts and offers on Packt books and eBooks.

Other Books You May Enjoy

If you enjoyed this book, you may be interested in these other books by Packt:

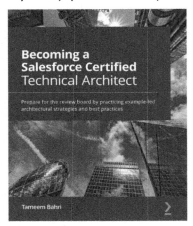

Becoming a Salesforce Certified Technical Architect

Tameem Bahri

ISBN: 978-1-80056-875-4

- Explore data lifecycle management and apply it effectively in the Salesforce ecosystem
- Design appropriate enterprise integration interfaces to build your connected solution
- Understand the essential concepts of identity and access management
- Develop scalable Salesforce data and system architecture
- Design the project environment and release strategy for your solution
- Articulate the benefits, limitations, and design considerations relating to your solution
- Discover tips, tricks, and strategies to prepare for the Salesforce CTA review board exam

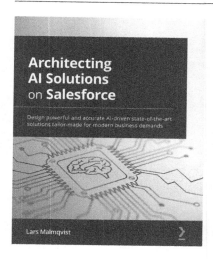

Architecting AI Solutions on Salesforce

Lars Malmqvist

ISBN: 978-1-80107-601-2

- Explore the AI components available in Salesforce and the architectural model for Salesforce Einstein

- Extend the out-of-the-box features using Einstein Services on major Salesforce clouds

- Use Einstein declarative features to create your custom solutions with the right approach

- Architect AI solutions on marketing, commerce, and industry clouds

- Use Salesforce Einstein Platform Services APIs to create custom AI solutions

- Integrate third-party AI services such as Microsoft Cognitive Services and Amazon SageMaker into Salesforce

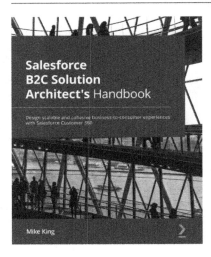

Salesforce B2C Solution Architect's Handbook

Mike King

ISBN: 978-1-80181-703-5

- Explore key Customer 360 products and their integration options
- Choose the optimum integration architecture to unify data and experiences
- Architect a single view of the customer to support service, marketing, and commerce
- Plan for critical requirements, design decisions, and implementation sequences to avoid sub-optimal solutions
- Integrate Customer 360 solutions into a single-source-of-truth solution such as a master data model
- Support business needs that require functionality from more than one component by orchestrating data and user flows

Packt is searching for authors like you

If you're interested in becoming an author for Packt, please visit `authors.packtpub.com` and apply today. We have worked with thousands of developers and tech professionals, just like you, to help them share their insight with the global tech community. You can make a general application, apply for a specific hot topic that we are recruiting an author for, or submit your own idea.

Share Your Thoughts

Now you've finished *The Salesforce CPQ Implementation Handbook*, we'd love to hear your thoughts! Scan the QR code below to go straight to the Amazon review page for this book and share your feedback or leave a review on the site that you purchased it from.

https://packt.link/r/1-801-07742-8

Your review is important to us and the tech community and will help us make sure we're delivering excellent quality content.

Made in the USA
Monee, IL
29 April 2022

95644490R00175